2 hr.

WHO PROSPERS?

*How Cultural Values
Shape Economic
and Political Success*

LAWRENCE E. HARRISON

BasicBooks
A Division of HarperCollins*Publishers*

Table 3.1 from Chi-ming Hou, "Strategy for Economic Development in Taiwan and Implications for Developing Economics," and Shirley Kuo, "The Achievement of Growth with Equity," in *Conference on Economic Development Experiences of Taiwan and Its New Role in an Emerging Asia-Pacific Area* (Taipei: Institue of Economics, Academia Sinica, 1988), pp. 57, 77. Reprinted with permission.

Table 6.2 from Kevin F. McCarthy and R. Burciaga Valdez, *Current and Future Effects of Mexican Immigration in California* (Santa Monica, CA.: RAND, R–3365–CR, 1985). Reprinted with permission.

Table 7.1 from Richard P. Freeman, *Black Elite* (New York: McGraw-Hill, 1976), p. 34. Reprinted with permission of the Carnegie Foundation for the Advancement of Teaching, Princeton, NJ.

Library of Congress Cataloging-in-Publication Data

Harrison, Lawrence E.
    Who prospers? : how cultural values shape economic and political success / Lawrence E. Harrison.
    p. cm.
    Includes bibliographical references and index.
    ISBN 0–465–01634–0
    1. Economic development—Psychological aspects. 2. Economic development—Social aspects. 3. Ethnopsychology. I. Title.
HD75.H36 1992
306.3—dc20   91–58597
                        HD 75   CIP
                        H36 1992

Designed by Abigail Sturgess

92 93 94 95 CC/HC 9 8 7 6 5 4 3 2 1

For Patsy

Contents

Acknowledgments

This book has benefited from the comments and help of a large number of people: Edward Banfield, Rodrigo Botero, Eliana Cardoso, John Hugh Crimmins, Gregory Curtis, David Dean, Jorge Domínguez, David Dugan, Richard Estrada, Richard Falknor, James Fallows, James Fox, Francis Fukuyama, Joel Garreau, Barbara Grady, Stephan Haggard, Mary Hansen, Amy Harrison Donnelly, Julia Harrison Grady, Beth Hastie, Ronald Inglehart, Neil Isaacs, Nicholas Lemann, Landon Lockett, Glenn Loury, Thomas Murphy, Dwight Perkins, Lucian Pye, John Ritchie, Riordan Roett, Gail Ross, Rafael Sagalyn, Reese Schonfeld, Albert Seligmann, David Simcox, William Sugrue, John Tanton, Jared Taylor, and Frederic Thomas. All personal communications, unless otherwise attributed, are from interviews I conducted between 1988 and 1990.

I am particularly indebted to Martin Kessler, president and editorial director of Basic Books, and Linda Carbone, development editor, for their most helpful suggestions about structure and precision and economy of language.

The book could not have been written without the support of the Laurel Foundation. I am also grateful to the Center for International Affairs at Harvard University, which provided an ideal base for research and writing.

Finally, I take this opportunity to express my gratitude for the help, companionship, and support of my wife, Patricia Crane Harrison.

Introduction

Progress and Poverty Without Marx

The central conservative truth is that it is culture, not politics, that determines the success of a society. The central liberal truth is that politics can change a culture and save it from itself.
—Daniel Patrick Moynihan, *The New Republic* (7 July 1986)

Why do some nations and ethnic groups do better than others? Climate, resource endowment, geographic location and size, policy choices, and sheer luck are among the relevant factors. But it is values and attitudes—culture—that differentiate ethnic groups and are mainly responsible for such phenomena as Latin America's persistent instability and inequity, Taiwan's and Korea's economic "miracles," and the achievements of the Japanese—in Japan, in Brazil, and in America.

Culture changes, for good and for bad. In the span of three decades, Spain has turned away from its traditional, authoritarian, hierarchical value system, which was at the root of both Spain's and Hispanic America's backwardness, and has immersed itself in the progressive Western European mainstream. During the same period, a racial revolution has occurred in America that has brought two-thirds of America's blacks into the mainstream—and the middle class. Yet, in the same three decades, the United States as a nation has experienced economic and political decline, principally, I believe, because of the erosion of the traditional American values—work, frugality, education, excellence, community—that had contributed so much to our earlier success.

The overriding significance of culture is the paramount lesson I have learned in my thirty years of work on political, economic, and social development. I lived for thirteen of those years in Latin America, serving as director of U.S. Agency for International Development (USAID) missions in Costa Rica, Guatemala, Haiti, and Nicaragua (during the first two years of the Sandinista revolution), and as deputy director in the Dominican Republic (during and after the 1965 revolution). I also worked for four years (1984–88) as vice president of the National Cooperative Business Association in charge of development activities in Asia, Africa, and Latin America. And I have spent four of the last ten years at Harvard University's Center for International Affairs, doing research on and writing about the relationship between culture and progress.

I started my career with USAID in 1962 in the Latin American Bureau, drawn by the promise and excitement of the Alliance for Progress, inaugurated by John F. Kennedy a year earlier. Like most Americans who worked on the Alliance, I believed that Latin America's authoritarianism, social injustice, and slow economic growth were the consequence of neglect by the United States. (Few of us subscribed to the Leninist "Yankee Imperialism" interpretation.) I well remember the sign in the office of Puerto Rico's Teodoro Moscoso, first U.S. Coordinator of the Alliance: PLEASE BE BRIEF. WE ARE TWENTY YEARS LATE.

But it soon became apparent to Moscoso and others, including myself, that there were internal forces at work in Latin America that were far more powerful than aid programs and rhetoric.* A USAID mission director is in a privileged position to learn what makes a society tick. I was involved in programs affecting all the key development sectors and activities: economic policy, government administration, education, health, agriculture, industry, infrastructure, and so on. I saw the problems through the eyes of presidents, cabinet ministers, mid-level bureaucrats, ambassadors, businesspeople, labor leaders, scholars, newspaper editors and reporters, the urban poor, and peasants.

It took many years of day-by-day experience in Latin America for me to appreciate how traditional Iberian values and attitudes impede progress toward political pluralism, social justice, and economic dyna-

---

*In 1966, Moscoso made a speech in which he said, "The Latin American case is so complex, so difficult to solve, and so fraught with human and global danger and distress that the use of the word 'anguish' is not an exaggeration. . . . The longer I live, the more I believe that, just as no human being can save another who does not have the will to save himself, no country can save another no matter how good its intentions or how hard it tries."[1]

mism. My two years in Haiti, 1977 to 1979, intensified my awareness of culture's powerful grip on progress—in Haiti's case, choking it. It was during those two years that I decided to write a book that would explore the relationship between culture and development. Published in 1985, *Underdevelopment Is a State of Mind—The Latin American Case* is, in essence, an analysis of how culture can impede progress. The reaction to it, as well as growing interest in the relationship between culture and progress evidenced by recent works by Peter Berger, James Fallows, Ronald Inglehart, Robert Putnam, Lucian Pye, and Thomas Sowell, among others, have encouraged me to examine some cases where culture has worked *for* progress. My concerns about what is happening to values and attitudes in the United States also contributed to my decision to write a second book. My resolve was strengthened by the recent extraordinary events in Eastern Europe and the apparent vacuum that the demise of Marxism-Leninism has left in understanding why some nations and ethnic groups do better than others.

THE COLLAPSE OF COMMUNISM

The collapse of communism in the last years of the twentieth century has brought stunning changes to Eastern Europe and the Soviet Union, as well as the rest of the world. The destruction of monuments to Marx and Lenin in Eastern European cities symbolizes the end of Marxism-Leninism as a credible explanation of progress and poverty within and among the nations of the world. All governments following the Marxist-Leninist model—including Cuba, Sandinista Nicaragua, and the Mengistu government in Ethiopia—have not only repressed personal freedoms and abused human rights but also failed to create material well-being for their populations. In 1990, open to scrutiny for the first time in forty years, Eastern Europe looked more like the Third World than the First.

Marx interpreted capitalism in the nineteenth century as a process in which an affluent few exploited a miserable many. Lenin extended this interpretation to explain why a few countries were rich and many were poor: national affluence was the fruit of "imperialism." The poor countries were the exploited "proletariat" of the world's nations. Thus, European countries were rich because they had exploited their colonies, principally in Africa and Asia. The United States was rich because it had engaged in a more subtle imperialism in Latin America.

History, particularly in the second half of the twentieth century, has confounded Marxist-Leninist analysis. Instead of the increasing pauperization of ever-larger lower classes predicted by Marx, a substantial movement from the lower classes to the middle classes has occurred in the advanced capitalist countries, accompanied and promoted by the emergence of democratic political systems. Britain's Canadian and Australian colonies prospered at least as much as the British Isles in the nineteenth century; and a current British colony, Hong Kong, has achieved "miraculous" economic growth in the last three decades. Most former European colonies in Africa are worse off, both economically and politically, than they were as colonies, however demeaning the colonial condition may have been.

Today, there are no ideologies that seriously contest the dominance and burgeoning popularity of democratic capitalism as the model best able to meet people's aspirations for the good life, even in regions as inexperienced with it as Eastern Europe, sub-Saharan Africa, and Latin America. Francis Fukuyama's thesis that humankind's ideological evolution has reached the end of the line with democratic capitalism appears valid indeed today, particularly after the spectacular collapse of communism in the Soviet Union in the summer of 1991.[2]

Marxist-Leninist theory most directly influenced the Soviet Union, its Eastern European satellites, and China. But it also profoundly affected the Third World, most of whose countries achieved independence after World War II. "Imperialism" has been a seductive explanation of national poverty for these countries: patterns of authoritarian government, social injustice, and economic stagnation were the "obvious" consequences of colonial exploitation. Good government and social justice would be "obvious" consequences of independence. The "obvious" economic prescription: self-sufficiency through the creation of import-substitution industries that would break the chains of "dependency" on the rich countries, coupled with broad state intervention in the economy. The best-known spokesman for this prescription was the Argentine economist Raúl Prebisch, who dominated Third World economic policy for three decades from his positions at the head of the United Nations Economic Commission for Latin America (ECLA) and the United Nations Conference on Trade and Development (UNCTAD).

The vast majority of Third World countries have experienced modest economic growth and sharp social inequalities under autocratic governments, and many of them have also experienced high levels of inflation, corruption, and misallocation of resources. The most inequitable countries in the world in terms of distribution of wealth, land, income, and opportunity are found in the Third World. The few who have done well economically and socially, most notably Taiwan, Korea, Hong Kong, and Singapore, have ignored Prebisch's prescription and have focused their economic policies on exports to the world market. In the process, they have exposed the myth of "dependency" and its corollary that only the advanced countries can compete as manufacturers for the world market.

If Marxism-Leninism, imperialism, and dependency are no longer viable explanations for affluence and poverty within and among nations, how, then, can these contrasts be explained? As I stated at the outset, numerous causative factors come into play, for example, climate, resource endowment, geographic location and size, policies, the vagaries of history. But alone or together, they are inadequate explanations. There are too many exceptions, cases where the indicated outcome fails to materialize.

Except for oil exporters, almost all the rich countries of the world are found in the temperate zone where, in early times, survival through the winter months depended on planning and saving. (The two tropical exceptions in the World Bank's 1990 listing of high-income economies are Hong Kong and Singapore. By the end of this century, Taiwan, which straddles the Tropic of Cancer, and temperate-zone Korea may well be added to the list.)[3] Yet within the tropical zone, there are sharp contrasts in economic well-being. Haiti, for example, had a per capita income of about $400 in 1988, while Barbados's was about $6,000.[4] We should note that Haiti, as a French slave colony, was the richest colony in the Caribbean in the eighteenth century.[5]

The relationship between national affluence and resource endowment is most apparent in the case of the oil-exporting countries of the Middle East. An example: the 1.5 million people who live in the United Arab Emirates had a per capita income of almost $16,000 in 1988. Yet other resource-rich countries have not done so well. Argentina, with an area five-sixths that of India but with only one-twenty-fifth of India's population, may be the most richly endowed country in the world in agricultural resources in proportion to its population; but its per capita income in 1989 was only about $2,200.[6] And some resource-poor countries do very well indeed, for example, Japan and Switzerland.

Geography is clearly relevant. It is obviously advantageous, as Mexico is learning, to be close to the world's most active markets, in North America and Europe. Thus, one might argue that Argentina's problems are in part a consequence of its remoteness. But in fact, Argentina reached its heyday during the last decades of the nineteenth and the first decades of the twentieth centuries mainly because of meat and grain exports to Europe. Moreover, Australia, also predominantly an exporter of primary products, is even more remote than Argentina. Its per capita GNP is over $14,000. And it is a stable democracy.

Economic policies that assure stability and continuity and nurture entrepreneurship correlate better with growth performance than do climate, resource endowment, or geography. But why have so many countries failed to pursue such policies with the necessary persistence to reap their benefits? Why, faced with the oil shocks of the 1970s, did Argentina and Brazil try to borrow their way out of trouble and end up mired in debt and galloping inflation, while Taiwan and Korea adopted austerity programs that led to rapid recovery? Why, within a multi-ethnic country, do some ethnic groups—for example, Japanese, Chinese, Koreans, and Jews in the United States—do better than others? Why are the Chinese uniformly high achievers in Taiwan, Hong Kong, Singapore, Malaysia, Thailand, Indonesia, the Philippines, the United States, and virtually every place they live *except* China?

In my view, it is impossible to answer these questions without examining the impact of culture on human progress—the values and attitudes of a nation, society, or ethnic group, and the institutions that both reflect and reinforce those values and attitudes. Nor is it possible to understand why some countries have succeeded in forging democratic institutions and social equality while most have not.

MARX WAS WRONG, WEBER WAS RIGHT

History has proven that Karl Marx was wrong; it may well be proving that Max Weber was right. Analyzing family income levels of Protestants, Catholics, and Jews in the German city of Baden in 1904–5, Weber found that Protestants did substantially better than Catholics and that Jews did better than either. The analysis led to Weber's masterwork, *The Protestant Ethic and the Spirit of Capitalism*, which explained why the values and attitudes inculcated by ascetic Calvinism were a more effective motivator of entrepreneurship, capital accumulation, and community responsibility than the values and attitudes inculcated by confessional Roman Catholicism.

Weber's emphasis on religion has prompted his critics to highlight two apparent anomalies: (1) the Catholic countries France, Italy, and Spain have grown more rapidly than most Protestant countries in Western Europe in recent decades; and (2) if "religion" (culture) is decisive, why are the Chinese so much more successful overseas than in China?

It is obvious that religion is but one of several roots of culture; after all, atheists and agnostics have values and attitudes. Moreover, Western Europe and North America have experienced a process of secularization, particularly in this century, that has reduced religion's impact on culture while expanding the impact of the education system and the media, above all, television. The integration of Europe, in addition to enlarging economic opportunity, has tended to homogenize the values and attitudes of Western Europeans, a point I will underscore in chapter 2, on Spain. As Ronald Inglehart points out, Weber's analysis was confirmed by the relative performance of Protestant and Catholic countries between 1870 and 1938.[7] The success of Catholic countries since can readily be explained by cultural change in those countries combined with the opportunities that arose because they—above all, Spain and Italy—had been so far behind non-Catholic countries in Europe at the end of World War II.

The value system of the Chinese—and indeed the Koreans and Japanese—is principally influenced by Confucianism, which is not a religion but an ethical code. In fact, there's a good possibility that Confucius and many of his disciples were agnostics. In chapter 3, on Taiwan and Korea, I analyze the cross-currents of the Confucian ethos that explain both the higher achievements of the Chinese outside of China and China's difficulties in achieving democracy.

LESSONS LEARNED, LESSONS IGNORED

The world has learned a lot about development in the half-century since World War II. We know that market-oriented economic policies are a prerequisite for sustained growth. We know that political stability is also an essential ingredient. We know that extensive governmental intervention in an economy often breeds fiscal and efficiency problems and suppresses private initiative. We recognize the crucial importance of saving, investment, and technology. And we have learned that human resources are more important than natural resources.

But for most poor countries, these lessons have had little impact, at least in terms of the access of the majority of human beings to the means of raising their standard of living; their ability to influence their governments' policies and actions; their equality before the law; and their equality of opportunity. What experts thought thirty years ago was going to be a fairly manageable, almost mechanical process of planned, stage-to-stage development has typically turned out to be vastly more complicated, slow moving, and in some cases even intractable. The Third World has repeatedly experienced famine, bloody insurgencies and civil wars, warfare between neighbors, dictatorship and extreme governmental corruption, and economic crisis and stagnation during the years since that early optimism. To repeat, the most inequitable countries in the world in terms of distribution of wealth, land, income, and opportunity are found in the Third World.

Latin America is a case in point. When John F. Kennedy proposed the Alliance for Progress in 1961, his advisers, flushed with the success of the Marshall Plan in Western Europe, were convinced that Latin America could be converted into a stable, democratic, and economically dynamic area in one, or at the most two, decades. In fact, Latin America's economic growth approximated 6 percent annually in the 1960s and 1970s, and, as population growth declined, the Alliance target of 2.5 percent annual growth of per capita GNP was substantially achieved. But broad-based development did not occur. The traditional patterns of authoritarianism and political fragmentation, polarization, and confrontation persisted, as did the traditional pattern of inequitable distribution of land, income, wealth, and opportunity. An unprecedented surge of democratization occurred in the 1980s, but it was accompanied by a prolonged period of economic instability and distress. Today, half of all Latin Americans live in the kind of poverty that makes poverty in the United States look like the middle class.[8]

Two hundred and fifty years ago, Spain's and Portugal's Latin American colonies were more affluent and powerful than the British colonies of North America. As we approach the end of the twentieth century, Latin America still has a long way to go in its efforts to achieve democratic stability, sustained economic dynamism, and social justice. I believe that culture is the principal explanation of this historic reversal.

HOW CULTURE INFLUENCES PROGRESS

Admittedly, the word *culture* is fuzzy and elastic. It can define group or national value systems, attitudes, religious and other institutions, intellectual achievement, artistic expression, daily behavior, customs, lifestyle, and many other characteristics. When we focus on the relationship between culture and progress, however, its definition becomes more manageable. In this book, I am addressing those aspects of culture that influence group or national political, economic, and social performance. Culture is a coherent system of values, attitudes, and institutions that influences individual and social behavior in all dimensions of human experience.

Clearly, cause and effect run in both directions in the relationship between culture and progress. Particularly in the short run, development can shape culture, as we shall see in the case of the Spanish "miracle." But in the long run, I believe that culture is usually a decisive cause, an assertion borne out by the cases of Spain, Portugal, and their former New World colonies over five centuries of political authoritarianism, sluggish economic growth, and social inequity.

In recent years, the term *political culture* has become popular, particularly with political scientists, but it is only a theoretical concept. Political scientists draw on those aspects of the coherent system of values, attitudes, and institutions that most influence the *political* dimension of human experience. Other aspects of that same system, and some aspects that affect political behavior, influence how people and societies act in the economic and social dimensions. Culture's impact is not confined to political development.

Some will argue that the word *development* itself is not useful because some cultures reject it or define it very differently than others. But the cataclysmic events of the past few years in Eastern Europe, the Soviet Union, China, and the Third World underscore what is now a substantially universal set of aspirations based on the democratic-capitalist model. That model nurtures human creative capacity, which is, I believe, the real engine of progress.

A society can encourage the expression of human creative capacity in many ways, just as it can suppress it. Creativity is likely to flourish where people expect and receive fair treatment, where justice is a substantial reality, be it in the courts, in government, in enterprise, or in the way the society opens opportunities to people. An effective and accessible education system—one that provides basic intellectual and vocational tools; nurtures inquisitiveness, critical faculties, dissent, and creativity; and equips people to solve problems—is indispensable. So is a health system that protects people from diseases that debilitate and kill.

Progressive societies encourage experimentation and criticism and help people both discover their talents and interests and mesh them with the right jobs. The idea of merit permeates such societies, and people are judged more by their performance than by their family background or class. Political pluralism and broad citizen participation are likely to evolve in such an environment. The freedom that nourishes the expression of human creative capacity also nourishes democratic political systems, stability, and continuity.

What has been demonstrated in this century, particularly in the last decade, is that democratic capitalism does a better job of promoting human progress and well-being than other systems. But, as the experience of most Third World countries in recent decades shows, the building of durable democratic capitalist institutions can be dauntingly difficult, particularly since cultural traditions that nurture progress are not likely to be in place.

What, then, are the cultural forces that facilitate or suppress the expression of human creative capacity and that influence movement toward or away from this increasingly universal aspirational model? There are, in my view, four fundamental factors: (1) the degree of identification with others in a society—the radius of trust, or the sense of community; (2) the rigor of the ethical system; (3) the way authority is exercised within the society; and (4) attitudes about work, innovation, saving, and profit. These factors flow from the overarching world view of a society, what social scientists refer to as "cognitive orientation" or "cognitive view." It is shaped by geographic and historical factors and, in the case of traditional societies, also by the idea, inculcated by stagnation that has persisted over centuries, that progress is possible only at the expense of others. In such societies, the time focus is the present or the past. In progressive cultures, the time focus is the future. An examination of these four factors will help clarify the link between values and progress.

The Radius of Trust

Identification with others in the society—the sense of community—is synonymous with social empathy and is a foundation of trust. Trust is of transcendental importance to the viability of pluralistic political systems. It comes crucially into play, for example, when power is transferred from the ins to the outs. It affects attitudes about cooperation and compromise, both indispensable to the smooth functioning of democratic politics. Where trust and identification are scant, political polarization, confrontation, and autocratic government are likely to emerge.

Trust is also important to the pluralistic, decentralized economic systems that have proved to be the most efficient and productive. Successful enterprise usually depends on effective organization and cooperation, which, in turn, depend on trust.

Commercial and industrial enterprises—and public administration—in low-trust countries are usually weighted down by centralization, including a variety of checking mechanisms and procedures designed, ostensibly, to assure conformity and to control dishonesty. Particularly in public administration, such controls not only stifle governmental creativity and private entrepreneurship but lend themselves to corruption and perpetuate privilege, as Hernando De Soto has documented so tellingly in the case of Peru.[9]

The radius of identification, or social empathy, is a key determinant of social equity and progress. If there is a relatively high degree of identification, as in Japan, the politically and economically powerful are more likely to concern themselves with the well-being of the masses. That concern is reflected, through budget allocations, in high levels of literacy and public health. Similarly, philanthropy, notably absent in most Latin American countries, is a likely consequence of an extended radius of identification. Countries like Costa Rica and Israel, which also show a high level of identification and empathy, are prone to democratic political systems that reinforce the claim of the masses to attention to their needs and aspirations.

In most poor countries, the radius of identification and trust is substantially confined to the family. What is outside the family is an object of indifference, even hostility. Familistic societies are usually characterized by nepotism and other forms of corruption, as well as antisocial behavior such as tax evasion, littering, and aversion to organization and cooperation for common purposes and causes.

The Rigor of the Ethical System

The ethical system often derives from religion, although that is not the case with the East Asian countries. In *The Protestant Ethic and the Spirit of Capitalism,* Weber focused on the link between religion and economic performance, particularly the impetus given to entrepreneurship, saving, and investing by a combination of Protestant asceticism and the Calvinist doctrines of calling and election. *Calling* requires an individual to discharge the personal and social responsibilities of his or her station in life; *election* is the doctrine that God has blessed a chosen few whose state of grace is apparent from their prosperity. But Weber also recognized the important link between ethics and economic performance, and he believed that the Roman Catholic emphasis on the afterlife and what he perceived as a more flexible ethical system put Catholics at a disadvantage to Protestants and Jews in this life: "The God of Calvinism demanded of his believers not single good works, but a life of good works combined into a unified system. There was no place for the very human Catholic cycle of sin, repentance, atonement, release, followed by renewed sin."[10]

The ethical system both reinforces and is reinforced by the radius of trust and identification to influence the degree of social justice and the fairness of the system of legal justice—for example, the extent to which independence of the judiciary and due process are a reality. Apropos of this observation, in a recent study, Keith Rosenn concluded that, in Latin America, judicial independence exists only in Costa Rica.[11]

The Exercising of Authority

Traditionally, authority has been seen in Hispanic America as a license. There is truth, albeit sometimes exaggerated and overgeneralized, in the stereotype of the Hispanic American male who sees life as a struggle to achieve the power that comes with authority, which, once achieved, is to be used in his own interest, unrestrained by concerns with the rights of others, constitutional checks and balances, or even prudence. Those who find the stereotype offensive and without foundation should ponder why the typical Latin American chief of state leaves office vastly enriched. I hasten to acknowledge that there are exceptions.

But beyond the costs in terms of the frustration of democracy and justice, diverted resources, bad policies, and quixotic adventures (for example, the decision of Argentina's military to attack the Falkland Islands), authoritarianism in Latin America—in the home, the church, school, government, business—probably also contributes to the suppression of risk taking, innovation, and entrepreneurship by constantly penalizing initiative.[12] The authoritarianism of the mandarins, including Mao, has, I believe, similarly suppressed economic growth in China.

Authoritarianism implies a hierarchical view of the world, one that nurtures paternalism, patron-client relationships, and social rigidity, conditions commonly found in the Third World. But authoritarianism is not peculiar to the Third World, as German history attests. It has traditionally flourished in Taiwan, Korea, and Japan, all of whose economic performance in recent decades has astonished the world. That apparent paradox demands examination, and chapters 3 and 4 in part address it.

Work, Innovation, Saving, and Profit

Positive attitudes about work may reflect religious influence, as Weber points out with respect to Protestantism. As we shall see in the two chapters on East Asian countries, religion is not the only source of such attitudes, which usually incorporate (1) the belief that rationality presents a tool with which the world can be manipulated and wealth increased, (2) a consequent high emphasis on education, and (3) an orientation toward the future that encourages planning and saving.[13] The implications of such attitudes for economic development are obvious. But the same attitudes also have important effects on political and social progress by influencing the way public officials go about their work: the extent of their vision, the significance they attach to planning, the effort and sense of responsibility they exert in shaping and executing policies.

Closely related to the value attached to work is the extent to which a society promotes creativity and entrepreneurship. David McClelland has argued that child-rearing practices are the principal reason some countries and ethnic groups produce proportionally more entrepreneurs than others. He believes that the years between five and twelve are crucial to a child's achievement motivation. He cites evidence that during this key growth period, moderate parental pressures are optimal and children's achievement tendencies are reinforced by: reasonably high parental standards at a time when a child can handle them; limited parental interference; and expressed parental pleasure in their children's achievements. McClelland believes that an authoritarian style of child rearing undermines a child's creativity, and he consequently believes that in most societies it is advantageous for mothers, rather than fathers, to take the leading role in child rearing.[14]

Support for McClelland's thesis can be found in the literature on Japan (see chapter 4) and Latin America.[15] Writing early in this century about Central America's "sickness," the Nicaraguan writer Salvador Mendieta focused his cure on child rearing: "To combat inconstancy, which is a common source of economic failure, explain to the child the inevitable relationship between time and human enterprise, and particularly in those kinds of undertakings that depend on science, experience, constancy, and tenacity; explain to him that beginnings are difficult; that by starting and not finishing things, one loses time, energy, and experience."[16]

To recapitulate, I believe that significant differences in political, economic, and social development among countries can usually be explained by differences in trust and identification, ethical codes, the way authority is exercised, and the value attached to work, innovation, and planning. To use the examples of *Underdevelopment Is a State of Mind—The Latin American Case,* the palpable differences between Nicaragua and Costa Rica, Haiti and the Dominican Republic, Haiti and Barbados, Argentina and Australia, and Latin America and the United States can be traced to these cultural factors, as can the striking parallels, at least until the past few decades, between Spain and the colonies it spawned in the New World.

Culture and Cooperatives:
An Illustrative Anecdote

In the summer of 1984, having just joined the Cooperative League of the USA—now the National Cooperative Business Association—to promote the cooperative form of organizing enterprises in Third World countries, I visited Thailand and the Philippines. It did not take me long to learn of the deplorable condition of most Thai cooperatives, many of which were initiated by the government with political rather than economic ends in mind (a genesis of cooperatives common to many poor countries). Toward the end of my visit in Bangkok, I met with two West Germans who had, with considerable frustration, been advising the Thai government on cooperative development. I asked them whether they could explain the poor record of Thai co-ops. One of them replied that they had just been talking about that a few days earlier and had come to the conclusion that cooperatives don't work well in Thailand because Thais don't trust one another, and they know how to relate to one another only in a hierarchical way.* I took careful note of the German adviser's words, because the same two cultural problems seemed to me to be an obstacle to cooperatives in Latin America.

A few days later, in Manila, I had a conversation with a Filipino cooperative leader who had spent several decades promoting co-ops in his country with very limited success and a lot of frustration. His first words to me were to explain that there are two fundamental cultural obstacles to cooperatives in the Philippines: Filipinos don't trust one another, and they know how to relate to one another only hierarchically. To this echo of the words of the German adviser in Bangkok, my Filipino host added, "and that is our inheritance from Spain," closing the circle for me.[18]

---

*My German interlocutor is not alone in perceiving cultural roots to the obstacles to cooperation in Thailand. The anthropologist Herbert P. Phillips notes in *Thai Peasant Personality* an "absence among village residents of any strong sense of identification with the needs of the community as a whole. Except for religious activities and the reciprocal work groups organized for rice transplanting and harvesting—the rewards for which are directly personal—the villagers are simply not predisposed to participate in communal projects."[17]

CULTURES THAT RESIST PROGRESS

Cultural relativism, which asserts that all cultures are essentially equal and eschews comparative value judgments, has been the conventional wisdom in academic circles for decades. Yet some cultures are progress-prone, while others are not. I believe that cultures that nurture human creative capacity and progress are better than those that don't. Some may be offended by this assertion, but it is, I believe, corroborated by the persistent flow of immigrants from cultures that suppress progress to those cultures that facilitate it.

A better understanding of how a culture can suppress progress may make it easier to understand why I think cultural relativism flies in the face of reality. Two analyses of progress-resistant cultures follow: the first by a Latin American who shares my view that Latin America's troubled history is principally the consequence of traditional Iberian culture; the second representing the views of a number of anthropologists who have found striking similarities in traditional peasant cultures around the world.

Mariano Grondona's Cultural Typology

The Argentine journalist and scholar Mariano Grondona is convinced that culture has been a dominant factor in his country's disappointing history, including the decline from what appeared to be substantial development early in this century.[19] Argentina's Golden Age, from about 1880 to 1930, was followed by militarism and the economic, political, and moral deterioration of the Perón period; several abortive attempts to restore democracy; seventeen years of military domination with thousands of "disappeared" persons and the Falklands debacle; and the plunge into four-digit inflation and bankruptcy that has apparently been arrested by the stabilization policies of the government of Carlos Saúl Menem. We should also note that the Golden Age was preceded by sixty-five years of independence—and more than two hundred years as a Spanish colony—in which authoritarianism, militarism, and brutality, particularly in the treatment of Indians, were commonplace.

Grondona has developed a typology that identifies some twenty cultural or ideological factors that operate very differently in development-prone and development-resistant societies.[20] Clearly, he has Protestant values in mind as typical of the former, Catholic values as typical of the latter. His typology expands on the four key factors I have discussed and forms a very helpful framework to capture both the relationship between values and progress and the contrasts between traditional and progressive societies.

Grondona believes that the way a culture views the value of the individual has an important influence on the degree of trust. The favorable culture respects and has faith in the individual, a faith on which egalitarianism and decentralization are based. The resistant culture is suspicious of the individual, and suspicion breeds mistrust, authoritarianism, and centralization.

He also believes that attitudes about "the lesser virtues"—a job well done, tidiness, courtesy, punctuality—are important elements of social identification and responsibility in a favorable culture, contributing to both efficiency and smooth human relations. They are unimportant in a resistant culture, partly because they impinge on the assertion of the individual's wishes.

Grondona also contends that a progress-prone society is characterized by an ethical system based on responsible self-interest and mutual respect. In the resistant culture, morality seeks perfection (altruism, self-denial), which exceeds the bounds of human nature and becomes utopianism. Humankind achieves salvation in the next world through good works in this world, in the favorable culture. In the resistant culture, "to be saved is to retire from the world, to keep away from its risks and dangers."[21]

In the favorable society, perfectibility is always present as a goal but is understood to be something to work toward, although unlikely to be completely realized. Imperfections and shortcomings are to be expected and are accepted. In the resistant culture, inevitable flaws are seized upon by spiritual and political leaders, often utopians, to induce guilt.

Respect for the law is a feature of progress-prone societies, and the law is the basis of authority, in Grondona's view. In the progress-resistant culture, the law is subordinate to, and often dictated by, the authority, who often achieves power through force. In the favorable culture, democracy is an inevitable outcome that dissolves the power of authoritarianism and consolidates pluralism. In resistant cultures, "democracy" becomes window dressing for new forms of authoritarianism.

Most of the values and attitudes in Grondona's typology affect the economic dimension of human progress:

- *Religion* explains and justifies success in a development-prone culture. In a development-resistant culture, religion relieves or explains suffering.
- *Wealth* is *created* as the product of human initiative and effort in the favorable culture. Wealth is the natural or physical resource that *exists* in the resistant culture, and life is a struggle to acquire (or redistribute) it.
- *Competition* is viewed in a progress-prone culture as a positive force that promotes excellence and enriches the society. The resistant culture discourages competition as a form of aggression that threatens the stability and solidarity of the society, in part because it nurtures envy.
- *Economic justice* demands saving and investment for the benefit of future generations in the progressive culture. In the resistant culture, economic justice demands equitable distribution to the current generation. Obviously relevant is the time focus of a society (see *time focus*).
- *Labor* is a moral, social duty and a central form of self-expression and satisfaction in a favorable culture. In a resistant culture, it is a burden, a necessary evil; real pleasure and satisfaction are attainable only outside the workplace.
- *Heresy,* or dissent, is crucial to progress, reform, and the search for truth in the favorable culture, which encourages innovation. The heretic is a criminal who threatens stability and solidarity in the resistant culture.
- *Education* nurtures inquisitiveness and creativity in a favorable culture. In a resistant, traditional culture, it transmits orthodoxy.
- *Pragmatism, rationalism, empiricism, and utilitarianism* are central values in a favorable culture, threats to stability, solidarity, and continuity in a resistant culture. Tradition, emotion, and chance substitute for rationality, with stagnating consequences.
- *Time focus* is the manipulable future in the favorable culture. The resistant culture focuses on the past, and the concept of future is one of destiny, reflecting a fatalistic world view.
- *The world* is a setting for action and achievement in a favorable culture; one approaches it with optimism. In the resistant culture, the world is controlled by irresistible forces ("God or the Devil, multinational companies, or the international Marxist

conspiracy," Grondona elaborates);[22] one approaches it with pessimism, if not fear.

- *Life* is "something I will do" in the favorable culture. In the resistant culture, life is "something that happens to me."*
- *Optimism* is nurtured in the favorable culture. In the resistant culture, survival is the goal and pessimism the mood.

Grondona, of course, had Catholic Argentina in mind as his example of a development-resistant society. But he believes that the same development-resistant, essentially Iberian cultural characteristics have been operative in virtually all Latin American countries. Mexico is three thousand miles away from Argentina and on a different continent; it has a large Indian and mestizo population; it is a third smaller in area but almost three times as populous; and it shares a border with the United States. But both Mexico and Argentina have had great difficulty in forging democratic institutions; both have repeatedly experienced high inflation (although Argentina's record in this respect is clearly worse); both have an acute debt problem; and both distribute income inequitably. Mexico fits Grondona's typology.

Universal Peasant Culture

A number of social scientists, the anthropologist George Foster perhaps foremost among them, have noted value, attitude, and institutional patterns that are both very similar in peasant societies around the world and evocative of Grondona's typology. The same zero-sum world view that Grondona emphasizes, Foster sees at the root of the phenomenon of universal peasant culture:

> Broad areas of peasant behavior are patterned in such fashion as to suggest that peasants view their social, economic, and natural universes— their total environment—as one in which all of the desired things in life such as land, wealth, health, friendship and love, manliness and honor, respect and status, power and influence, security and safety, *exist in finite quantity and are always in short supply,* as far as the peasant is concerned.

*I am reminded of the comment of a friend, a retired social worker in Boston, several of whose clients had been Haitian immigrants: "They are letting life happen to them."

Not only do these and all other "good things" exist in finite and limited quantities, but in addition *there is no way directly within peasant power to increase the available quantities.*[23] [Emphasis in original.]

Foster goes on to trace some of the implications of this world view. In the typical peasant society, an individual or a family can progress only at the expense of others. The typical peasant sees little or no relationship between work and technology on the one hand, and the acquisition of wealth on the other: one works to eat but not to create wealth. The Anglo-Saxon virtues of hard work and thrift are meaningless in peasant society because, given the limitations on land and technology, additional hard work does not produce additional income.

Peasants are individualistic, and each social unit sees itself in continual struggle with its neighbors for its share of scarce wealth. An individual or family who advances is viewed as a threat to the stability of the community, which behaves like crabs in a barrel. Similarly, the peasant avoids leadership roles, fearing that his motives will be suspect. In this kind of environment, it is not surprising to find that peasants seek wealthy and powerful patrons.

Peasant societies are cooperative only insofar as they honor reciprocal obligations. The concepts of community welfare and social responsibility are alien. Mutual suspicion limits cooperative solutions, including agricultural production and marketing cooperatives. The anecdote about the comments I heard in Thailand and the Philippines is a case in point.

The value and attitude system that Foster describes finds remarkably consistent corroboration in the work of a number of social scientists. In his milestone work, *The Moral Basis of a Backward Society,* Edward Banfield analyzes the social pathology of the then backward southern Italian town of Chiaromonte ("Montegrano") and arrives at a diagnosis strikingly similar to Foster's model.[24] The anthropologist Melville Herskovits's classic *Life in a Haitian Valley,* first published in 1937, describes a peasant society that functions very much according to the universal model. Moreover, Herskovits notes the close cultural parallels between Haiti and the West African region from which the ancestors of the Haitian people were imported by the French as slaves.[25] Henry Wells, a political scientist, describes Puerto Rico as profoundly influenced by a traditional Hispanic culture similar in many respects to the universal peasant model.[26] David

Korten uses the Foster model as the basic structure of his 1972 study of Ethiopian peasants.[27] Herbert Phillips's conclusions on the limits of cooperation of peasants in Thailand are virtually identical to Foster's model.[28] Finally, Frank Moya Pons, a historian, sees not only peasants in the Dominican Republic as conforming to the universal model but also urban dwellers, including the elite.[29]

Many anthropologists believe that peasant value systems have their roots in the cities. Foster says, "if we examine the content of any peasant community, we are struck by how many of its elements represent simplified, village manifestations of ideas and artifacts which originated in the city at an earlier period: Religious beliefs and practices, linguistic forms, costumes, house furnishings, forms of social organization."[30] Whether traditional, static culture was propagated from the cities to the rural areas or vice versa, it is clear that the value and attitude systems that resist progress permeate the entire underdeveloped society, from the barefoot, illiterate peasant to the ostensibly urbane, educated city dweller. Notwithstanding the close parallels between Foster's and Grondona's observations, Grondona was principally describing the culture of cosmopolitan Buenos Aires.

The cultural pathology of underdevelopment is a vital backdrop for this book, in which the principal objectives are to develop a better appreciation of the array of factors that have contributed to national and ethnic group *success;* the relative importance of cultural factors, traditional or recent; what those cultural factors are; the way they may have changed; and the way they have promoted progress or stood in its way.

CULTURAL DETERMINISM?

The collapse of communism in Eastern Europe has driven the final nail into the coffin of Marx's theories of economic determinism. The word *determinism* has acquired a bad odor because of its link to Marx, and rightly so. It is abundantly apparent that no one factor can fully explain or predict the variations in human and societal behavior and progress. In the process of rejecting various "determinisms," Ronald Inglehart says, "we do make a more limited claim, however: that culture is an essential causal element that helps shape

society—and a factor that today tends to be underestimated."³¹
There is a further question, however. What if culture is the most
important of the several factors?

I believe that to be true in all the examples addressed in this book.
Chapters 1–4 look at five national success stories that have at one
time or another been described as "miracles": Brazil, Spain, Taiwan,
Korea, and Japan. Brazil's economic performance over the past century has been extraordinary, yet its lagging political and social evolution are not all that different from the Latin American mainstream.
Spain, after centuries of authoritarianism, social injustice, and economic stagnation highly evocative of the experience of its former
colonies in the New World, has, in a period of three decades, vaulted
into the ranks of the advanced Western European democracies.
Taiwan and Korea were backward Japanese colonies during the first
half of this century, fairly faithful replicas of China before that.
Perhaps least surprising of the "miracles" for students of history is
Japan. Japan's remarkable performance since its disastrous defeat by
the United States in World War II was presaged by Japan's remarkable performance during the Meiji Restoration, following the appearance of the American fleet in Tokyo Bay in 1853.

In each case, I believe that cultural factors have been crucial: the
values and attitudes of European and Japanese immigrants in the
case of Brazil; Spain's post–World War II opening to the West, the
Enlightenment, and the Industrial Revolution, after centuries of
self-imposed isolation; and the power of the Confucian ethos in the
cases of Taiwan, Korea, and Japan.

The list is obviously not comprehensive. The progress of West
Germany, Italy, Hong Kong, Singapore, and other countries has also
been called miraculous. But the five countries I have selected speak
for more than just themselves. Taiwan and Korea are good proxies
for Hong Kong and Singapore (the quartet is often referred to as "the
four dragons"), as well as for the overseas Chinese. Although there
are major differences in the two cultures (and maybe some important
similarities too, for example, in work ethic), Japan and West Germany have both risen from the ashes of World War II to become
international economic powerhouses. Spain is to some extent a latter-
day surrogate for Italy and quite possibly a precursor of Portugal and
Latin America.

Chapter 5's discussion of three ethnic groups in the United
States—the Chinese, the Japanese, and the Koreans—is in one re-

spect a corroboration of the findings of the previous two chapters, in another an important backdrop for the two ethnic groups discussed in chapters 6 and 7: Mexican-Americans, whose acculturation to the American mainstream has been disturbingly slow; and black Americans, two-thirds of whom have made it into that mainstream, while the one-third in the ghetto live isolated from it, as did their ancestors under slavery and Jim Crow.

I am profoundly troubled by the mounting evidence of decline in the United States: the budget and trade deficits, the savings and loan debacle, the penury of our states and cities, the drug and crime epidemics, the sleaze on Wall Street and in Washington, the disturbing condition of our education system, the inferior quality of some American products, a lifestyle of rapid gratification and self-indulgence, intensifying racial and ethnic divisions. I believe that value erosion is at the root of these problems. In the final chapter, I pull together the main threads of the preceding chapters and offer a personal essay on the condition of the United States that attempts to be both diagnosis and prescription.

PART I

SUCCESS STORIES

1

Brazil

Immigrant Entrepreneurs Drive Growth

*Between 1920 and 1988 the average growth rate of GDP per capita
in Brazil was 3.4 percent [among the highest in the world].*
—Eliana Cardoso, "Debt Cycles in Brazil and Argentina," 1991

*Brazil's social welfare indicators are strikingly low. . . . In the
northeast of Brazil [infant mortality] is higher than in much of
Sub-Saharan Africa. . . . Only 21 percent of Brazilian children
attend secondary school, compared to 90 percent in Korea.*
—Ibid.

*Despite narrowly oligarchic and corrupt government, Brazil pros-
pered. Following the abolition of slavery, immigration flowed from
Europe. . . . Their numbers were never comparable to those going
to the United States . . . and . . . Argentina, but they were largely
responsible for the growth of industry.*
—Robert Wesson and David V. Fleischer, *Brazil in Transition*
(1983)

Since I started working with development problems in Latin America in the early 1960s, people have been telling me that Brazil is
different. It is obviously different by virtue of its size: larger than the
forty-eight contiguous American states; larger than Australia; more
than two-and-a-half times larger than India; three times larger than
Argentina. But what people who know Brazil usually mean is that
Brazilians have certain qualities that make them different from other
Latin Americans. A senior American diplomat describes dealing with
Brazilian foreign ministry officials as comparable to dealing with
Western European professionals. An American businessman who
experienced great frustration in other Latin American countries calls
his visits to Brazil a breath of fresh air, comparable to working with
private-sector people in the most advanced countries. The *New York
Times*'s Marlise Simons, who has lived in Brazil and Mexico for a
number of years, described Brazilians to me as being like Americans
in their optimism, can-do attitude, and belief in the future—and

unlike Hispanic Americans, for example, the Mexicans, who are so focused on the past. And Landon Lockett, an American who taught for five years in a Brazilian university, told me "Hispanic Americans are a bundle of complexes, preoccupied with 'dignity.' Brazilians are casual."

The indicators of progress, however, are not so clear-cut. They give a decidedly mixed picture of where Brazil stands with respect to the rest of Latin America.[1] With a 1989 per capita GNP of $2,540, Brazil falls in the World Bank's "upper-middle-income" category, above Argentina and Venezuela. Life expectancy in Brazil, at sixty-six years, is about average for Latin America. A reported adult literacy rate of 78 percent in 1985 is also about average for Latin America.[2] Brazil's income distribution, reported for 1983 but probably not significantly different today, is the most inequitable of the forty-one countries around the world that provided data to the World Bank: the most affluent 10 percent of the population accounted for 46.2 percent of the nation's income.

Unlike most other Latin American countries, Brazil achieved independence peacefully, with a member of the Portuguese royalty as monarch. But since the almost simultaneous end of monarchy and slavery a hundred years ago, Brazil's political evolution has been more or less typical of Latin American authoritarian patterns. The traditional oligarchy, rooted in plantation agriculture, dominated politics during most of the period; chiefs of state have usually gained power through means other than open elections; democratic institutions are fragile; due process is the exception rather than the rule; and the military, who ruled Brazil from 1964 to 1985, remain the ultimate arbiters of the political process.

But Brazil's economic performance since the early 1900s has outstripped that of all other Latin American countries, including oil-rich Mexico and Venezuela. Indeed, for much of this century, Brazil has grown faster than any other large country in the world except Japan. Between 1965 and 1980, Brazil's GNP growth averaged 9 percent annually. In 1965, Brazil's was the fifteenth largest economy in the world; in 1987, it was the eighth largest, having overtaken Australia, China, India, Mexico, the Netherlands, Spain, and Sweden. In 1987, Brazil, with a population of about 145 million, produced more than did China, with a population over one billion.[3]

In terms of its economic performance, then, Brazil qualifies as a success story, at least through 1980. Since then, growth, burdened by Brazil's heavy debt overhang, among other factors, has slowed to below 3 percent annually; inflation had accelerated to triple- and even quadruple-digit levels prior to the installation of the Collor de Mello government in 1990; the democratic experiment continues but still must be regarded as fragile; and the normally optimistic Brazilians have been sending their capital out of the country and even emigrating, particularly to the United States. Several of the Brazilians with whom I spoke during a visit late in 1988—people who had talked of the Brazilian "miracle" fifteen years ago—observed either that God was not, after all, a Brazilian or that Brazil would be more aptly discussed in *Underdevelopment Is a State of Mind* than in this book.

Brazilian politics and Brazilian society, then, appear clearly to be in the Latin American mainstream—more of the nineteenth century than of the twentieth—but Brazil's economic growth in this century is quite another story.

HISTORICAL OVERVIEW

A review of Brazilian history shows fairly close parallels between its political, economic, and social evolution as a colony and that of the Spanish colonies. Pedro Álvares Cabral discovered Brazil in 1500, six years after Spain and Portugal signed the Treaty of Tordesillas, which established a north-south line 370 leagues west of the Cape Verde Islands as the demarcation between Spain's (to the west) and Portugal's (to the east) colonial rights. Brazil's colonization until the gold rush of the eighteenth century was largely confined to the Atlantic littoral, and its early economy was dominated by sugar production on slave plantations in the northeastern region of the country. Most of the slaves were imported from the Portuguese colonies in Africa, but there were also internal slaving operations whose quarry was the Indian, particularly in the sixteenth and seventeenth centuries. The slave-hunting parties, or *bandeiras*, were mostly organized in São Paulo and were the first significant source of income for what would become the richest state, and the largest city, in Brazil. Members of the *bandeiras* were referred to as *bandeirantes*, and it is they whom Clodomir Vianna Moog compares with "pioneers" as the symbol of the fundamental cultural differences between Brazil and the United States in his fascinating book *Bandeirantes e Pioneiros.* [4]

Portugal's economic policies were similar to the mercantilist policies of Spain. That meant that Brazil exported what it produced—principally sugar, gold, and gemstones during the colonial period—to Portugal and increasingly to England, with which Portugal had a special trading arrangement from early in the eighteenth century, one that endured in Brazil even after independence. Brazil imported from Portugal and England everything it needed but didn't produce. Mercantilism also meant the Portuguese tried to control agricultural, commercial, and industrial activity in the colony, part of a general policy of suppression of Brazilian competition with the homeland, although not as suffocating as in the Spanish colonies.

A further brake on economic development was the Ibero-Catholic anti-entrepreneurial, antiwork tradition. (The Brazilian expert Charles Wagley cites the "old and popular" Brazilian saying *Trabalho e para cachorro e negro*—"Work is for dogs and blacks.")[5] Current evidence of this tradition is found in the World Bank's World Development Report. In 1987, Portugal's per capita GNP was $2,830, the lowest in Western Europe and only $800 higher than Brazil's. (Spain's per capita GNP was more than twice Portugal's but was nonetheless the third lowest in Western Europe.) The World Bank grouped Portugal (also Brazil and Greece) with the upper-middle-income countries,[6] not with the industrial-market economies of Western Europe, North America, and Japan.[7]

Colonial social policy was strongly influenced by the church. A well-known Brazilian lay Catholic anthropologist, Thales de Azevedo, has written, "Brazilian Catholicism inherited from Portuguese culture a certain softness, tolerance and malleability which an exalted, turbulent and hard Spanish religious character did not know."[8] One consequence was a less harsh treatment of Jews at the time of the Inquisition. But except for the Jesuits, the Portuguese priests were committed to a status quo that endorsed slavery, perpetuated and exploited ignorance, participated in an economic system that concentrated land, wealth, and power in a few hands, and countenanced violence and bloodshed. The priests also indulged in worldly pleasures.[9] The church became an institution of wealth and power intimately linked to the plantation power structure through the custom of one of the plantation owner's sons joining the priesthood.

As in the Spanish colonies, the church controlled ("suppressed" may be more accurate) education. This meant heavy emphasis on classical studies and religion for the tiny fraction of the population, mostly children of the elite, who had access to the only schools—church schools.[10] Portuguese mercantilism extended to education: the printing press was not legalized until 1808, when the Portuguese court emigrated to Brazil ahead of Napoleon's occupation.

A Peaceful Independence

In 1822, Brazil passed peacefully from colony to independent Brazilian Empire under the leadership of the Portuguese Prince Regent, Dom Pedro, who became Emperor Pedro I, and his Austrian wife, Leopoldina von Hapsburg. The peaceful passage to independence contrasts with the violence that marked the dissolution of the Hispanic American empire and is often cited by Brazilians as both evidence and a cause of their more "peaceful" national temperament.

But, as in the former Spanish colonies, independence in no fundamental way altered the traditional colonial patterns of authoritarianism, concentration of economic power, and social injustice. The authoritarianism was diluted only by strong regional decentralizing pressures from the authoritarian "colonels" of the landed aristocracy, who generated a continuing tension with the authoritarian crown, a tension that occasionally erupted in separatist violence. The monarchy continued under the enlightened, scholarly, and development-conscious Pedro II until 1889, its downfall precipitated in part by the emancipation of the slaves the preceding year. The rigidity of the social system is apparent from the continuing elitism in education. Wagley observes that, in 1871, when Brazil's population totaled about ten million, "only about 150,000 were receiving an elementary education and less than 10,000 a secondary education."[11] The implications for social mobility are obvious.

For forty years following the demise of the empire, Brazil experimented with republican institutions—the period is often referred to as "the Old Republic." During this period, civilian politicians, for the most part representing the landed aristocracy, were dominant, although the military was the ultimate arbiter of politics. Robert Wesson and David V. Fleischer observe, "After administering the country fairly well for a couple of decades, the political elite had failed entirely to absorb the new forces of the growing nation. The oligarchy, to the contrary, narrowed itself: the percentage of the population voting actually decreased, from 2.5 percent in 1894 to 2 percent in 1926, and leaders refused to consider such an elementary step toward democracy as the secret ballot."[12]

In a break with prior political traditions, the populist Getulio Vargas came to power as a dictator through the Revolution of 1930, ruling his "new state" autocratically until 1945 and presiding over an industrial surge. Vargas was ousted by the military in 1945, and a democratic constitution was passed in 1946 that was clearly designed to rein in the power of the chief executive. Vargas was returned to office by free elections in 1951 but committed suicide in 1954 when the military insisted that he resign. With the 1946 constitution still in effect, Juscelino Kubitschek was elected for a five-year term in 1955, and the economy, particularly the industrial sector, continued to flourish.

With the resignation of Kubitschek's successor, Janio Quadros, after seven months in office, Vice President João Goulart, a left-leaning populist, moved up to the presidency. From the outset of his three and one-half years in power, the military, along with conservative and moderate elements, were uneasy with the direction in which he was taking the country. When, in 1964, Goulart attempted to go over the heads of the military commanders in a direct appeal to enlisted personnel, the military ousted him, commencing twenty-one years of military rule, which fostered the economic miracle but had limited impact on Brazil's chronic, extreme social injustice.

The Military Departs

Brazil has the largest Catholic population of any country in the world. Since Pope John XXIII shifted Catholicism's emphasis from the afterlife to this life, the Church has become a major force in Brazilian politics. Some 70,000 church-based communities have been created in the past twenty-five years, "a network . . . that reached the people as no other organization in Brazil could."[13] In 1964, the Church, in opposition to "godless communism," supported the ouster of Goulart. But by the end of the decade, when the Church openly opposed the military government, many priests, nuns, and lay Catholic activists were arrested. Some were tortured.

Through the years of military government from 1964 to 1985, the Church was the best-organized, most effective critic and opponent of the military's human rights abuses and the trickle-down growth policies responsible for Brazil's economic miracle. The Church's center of gravity shifted steadily leftward, to the point where private property and capitalism had become equated with evil. Considering Brazil's extreme social inequities, it should not be surprising that it has become a bastion of Liberation Theology, a splinter movement rooted in Marxist-Leninist redistribution. The Church was to play an important role in the electoral victories of the left in 1988, and many priests and nuns worked for the candidacy of the leftist Luis Inácio da Silva ("Lula"), who narrowly lost the 1990 presidential election to Fernando Collor de Mello.

Indirect elections were held early in 1985, but the winner, Tancredo Neves, representing antimilitary forces, died soon after he was inaugurated, and his vice president, José Sarney, took over. Heir to expansionary economic policies continued by the military despite the oil price shocks of the 1970s—policies that were dependent on heavy borrowing from abroad—Sarney presided over a period of record inflation, reduced economic growth, chronic social problems, and growing popularity of populist and Marxist politicians.[14] Symbolic of the disaffection of the electorate was the victory of the Workers' Party's Luiza Erundina in the November 1988 mayoral elections in São Paulo, the hotbed of Brazilian capitalism and the principal engine of the economic miracle. Erundina, a fervent admirer of Sandinista Nicaragua,[15] won with the support of the poor, the Liberation Theology wing of the Catholic Church,[16] and a significant number of centrist and conservative voters alienated by the ineptness and corruption of the national government.

By 1989, the last full year of his administration, Sarney had been totally discredited, and the durability of the renewed Brazilian experiment with democracy was in doubt. Against a backdrop of four-digit inflation, the conservative populist Collor de Mello, with about 53 percent of the vote, defeated the Workers' Party candidate da Silva, with about 47 percent of the vote, in elections early in 1990. Collor de Mello moved quickly against inflation by imposing monetary and fiscal austerity, including the privatization of state enterprises, but two years later the stabilization program was in serious trouble. Collor de Mello's popularity has plunged, and it is far from certain that Brazil's still-fragile democratic institutions will survive the prolonged economic distress.

This brief overview of Brazilian history should make it clear that Brazil's political and social evolution is similar to the Hispanic American mainstream. Brazil's "patrimonial politics," controlled by an authoritarian (albeit muted, by Hispanic standards) and paternalistic elite that has nurtured the dependency psychology of patron-client relationships and discouraged popular participation,[17] smacks strongly of traditional Hispanic American politics. But Brazil's economic performance stands out.

Economic Dynamism

Brazil is richly endowed with natural resources. It possesses large reserves of iron, manganese, nickel, tin, chromium, bauxite, beryllium, copper, lead, tungsten, and zinc. Gold, silver, and precious and semiprecious stones are extracted in commercial quantities. Although Brazil's production of petroleum has increased significantly in the last decade, it still must import about 50 percent of the petroleum it needs. Its coal deposits are low-grade, but its hydroelectric resources now account for 90 percent of its electricity generation.

Brazil also boasts vast agricultural resources. From the mid-sixteenth to the mid-seventeenth centuries, the plantations of northeastern Brazil dominated world sugar production, and sugar continues to be a major crop to this day, both for export and domestic table consumption and for conversion to alcohol for vehicle fuel. Coffee was introduced in Brazil in the first half of the nineteenth century and soon became Brazil's principal export. Today, Brazil is the world's largest exporter of coffee and orange juice concentrate; the second largest exporter of cocoa and soybeans; and a major exporter of sugar, meat, and cotton. It is substantially self-sufficient in food, wheat being the exception. Yet subsistence agriculture continues as a way of life for millions of *camponeses,* particularly in the northeast.

Moreover, there is a lot of room for expanding acreage dedicated to agriculture. While the underdeveloped Amazon basin, particularly its rain forests, is best known outside Brazil because of preoccupation with the worldwide ecological implications of its development, the recent cultivation of new land in other areas away from the coast— Goiás, Mato Grosso, Mato Grosso do Sul—has made possible Brazil's soaring soybean production.

Brazil achieved extremely high economic growth rates from the late 1960s through the 1970s: between 1968 and 1973, its annual GNP growth averaged more than 11 percent annually; it averaged 8.4 percent from 1970 to 1981. But this performance must be viewed against the historical backdrop. As we noted at the outset of this chapter, the economist Eliana Cardoso has observed that, between

1920 and 1988, the average annual per capita GDP growth rate was 3.4 percent, implying an average annual GDP growth of about 6 percent sustained over a sixty-eight-year period, probably the most rapid economic expansion in the world, except for Japan, during that time.[18] During those same sixty-eight years, Argentina's per capita GDP grew at a 1 percent annual rate. And, we should note, Brazil's population growth rate, which approximated 3 percent annually during the 1950s and 1960s, was much higher than Argentina's for most of the period. (Brazil's population growth rate is now below 2 percent.)

Brazil's industrial production expanded at an annual rate of 9.9 percent from 1965 to 1980, even faster than Japan's.[19] From 1930 to 1940, the number of Brazil's industrial plants tripled; industrial production increased at an average annual rate of 11 percent from 1933 to 1939.[20] The growth had been initiated largely by immigrants, starting in the late nineteenth century. Further impetus was provided by the scarcity of imported goods during world wars I and II, and by the decreasing influence of the aristocracy, particularly after Vargas put an end to the Old Republic.[21]

While Brazil sustained a 7.1 percent annual GNP growth rate from 1947 to 1974, the economist Edmar Bacha notes that an important pause occurred as a result of the political turmoil during 1961–67, and, with Brazil's long-sustained economic dynamism in mind, he correctly observes that "the . . . growth experience under military rule is better described as a vigorous economic recovery than an 'economic miracle.' "[22] That something less than an economic revolution was occurring is also suggested by the modest changes in the composition of Brazil's overall production. In 1960, agriculture accounted for 16 percent, industry 35 percent, and services 49 percent;[23] in 1986, agriculture accounted for 11 percent, industry for 39 percent, and services for 50 percent.[24]

The only unprecedented change in the Brazilian economy during the past few decades has been the explosive growth of industrial exports. The value of industrial exports was $134 million in 1965, $11.8 billion in 1987. In 1965, the value of exports of primary products exceeded the value of industrial exports by a ratio of 9 to 1. In 1987, the ratio was 5.5 to 4.5.[25]

Brazil's economic growth in this century has thus been extraordinary, but it is far from a recent phenomenon. We must inquire into the forces that have generated this dynamism, which is atypical of Ibero-American countries. But as we do, we should keep in mind another Brazilian phenomenon. Sustained high levels of GNP growth, particularly involving rapid industrial expansion, usually lead to significant improvements in the standard of living of the lower classes, as in East Asia. This has not happened in Brazil, where today "64.7% of the economically active population . . . lives at levels that vary from misery . . . to extreme poverty."[26]

BRAZILIAN CULTURE

Brazilians, and foreigners who have lived in Brazil, often emphasize the differences between Spanish and Portuguese culture as central to the differences between Hispanic American countries and Brazil. These differences are often framed in words that imply Brazilian superiority, a self-image that was repeatedly communicated to me during my 1988 visit, a self-image that says, "We're really much more like you North Americans than we are like the Hispanic Americans."

Live and Let Live

The Brazilian sociologist Gilberto Freyre wrote extensively of the Portuguese influence on Brazilian culture and "has portrayed the Portuguese as an especially adaptable, racially tolerant, and malleable people."[27] Evidence of Portuguese resilience and tolerance, particularly in comparison with Spain, appears throughout modern history and has been touched on earlier in this book: the far less cruel treatment of the Jews in Portugal than in Spain during the Inquisition; Portugal's successful relationships with the xenophobic Japanese in the sixteenth century; the relatively enlightened management of Portugal's African colonies; Brazil's peaceful transition to independence. In Portuguese bullfights, the bull is not killed (the same is true, by the way, in Costa Rica). And as a final example of Portuguese flexibility, pragmatism, and humaneness, there is the story, perhaps apocryphal, of the Portuguese admiral who, at the moment of engagement with a Spanish fleet, requested a meeting with the Spanish admiral. "How many ships do you have?" he asked the Spaniard, who replied, "Two hundred." The Portuguese then said, "I have one hundred. You win." Whereupon he withdrew his fleet.

Fernando Díaz-Plaja, author of the Spanish best-seller *El Español y Los Siete Pecados Capitales (The Spaniard and the Seven Deadly Sins)*, finds the essence of Spanish national character in *soberbia*— pride, with overtones of arrogance, haughtiness, and vanity.[28] "Honor" and "dignity" drive the Spaniard, particularly the male, to confrontation and extremism, a point driven home by Cervantes in *Don Quixote*. By contrast, the "softness" in what Freyre calls "Luso-tropical" temperament is reflected in the oft-mentioned tendency of Brazilians to be less prone to confrontation and violence than Hispanic Americans. "Brazilians believe in 'live and let live,'" John Hugh Crimmins, U.S. ambassador to Brazil from 1973 to 1978, who has also served in Hispanic America, told me. One often hears, from both Brazilians and foreigners, that Brazilians have a knack for solving problems, for cutting deals, for *jeito*—doing what's necessary to fix things. (Interestingly, however, as in Spanish, there is apparently no Portuguese word that accurately translates the English *compromise*.)[29] Freyre, who studied for many years in the United States and had an excellent command of English, says: "The secret of Brazil's humane, Christian and modern civilization in tropical America has been her genius for compromise. While the British, as no other people, have had this genius for compromise in the political sphere . . . the Brazilians have been successful in using this same power of compromise in the cultural and social spheres."[30]

Freyre's view of Brazilian society is, however, romanticized and aristocratic, as María Alice Aguiar de Medeiros points out in her trenchant book, *O Elogio da Dominação (In Praise of Domination)*.[31] In de Medeiros's view, which contemporary data bear out, the plantation relationships that Freyre described in his best-known work, *Casa-Grande e Senzala* (the English version is titled *The Masters and the Slaves*), and that he implies typify Brazil generally, are not humane, Christian, or modern. De Medeiros focuses on the authoritarian and exploitative nature of those relationships and on their rigid hierarchy, factors that evoke the strikingly similar characteristics of Hispanic America and, indeed, plantation slavery wherever it occurred. She also exposes the disguised racism that is a fact of Brazilian life, a reality underscored by outspoken criticism of their second-class citizenship by Brazilian blacks during the centennial of emancipation in 1988.[32]

The highly skewed pattern of income distribution I mentioned is one indicator supporting de Medeiros's conclusions. More recent analysis of social conditions in Brazil provides further support for her views. Table 1.1 is, in my view, an indictment of those who have exercised political and economic power over the centuries. "Live and let live" for those with power has been a license for social irresponsibility, for social narcissism, in stark contrast with the tradition of noblesse oblige that has played such an important role in the evolution of the far more equitable societies of Western Europe, Canada, the United States, Australia, and East Asia.[33] The comment of a Presbyterian Brazilian to a friend of mine is apt: Brazilians are not tolerant; they're indifferent. In this connection, it is noteworthy that there is virtually no significant tradition of philanthropy in Brazil, nor, for that matter, anywhere else in Latin America.

Essentially, table 1.1 shows that social conditions in Brazil as a whole are slightly worse than in Chile, Mexico, and Colombia, and dramatically worse than in Korea. It also substantially debunks the oft-heard notion that the appalling social conditions in the northeast disguise the highly progressive conditions in the rest of the country (although there is obviously a large gap between the two regions).

I believe that there is truth in the generalization that Brazilians (and Portuguese) are more resilient and tolerant than Hispanic Americans (and Spaniards). As we shall see, those qualities have played a crucial role in Brazil's response to the more progressive values and attitudes of immigrants. But Brazil's resilience and tolerance clearly have not expressed themselves in social progress and equity, although there has been some improvement in recent years,

TABLE 1.1
SOCIAL INDICATORS

	Infant Mortality Rate (per 1,000 live births)		Life Expectancy at Birth		Secondary School Enrollment[a]	
	1965	1985	1965	1985	1965	1985
Northeast Brazil	125 (1976)	116	46	49 (1978)	3	15
Rest of Brazil	75 (1976)	52	58	64 (1978)	11	25
BRAZIL	104	67	55	65	6	21
CHILE	107	22	57	67	34	66
MEXICO	82	50	58	64	16	35
COLOMBIA	96	48	54	63	17	49
KOREA	63	27	55	65	35	91

[a]Percentage of secondary school–age youths attending secondary school.
Source: World Bank, Brazil: Public Spending on Social Programs: Issues and Options (Washington, D.C., 27 May 1988), p. 1.

as in most Latin American countries. Brazil's social inequity places it in the mainstream of Latin America, and the roots of that inequity are to be found in the same place as those of Mexico, or Guatemala, or Peru: in the traditional Iberian world view and the values and attitudes that flow from it.

Familism, Authoritarianism, and Catholicism

Let's look at Brazilian culture in terms of the four factors discussed in the introductory chapter: radius of trust and identification; rigor of the ethical system, particularly its religious roots; exercising of authority; and attitudes about work and innovation.

Wagley begins his discussion of the Brazilian family with these statements: "There seems to be unanimous agreement among students of Brazilian social history that the family has been in the past the most important single institution of Brazilian society. . . . While in other Latin American cultures familism has been an important aspect of social life, in Brazil, there has been almost a cult of the family."[34] Gilberto Freyre was a high priest of the cult: "The family and not the individual, much less the State or any commercial company, was from the sixteenth century the great colonizing factor in Brazil, the productive unit, the capital that cleared the land, founded plantations, purchased slaves, oxen, implements; and in politics it was the social force that set itself up as the most powerful colonial aristocracy in the Americas."[35]

The social consequences of familism in Brazil follow what appears to be a universal pattern, a pattern evident throughout Hispanic America: a limited radius of social identification resulting in lack of concern for the interests and well-being of people outside the family, and for the society as a whole; the generalized absence of trust throughout the society; the absence of due process in a judicial system in which *jeito* plays a prominent role;[36] fragmentation of politics and low incidence of organized group solutions to common problems; nepotism and corruption; tax evasion; absence of philanthropy; and, with respect to what Mariano Grondona refers to as "the lesser virtues," daily small antisocial acts such as the indiscriminate disposal of trash in vacant lots and gutters.

Familism, particularly among Freyre's elite, nurtures a self-absorption and narcissism that closely parallel the traditional Spanish self-caricature, *Que viva yo!*— "Long live I!" The narcissism is linked to

the highly authoritarian relationships in the family, indeed throughout the society, with the father in the role of the *caudillo* (dictator)
and the sons raised to emulate the father.[37] Listen to the comments
of several writers who know Brazil well:

- The Brazilian social anthropologist Roberto DaMatta, the author of *A Casa e a Rua (At Home and on the Street)*, which
  describes the sharp contrasts between the Brazilian's behavior
  within the family and with strangers, says: "If I am buying from
  or selling to a relative, I neither seek profit nor concern myself
  with money. The same can happen in a transaction with a
  friend. But, if I am dealing with a stranger, then there are no
  rules, other than the one of exploiting him to the utmost."[38]
- J. O. de Meira Penna, a retired Brazilian diplomat, social commentator, and columnist, observes: "in Brazil, the public service is not popularly thought of as an institution that offers and
  receives *services,* rather one that offers and receives *favors.* "[39]
- Charles Wagley: "In keeping with the important role of kinship
  in political life, it is not strange that nepotism was rife in
  Brazilian government service."[40]
- The Brazilian sociologist María Lucía Victor Barbosa: "The
  governing classes are characterized by corruption, nepotism,
  ideological inconsistency, absence of a vision of the common
  good, demagogy, opportunism. . . . The exercise of public power
  in Brazil . . . implies chronic incompetence combined with
  crookedness."[41]
- The president of the Confederation of Industries of São Paulo,
  Mario Amato: "Brazil is characterized by lack of respect for
  human life, by systematic violation of the law, by neglect by the
  authorities, by generalized corruption, and by the decadence of
  its customs."[42]

The best Brazilian universities are the state universities, which are
free. But to enter, one must pass a rigorous test, one that few who
attend public primary and secondary schools can pass. More than 90
percent of the students at the state universities are graduates of
private secondary schools, which are usually expensive. In most cases,
graduates of *public* secondary schools can only get into *private* universities that require tuition payments and are in most cases inferior
to the free state universities.

As is strongly implied by the foregoing, the Brazilian ethical code, principally a derivative of traditional Iberian Catholicism, is less morally exigent than Protestant or Jewish ethical systems. We are again reminded of Weber's words: "The God of Calvinism demanded of his believers not single good works, but a life of good works combined into a unified system. There was no place for the very human Catholic cycle of sin, repentance, atonement, release, followed by renewed sin."[43] The moral flexibility of traditional Iberian Catholicism is reinforced by familism, which sanctifies a double ethical standard for dealings within the family, on the one hand, and with the broader society, on the other.

Given the pervasiveness of familism and traditional Ibero-Catholic ethics in Brazil, it is not difficult to understand how Brazilian society as described in table 1.1 came about.

African Cults and Protestantism

Large numbers of Brazilians of African ancestry practice traditional African cults that slaves brought to Brazil. They are particularly popular in the larger cities. The cults—known by regional names such as *candomble, xango, and macumba*—derive principally from West African folk religions akin to Haitian *vodun* (voodoo). As in Haiti, they tend to merge with Catholicism. The cult spirits, for instance, are commonly identified with Catholic saints. There is little or no ethical content to most of the cults, and they perpetuate a superstitious world view that tends to shackle their adherents to the lower economic and social levels of Brazilian society.

As in a number of other Latin American countries, Protestantism has burgeoned in Brazil in recent decades. There were 1,741,000 Brazilians who identified themselves as Protestants in a 1950 census; today the number may exceed twenty million.[44] "They are thought of as perhaps more moral than others; Protestants do not generally drink alcohol or smoke, and they are known to have a stable and worthy family life . . . conversion to Protestantism is generally a resultant and concomitant of social mobility. . . . it stresses hard work."[45]

The spread of Protestantism has reinforced the previously mentioned Portuguese tradition of exercising authority and power with greater moderation, resilience, and tolerance than is customary in

Hispanic societies. The historic wellspring of Protestantism has been European—above all, German—immigration, although immigrants from the American South following the Civil War and American missionaries have also had some impact, the latter particularly in recent years.

EXPLAINING BRAZIL'S ECONOMIC DYNAMISM

Clearly, Brazil's immensity and rich resource endowment are relevant to its economic performance in this century. I believe that its size has a lot to do with the optimism that has characterized Brazilians until recently; with the Brazilian focus on the future; with the perhaps not-altogether-tongue-in-cheek assertion that God is a Brazilian. Brazilians perceive that the size of their country and its richness should assure a promising future, that Brazil should become an increasingly powerful and affluent actor on the world scene.

But Brazil's size and resource endowment are not enough to explain the economic success. If it were, Argentina, one-third the size of Brazil but almost as large as India and blessed with vast amounts of very fertile land and substantial mineral resources, would be resoundingly successful. Indeed, early in this century, when Brazil was a very poor, backwater country, Argentina was considered a developed country because of its high rates of growth, driven by its rich resource endowment, immigration, and foreign investment, principally British. But the subsequent relative decline of Argentina placed it in a lower World Bank category—"lower middle income"—in 1989, and Argentina's per capita GNP in 1989 was almost $400 lower than Brazil's. While Argentina's political problems have clearly hampered economic growth, Brazil's political history, although less violent, has not been all that different: neither country has demonstrated a vocation for democracy, and the military in both has played a dominant political role in recent decades. Perhaps the most important political difference has been the tendency of Brazilian governments, civilian and military, to concern themselves more purposefully with economic growth.[46]

But the principal explanation of Brazil's economic success resides, I believe, in the emergence of a large and dynamic Brazilian entrepreneurial class, industrial *and* agricultural, particularly in São Paulo and the states of the South. No such phenomenon has occurred in

Argentina, where "entrepreneurship" has usually taken the typical Hispanic American mercantilist form of a preference for commerce over industry, dependence on governmental protection, avoidance of competition, concentration on the domestic market and low export growth, emphasis on low volume and high prices, reluctance to innovate, and a generalized mistrust that has kept businesses at family scale. Behind these manifestations lies an authoritarian, individualistic, present-time-focused, antiplanning, and antiwork value and attitude system typical of Hispanic America.[47]

The overarching question is, Why did a large and dynamic entrepreneurial class emerge in Brazil? Surely, given Portugal's economic performance in the last two centuries, it would be difficult to make a case that the differences between Spanish and Portuguese culture are the explanation. In the case of Brazil, there is evidence that the principal impetus has come from immigrants from Europe and Japan.

The Positive Contribution by Immigrants

Until 1818, Portugal forbade the migration to Brazil of other than Portuguese nationals and slaves. In that year and the next, colonies of German-speaking Swiss were established in what were to become Rio de Janeiro and Bahia. By the middle of the nineteenth century, increasing pressure against slavery led São Paulo coffee growers to look to Europe for laborers for the booming coffee industry. Until that time, German-speaking Europeans constituted the bulk of immigrants. But they were found to adapt poorly to plantation work, and Brazil made an effort to attract immigrants from other parts of Europe, particularly southern Europe. From 1884 to 1939, more than four million people migrated to Brazil. Italians were the largest single ethnic group, accounting for 34 percent. Portuguese, Spaniards, Eastern Europeans, Japanese, and Germans all came in significant numbers.

In the early 1950s, the United Nations Educational, Scientific and Cultural Organization (UNESCO) sponsored a symposium on immigration that focused on five countries: Argentina, Australia, Brazil, the United Kingdom, and the United States. The symposium was coordinated by Professor Oscar Handlin of Harvard University, and the Brazil rapporteur was Dr. Emilio Willems. The proceedings were published by UNESCO as a book, entitled *The Positive Contribution by Immigrants*, in Paris in 1955. Unless otherwise noted, the information in this section derives from Dr. Willems's chapter on Brazil.

Some 55 percent of these immigrants settled in the state of São Paulo. That included more than 70 percent of the Italians, most of whom were from northern Italy,[48] and virtually all the Japanese. The bulk of the Germans and Eastern Europeans settled in the southern states of Rio Grande do Sul, Santa Catarina, and Paraná.[49]

Most of the German and Eastern European immigrants started in small-scale agriculture, particularly in new crops, such as potatoes, wheat, and vegetables. Gradually, they transformed Brazilian eating habits. But many of the German immigrants were artisans, and the virgin Brazilian market offered many opportunities to move out of cottage industries and into manufacturing plants. The economic division of labor that has endured since is described by Willems: "Germans and German-Brazilians still hold their positions as producers, whereas distribution and consumption is carried on mostly by Luso-Brazilians, on a nationwide basis."

The German artisans first turned to tanneries, saddleries, and shoe factories. In 1920, for example, 55 percent of Brazilian plants producing leather goods were owned by German-Brazilians. Germans also started the first textile mills, in 1874, and the first mechanical looms, in 1880. A 1950 census of industrial activity in the states of Rio Grande do Sul and Santa Catarina showed that almost 80 percent of the owners were not of Portuguese extraction, Germans, at 46 percent, being by far the largest single ethnic group. While there are no data to tell us what percent of the population was of German extraction, Willems observes, "it is safe to conclude that the 46% referring to entrepreneurs of German extraction far exceeds the proportion of both native and foreign-born Germans in those two states."

Italian immigrants in São Paulo, who numbered almost one million in 1940, also moved rapidly into industry, starting in the last decades of the nineteenth century. By 1950, Italians accounted for almost 48 percent of all industrial activity in the São Paulo metropolitan area, while those of Portuguese extraction accounted for 15 percent. Germans accounted for 2 percent of the São Paulo population but 10 percent of the industry, and Willems adds, "It is also safe to say that the participation of the Italians, Syrians and Lebanese as well as the category of 'others' (mainly Americans, British, Eastern European Jews, and French) . . . surpasses their proportions of the total population."

The experience of Japanese immigrants, the first 781 of whom arrived in 1908, has been similar. Today, there are almost one million

Brazilians of Japanese extraction. Most of the early settlers started on coffee plantations but moved rapidly into small farm operations of their own. Farmers of Japanese extraction started a cooperative in the 1920s that today counts more than fifteen thousand members in fifteen states. The co-op exports soybeans, fresh fruit, coffee, tea, cacao, and cotton, mostly to Japan.[50]

But Japanese farmers are also major suppliers of the domestic market. They produce about 70 percent of the fruit and vegetables eaten in São Paulo. They are also disproportionately influential in industry, banking, and—which will not come as a surprise in the light of the success of Japanese American students in the United States— the universities. They have also been successful in interesting home- land Japanese in investing in Brazil. Today, Japan is the third most important foreign investor, after the United States and Germany. The Japanese have invested in more than three hundred Brazilian enterprises.[51]

Brazil's extraordinary economic performance in this century can be attributed in large part to the creative capacity of immigrants from countries (including the northern part of Italy) that have sub- stantially outperformed Portugal over the past few centuries.

The Contrasting Immigration Experiences of Brazil and Argentina

Argentina has sometimes been referred to as a "European" country because of the large immigrant component in its population. Tomás Roberto Fillol makes the point that this thinking is deceptive; more than 80 percent of the Argentine people are of either Spanish or Italian extraction, and the cultural parallels between Spain and Italy are very close.[52] But in fact, the immigrant waves of the second half of the nineteenth century played a major role in the rapid develop- ment of Argentina's vast resources during its Golden Age, along with foreign capital, principally British. Robert Foerster wrote in 1919 that, "Without the immigration of the past half century the gigantic strides of Argentina would not have been taken. Without the coming of the Italians, the forward movement must have been slow."[53] Among other things, the Italians were chiefly responsible for the development of crop agriculture; prior to their arrival, virtually all land had been dedicated to livestock.

Moreover, there are also significant German, British, and Jewish immigrant communities in Argentina. (Half a million Jews live there, making it the fifth largest Jewish community in the world, after the United States, Israel, the Soviet Union, and France.) In fact, both Brazil and Argentina received on the order of four million immigrants of similar ethnic profile from the mid-nineteenth to the mid-twentieth century. Immigrants therefore represent a far larger percentage of Argentina's far smaller total population. Is it then logical to point to immigration as the primary explanation of Brazil's extraordinary economic performance in this century? Or to pose it as a former U.S. Ambassador to Brazil, Harry Shlaudeman, did in a 1988 conversation with me: "Why have Brazil's Italians done so much better than Argentina's Italians?" (Shlaudeman has also represented the United States in Buenos Aires.)

Part of the explanation may lie in the fact that the large majority of Italians who migrated to Brazil were from northern Italy, traditionally more progressive and entrepreneurial than the south. Until about 1905, the bulk of Italians who migrated to Argentina were also from the north. Early in the twentieth century, however, sharp rises in agricultural land values put land beyond the reach of immigrants, and the composition of Italian immigrants shifted dramatically. Thereafter, in Foerster's words, "the South Italians . . . flooded to . . . Buenos Aires . . . without much rising from the humble places, they have been excavators, street pavers, teamsters, porters, barbers, shoemakers, and petty shopkeepers. Their concentration in the vast seaport city is less a reflection of poverty on arrival than of their somewhat unenterprising or ignorant dependence upon a great employment market."[54] Today there is roughly an even division between Argentines of northern and southern Italian origins.

The main difference between the two countries with respect to immigration, however, appears to lie in the acculturation balance— the extent to which the immigrants influenced and were influenced by the host culture. In both countries, indeed in traditional societies throughout the world, the value system is largely determined by the upper classes. The traditional Iberian values of Argentina's landed aristocracy, particularly their negative attitudes toward work, entrepreneurship, and business in general, have remained dominant in this century, even as the grip of the aristocracy on political power has slipped, starting in 1916. Fillol employs the analysis used by Everett Hagen[55] in explaining why the early immigrant dynamism dissipated in the face of the rigidity of these values:

[A]n immigrant who succeeds in attaining an economic position considerably above the one he held in his country of origin logically expects the new society to accord him the social status which people of comparable wealth and income held in his original society. In Argentina, however, the values attached to money and wealth are not those of other, less mobile societies. . . . It is therefore logical to expect that the successful immigrant must have felt deprived of the social position he believed rightfully his own. . . . Over the generations, if one's prowess cannot gain for one the recognition one feels he deserves, and if no route of escape from the trap seems open, a pervasive apathy associated with some degree of "retreatism" will become steadily more apparent . . . active value orientations will be progressively abandoned as a result of the individual's feeling of impotence . . . *we can conclude that the Argentine society has assimilated the impact of massive immigration without undergoing a noticeable change in its value-orientation profile.* [56] [Italics added.]

Fillol's analysis may appear esoteric, but it is strongly supported by a prominent Argentine social scientist, Carlos Escudé. In *The Failure of the Argentine Project,* Escudé documents how the traditional Argentine aristocracy, "possessed [of] a culture conditioned by the Hispanic social structure that nurtures great economic, political, social, and ethnic inequality," undertook a conscious campaign to de-Europeanize the immigrants. The principal instrument was a chauvinistic, militaristic, antiliberal educational philosophy that has dominated the Argentine education system since 1908; a similar philosophy was also dominant during the first half of the nineteenth century. Escudé concludes:

The native aristocracy always had the critical mass necessary to impose its own value system on the immigrants. . . . Obviously, the critical mass is not just a question of numbers. . . . Compare the Argentine case with the contrasting case of the native element in Texas, the Chicanos: After Mexico's defeat, the Chicanos lost their critical mass, and the Anglo-Americans, who held the political power and eventually the numerical majority, imposed their culture. . . . In Argentina, the reverse occurred, and the descendants of Germans and Irishmen, ethnically identical to many Texan "Anglos," were transformed into native Argentines.

. . .

[S]tudies like this book should serve to underscore the importance of the study of culture . . . not only as a means of understanding socio-economic and political processes but also decisions of enormous importance. [57]

That Argentina's traditional Hispanic value system is largely intact today is apparent from Grondona's typology of societies resistant to development. He is an Argentine, and Argentina was his model.

Thomas Skidmore recently observed, "It is impossible to study Argentina and Brazil over the last three decades and not be impressed by differences in their national psychologies."[58] With respect to evolution of values, Charles Wagley perceives a very different process under way in Brazil from that in Argentina. He confirms the applicability in Brazil of the universal pattern of the upper class establishing the value system for the rest of society,[59] but he describes a process of social and cultural amalgamation that is both in stark contrast to Fillol's description of Argentina's rigidity and evocative of the "softness" and "resilience"—the "live and let live" outlook—that repeatedly appear in the literature on Brazilian society and culture:

> [P]art of the old elite have lost their upper class connections in the metropolitan centers. . . . Another portion of the group, the big-city bureaucrats and professionals, have diverged from the elite and merged with the upper echelons of the expanding middle class. Yet another portion, by diversifying investments, industrializing and nationalizing their rural holdings, and intermarrying with the industrial capitalist elements who now dominate the upper class, have managed to preserve their influence and power on the national scene . . . during the last twenty years [roughly 1943–63] an increasing number of people from the middle class have moved into the upper class through acquired wealth, political influence, education, or professional competence. The Vargas regime brought many new names to national prominence.
>
>   . . .
>
> This process is not a new one in Brazilian society, for the traditional upper class has never been a truly closed social class; it has always been fed through the assimilation of newcomers from the lower and middle classes and from abroad. Nowadays, newcomers into the upper economic and social echelons of society are more numerous than ever before. As a consequence, the dominant segment of Brazilian society may take a new form, one more like that which prevails in the United States, where the values of the power group derive from commerce, industry, and capital, rather than from politics and land-owning.[60]

A part of the explanation for the differences between Brazil and Argentina probably also lies in Brazil's greater size (three times) and, particularly, its greater population (five times). With the sixth largest population in the world (after China, India, the Soviet Union, the United States, and Indonesia), Brazil has a domestic market that offers opportunities for diversification and economies of scale that far exceed Argentina's. It is also true, as noted, that Brazilian chiefs of state, particularly since Vargas, have usually concerned themselves more with economic development than their Argentine opposite numbers. And, as Eliana Cardoso concludes, while Brazilian economic policies have been far from impeccable in this century, they have nonetheless been more conducive to stability and growth than have Argentina's. For example, while both have experienced repeated inflationary episodes, price fluctuations in Argentina have tended to be more violent.[61]

But the geography and the policies are not enough to explain sixty-eight years of growth at above 6 percent annually. That growth has had to have an important source in entrepreneurial energy. Although the "live and let live" philosophy has had negative consequences for social justice, it does, after all, approximate laissez-faire. And this Brazilian characteristic, so different from Hispanic American culture, appears to have nurtured a set of values and attitudes, initially those of immigrant achievers and now permeating the entire society, that may be the real engine of Brazil's economic miracle.

BRAZIL ASSESSED AGAINST GRONDONA'S TYPOLOGY

Viewing Brazil against Mariano Grondona's typology of development-prone and development-resistant societies will help us both to recapitulate and to draw some conclusions about the implications of the interplay of Brazilian cultural currents for Brazil's future.

It is clear that Brazilian values and attitudes diverge in some important respects from the Hispanic American mainstream. This is above all true with respect to those factors affecting economic performance, in which Brazil has excelled: orientation toward the future, the expandability of wealth, the utility of competition, the rewards of achievement and success, the goodness of work, and to some extent the exercising of authority. It is much less true of the factors affecting political and social progress, in which Brazil has lagged: the value of the individual, morality, economic justice, education, and the "lesser virtues" (tidiness, courtesy, punctuality). Moreover, with respect to the values and attitudes that affect economic performance, there are still strong currents, particularly in the Liberation Theology movement and other left-wing political groups, that see the world through a utopian, "limited good," or "zero-sum" authoritarian prism.

These cross-currents and contradictions came to a head in the 1980s. Economic growth has decelerated, and high levels of inflation threaten unprecedented economic decline. In Eliana Cardoso's worst-case projection, "the economic scenario for Brazil in the 1990's is the Argentine scenario of an economy that grows at a very moderate rate, with capital flight, emigration, frequent bouts of inflation and financial instability, low investment and declining real wages. The economic pie will shrink and the infighting will become fiercer. . . . fudging distribution through growth worked in the past but might not be possible in the future."[62]

Brazil's political future is particularly uncertain. The mixture of high degrees of social inequality, economic distress, and instability that have precipitated draconian policies, and fragile institutions of pluralism could lead to political paralysis and a return of authorative government. What appears to be necessary for Brazil to consolidate itself as a modern democratic capitalist nation is the kind of stability and growth-stressing-equity strategy that Helio Jaguaribe proposes in *Brasil 2,000.* [63] But this may well not be feasible without profound change in Brazilian values and attitudes.

I conclude this chapter with the words of Clodomir Vianna Moog, written a quarter of a century ago:

> Agrarian reform, economic reform, financial reform, constitutional reform? Certainly, Brazil needs reforms and achievements of all kinds— railways and highways, hydroelectric energy, immigration of pioneers, not *bandeirantes.* . . . but what is really needed is a reform within the Brazilian mind. Don't have any illusions: without a reform within the mind, without reacting against the past, without an examination of the national conscience . . . that makes us shape within ourselves, not only intellectually but . . . above all emotionally, a radical shift of concepts and attitudes about life, Brazil, and the universe . . . we shall continue to be what we are: a country that progresses but does not ennoble itself, a country without a message for the world, a disorganized collectivity that lacks moral initiative and public spirit . . . that permanently awaits miracle workers or caudillos to solve the problems that only spiritually, morally, and organically integrated communities can really resolve.[64]

2

Spain

The Enlightenment and the Industrial Revolution Finally Arrive

*There is a new Spain and . . . a new kind of Spaniard very different
from the intolerant, intemperate figure of legend and history.*
—John Hooper, *The Spaniards: A Portrait of the New Spain*
(1987)

Tortura no es arte ni cultura ("Torture is neither art nor culture").
—Hand-printed sign beside a bullfight poster
at a stadium in Gijón, Spain

[I]n its rush to become European, Spain is becoming less Spanish.
—Alan Riding, *New York Times*, 17 June 1991

Suppose an extraterrestrial social scientist visited all nations of the
world in 1950, duly taking notes on their political, economic, and
social condition. Forty years later, he returns to measure the changes.
His mind is, of course, boggled by the collapse of communism in
Eastern Europe. He also sees a clear new pattern: Germany, in poor
shape at the time of his first visit, has reunified and become the
powerhouse of Western European democracies; Japan has transformed itself from a devastated militarist nation humiliated by defeat
into the world's most dynamic economy, and a democracy to boot;
the four East Asian "dragons"—Taiwan, Korea, Singapore, and
Hong Kong—have startled the world with their sustained high levels
of economic growth. (As we shall see in the next two chapters, there
are historic antecedents and cultural forces that make these East
Asian "miracles" not all that astonishing.) But the extraterrestrial
might be most surprised by what had happened to Spain in those
forty years between visits.

In 1950, Spain was a closed, isolated, economically backward,
inequitable, rigid, and traditional authoritarian society run by the
quintessential *caudillo*, Francisco Franco. In 1990, Spain was an

open democracy with ample social mobility, the highest economic growth rate in the European Community, and liberal Felipe González as prime minister, his Socialist Party having won three successive elections.

How can one explain the transformation of Spain, which had until recent decades failed to create political pluralism, social equality, and economic dynamism, following essentially the same authoritarian, traditionalist path as its former colonies in the New World? A number of factors come into play, but the principal one, I believe, is Spain's decision to open itself to the mainstream ideas of the West— to permit the Enlightenment and the Industrial Revolution to cross the Pyrenees, albeit two centuries late.

THE POWERFUL MOMENTUM
OF HISPANIC CULTURE

A striking feature of Spanish history during the nineteenth century and the first half of the twentieth century is the close parallel of its political, economic, and social development with that of its former colonies in Latin America.[1]

While Western Europe and North America were, in most cases, fashioning increasingly open, participatory, pluralist societies, *la madre patria* and its offspring (with a few exceptions, most notably Costa Rica) were unable to evolve stable institutions of democratic government; authoritarian rule, often disguised by constitutional fig leaves, was the norm. Octavio Paz observes, "In Spanish America, liberal democratic constitutions merely served as modern trappings for the survival of the colonial system. This liberal, democratic ideology, far from expressing our concrete historical situation, disguised it, and the political lie established itself almost constitutionally. The moral damage it has done is incalculable."[2]

Neither Spain nor its former colonies were able to institutionalize civilian control of the military, who typically saw themselves as above the constitution (which was usually not respected by other elements in the society in any case). Between 1814 and 1876, the Spanish military tried to overthrow the government on thirty-five occasions, succeeding eleven times. The latest—and, it is hoped, the last— *pronunciamiento,* to use the Spanish word for an intervention by the military to dictate a change of government, occurred in 1981. As recently as 1990, elements of the Argentine army attempted to overthrow the democratically elected government of Carlos Saúl Menem. Costa Rica succeeded in suppressing militarism by constitutionally prohibiting the existence of a military institution. In Spain and elsewhere in Hispanic America, the military spawned many of the dictatorships.

Spain is amply endowed with agricultural and mineral resources. Yet its economic development, burdened by mercantilist policies and institutions whose roots go back to the sixteenth century, was so slow—and so inequitable— that, as recently as 1950, it could reasonably have been labeled an underdeveloped country. Its per capita income was lower than that of its former colonies Venezuela, Uruguay, Argentina, Cuba, Panama, and Colombia, all of which, by the way, still exhibited manifestations of the mercantilist mindset[3] and all of which were considered underdeveloped countries.

In 1950, when illiteracy in Western Europe averaged 4 percent, Spain's illiteracy rate was 18 percent, higher than Argentina's and Uruguay's, and just a few points lower than those of Chile, Costa Rica, and Cuba. Life expectancy in Spain in 1950 was sixty years, ten years less than the Western European average and lower than that in Argentina and Uruguay. Distribution of land, income, and wealth in Spain paralleled the extreme inequality characteristic of Latin American countries.

As one might expect, the absence of democratic political institutions in Spain and its former colonies was accompanied by the absence of due process in judicial institutions and their domination by the executive. As I mentioned in the introduction, a recent study of Latin American judicial institutions concluded that Costa Rica is the only Latin American country where the judiciary is truly independent.[4]

Spain was the richest country in the West in the sixteenth and seventeenth centuries. As late as the eighteenth century, its colonies were far richer, and were generally considered more promising, than the British colonies of North America. Yet in 1950, Spain and its former colonies were a half century or more behind Western Europe, Canada, and the United States in terms of economic development, the forging of democratic institutions, and social justice. Why?

Some of the explanation may be found in geography and natural resource endowment. Spain, Mexico, the Central American countries, and the Andean countries suffer from topography that tends to fragment and isolate (the Pyrenees have long been a symbol of Spain's isolation from Europe), and they have few navigable rivers. Canada and the United States may also have an edge in mineral and land endowment, although Latin America has a considerable advantage in petroleum, iron, copper, bauxite, tin, and manganese, and Argentina may be the richest country in the world in proportion to its population. Surely geography and resource allocation were not an impediment to Spain's and Latin America's economic progress in the sixteenth and seventeenth centuries. Moreover, there are a number of contemporary success stories, such as Japan and Switzerland, in which geography and resource endowment are less favorable than Spain's and Latin America's.

Climate may also be relevant. A temperate climate may be optimal for encouraging habits (austerity, saving, planning) that promote economic development, and much of Latin America is in the tropical zone. On the other hand, all of Uruguay, most of Argentina and Chile, a good part of Mexico and Uruguay, and Brazil just south of Rio de Janeiro are in the temperate zone, and many Latin American capitals (Mexico City, Bogotá, Caracas, Quito, Brasilia, and all the Central American capitals except Managua) are at altitudes that afford temperate climates. Spain shares its northernmost latitude with Maine, its southernmost with North Carolina.

Obviously, Spain and most Latin American countries pursued policies that did not facilitate pluralism, economic growth, and social equity. But why did they persist in these policies, in many cases right up to the present, as the success of democratic capitalism became increasingly apparent?

Soberbia: Spanish Individualism and the Limited Radius of Identification

Viewed over the sweep of centuries, the lagging development of Spain and its former colonies can be explained, I believe, only by powerful and persistent cultural forces. With respect to the economic dimension, Eléna de la Souchère's basic diagnosis is highly relevant:

> Coordination, foresight, method: these were the conditions indispensable to the achievement of prosperity. And it was precisely these conditions which the Iberian character found the most repugnant. At the very root

of Spanish poverty, there is a divorce between man and the soil, between the individual energies of men and the collective discipline required for cultivation of the soil.[5]

The cultural and psychological pathology that lie behind Spain's underdevelopment has been analyzed by several prominent Spanish writers, going back to the utopian extravagance of Cervantes's Don Quixote. More recently, Fernando Díaz-Plaja devoted a third of his best-selling *El Español y Los Siete Pecados Capitales* to *soberbia* (pride, with connotations of arrogance, haughtiness, and vanity) and attributed the Spaniard's excessive individualism (he uses the word *superindividualism*) to excessive pride.[6] José Ortega y Gasset uses the word *particularism,* which he calls "the most widespread and dangerous characteristic of modern Spanish life," to capture a related phenomenon:

> that state of mind in which we believe that we need pay no attention to others. . . . Taking others into account implies at least an understanding of the state of mutual dependence and cooperation in which we live. . . . Among normal nations, a class that desires something for itself tries to get it by agreement with the other classes. . . . But a class attacked by particularism feels humiliated when it realizes that in order to achieve its desires it must resort to these organs of the common will.[7]

Díaz-Plaja adds, "The Englishman says that his house is his castle, referring to his rights as an individual against government intrusion. The Spaniard also considers his house his castle, but against everyone, a castle bristling with cannon and surrounded by deep moats."[8] A Spanish epigram of unknown source reads, "For the Spaniard it is not enough to have heaven guaranteed for himself; he must also have hell guaranteed for his neighbor."[9] There are other factors that explain the difficulties Iberian societies have had in forging democratic institutions—remember, for example, that analysts of Spanish culture have emphasized a narrow radius of trust and the centrality of the family to the exclusion of the broader society—but I would argue that the *soberbia* of traditional Hispanic culture has nurtured authoritarianism, eschewed compromise (a word for which there is no accurate Spanish synonym), and made stable democracy virtually impossible. As Díaz-Plaja explains:

> When the Spaniard gets together with others to form a political party, he is doing nothing else than extending his ego to that party . . . thus the party is just as vociferous and intransigent as each one of its members; the rules of the democratic game that are supposedly accepted by all the

parties are generally scorned. Before the elections of 1936, the leader of
the Spanish Socialist Party, the leader of the National Monarchy Bloc,
the leader of the Communist Party, and the Anarchists all publicly
affirmed that they would respect the results of the elections if they won,
but never—loud applause—if they lost.[10]

Traditional patterns of male child rearing have a lot to do with the
Spaniard's *soberbia* and rigid authoritarianism, and with comparable
patterns of behavior in Latin America. In describing an encounter
in Madrid with a boy who broke a bus stop waiting line to reserve
seats for his mother and himself, Díaz-Plaja explains his lack of
respect for the rights of others: "the fault wasn't [the boy's]. His
parents, his older brothers, his uncles had taught him that society is
a jungle and that you don't get anywhere unless you think only of
yourself." He closes his chapter on *soberbia* by explaining that "the
Spaniard is very much a child . . . like a child, he is an egoist; like
a child, vain; like a child, he always wants what he wants. And like
a child, he loves to be the center of attention."[11]

Díaz-Plaja's observations on the immaturity of the Spaniard re-
mind us of similar observations in other settings: David Landy, in a
study of a Puerto Rican peasant village, concludes that the way boys
are reared results in "dependent and insecure adults."[12] In a study
of the mountain city of Constanza in the Dominican Republic,
Malcolm T. Walker notes, "Even at the risk of making value judgments, it does strike one that Constanza men are emotionally imma-
ture; in large measure this immaturity stems from the nature of
socialization of the male. . . . Boys . . . are treated with extreme
indulgence."[13] And, perhaps coincidentally, in his analysis of a town
in southern Italy that was part of a Spanish colony for more than two
centuries, Edward Banfield emphasizes "the indulgence of parents
toward children and their willingness to allow children to be selfish
and irresponsible. . . . Montegranesi act like selfish children because
they are brought up as selfish children."[14]

The Ethical Code, Authoritarianism, and
Attitudes About Work and Innovation

Moving from radius of trust to the second major cultural factor
affecting progress, the rigor of the ethical code, I have already dis-

cussed in chapter 1 the elasticity of the traditional Ibero-Catholic ethical system, particularly what Weber described as "the very human Catholic cycle of sin, repentance, atonement, release, followed by renewed sin."[15] The authoritarian, hierarchical structure of the traditional Church reinforced similar tendencies in the family and the society at large. The ethical elasticity, the family-limited radius of trust, and excessive individualism have combined to shape antisocial behavior—including degrees of corruption, nepotism, and tax evasion generally conceded to be far in excess of the norms of the developed countries of the West—as well as rigid authoritarianism, the third cultural factor, which has dominated politics and administration, and suppressed dissent and creativity, in Spain and Hispanic American countries.

As discussed with regard to Brazil, the traditional Ibero-Catholic view of work, innovation, and profit, the fourth key cultural factor, is essentially negative. The upper classes in Spain and Latin America have displayed "disdain for physical labor, money-making, technological skills, and non-humanistic learning."[16] Ortega y Gasset adds, "All occupations in which we engage out of necessity are painful to us. They weigh down our life, hurt it, tear it to pieces. . . . The man who works does so in the hope . . . that work will lead to liberation, that some day he will stop working and start really living."[17] Sima Lieberman observes, "Agriculture, crafts and commerce took second place to armed conquest as sources of wealth in the eyes of both Castilian *hidalgos* [people who were 'someone'] and peasants," and cites the view of S. G. Payne: "Thus in Castilian society, riches were commonly considered not as something that one created or built, that is, worked for, but as something one conquered or enjoyed because of one's status as a warrior conqueror, a nobleman."[18]

As Weber noted, traditional Catholic fatalism has contributed to a focus on the present rather than the future, with obvious negative implications for planning, saving, and investment. Díaz-Plaja notes, "For the Spaniard, everything is instantaneous, and there are few countries where people concern themselves less with the future."[19]

Innovation, moreover, particularly when it comes from the outside, threatens the *soberbia* of the traditional Spaniard. Ortega y Gasset observes, "The perfect Spaniard needs nothing; more than that, he needs nobody. This is why our race are such haters of novelty and innovation. To accept anything new from the outside world humiliates us. . . . To the true Spaniard, all innovation seems frankly a personal offense."[20] Lieberman adds, "The Spanish social elite persisted in viewing technological and organizational changes as possible threats to a divinely mandated traditional social order."[21]

HISTORICAL OVERVIEW:
THE MIRACLE UNFOLDS

I cannot see any other satisfactory explanation for Spain's—as well as Hispanic America's—political, economic, and social backwardness through the first half of this century than these cultural/psychological factors that the various writers I have quoted have illuminated. But Spain has become a vastly different country: the democratic process that started after Franco's death in 1975 now appears irreversible; the Spanish economy has for almost three decades demonstrated a dynamism that has moved Spain into the ranks of the developed countries; and social justice has made comparably impressive strides. How did it happen? To what extent has traditional Spanish culture changed? And what has been the role of cultural change in the Spanish miracle?

The Trauma of the Civil War

There is a tendency in the United States, shaped strongly by Ernest Hemingway, to view the carnage that bled Spain from 1936 to 1939 as the work of the bad guy Fascists, supported by Hitler and Mussolini. The good guys were the Left, supported by Stalin, and liberals, Socialists, and Communists from around the world, including the famous American Lincoln Brigade. The good guys were assumed to be defending the liberal democratic constitution of the Second Republic, ratified in 1931. And indeed, many of them had the vision of the Spain that has emerged in the last few decades, and particularly since the death of Franco. But many did not. *Soberbia*, authoritarianism, and the penchant for violence were scarcely the monopoly of the right, and it is far from clear that a liberal democracy would have emerged had the Republican side won; a Stalinist dictatorship might easily have been the outcome.

The Left came to power in 1931, initiating the "Red biennium" in a climate of what E. Ramón Arango has described as Pentecostal politics.[22] The Church, the military, and the Basques, who were generally conservative and pro-Church, were the principal targets. So much energy was spent on campaigns *against* them that little was accomplished *for* the Left's principal constituency, the land-hungry poor.

Not surprisingly, then, the Right won an overwhelming victory in the elections of 1933, initiating the "Black biennium." The reactionary policies pursued by the Right were within constitutional bounds, but when a rightist party that was anathema to the Left was brought into the governing coalition in 1934, leftist leaders effectively renounced the constitution. "They did not content themselves with declaring their opposition to the *program* of the right, a stance within the concept of loyal democratic opposition; they declared themselves against the *existing institutions of the country*—institutions they themselves had created."[23] The Left's response was a violent, destructive insurrection. The Spanish writer Salvador de Madariaga observes, "With the rebellion of 1934, the left lost every shred of moral authority to condemn the rebellion of 1936."[24]

The 1936 elections were held in a climate of chaos. As Díaz-Plaja observed, each of the principal parties publicly stated that it would not respect the outcome if it lost. The Left won with a substantial majority. The Socialist Party leader Francisco Largo Caballero, whom Brian Crozier identifies as bearing more responsibility for the civil war than anyone else[25] and who was referred to as the Spanish Lenin, prodded the new government into increasingly radical policies (we are reminded of Salvador Allende's contribution to his own demise in Chile in 1973). When a prominent rightist was killed by the police on 12 July 1936, civil war erupted.

The war was astonishingly bloody and costly. Approximately half a million Spaniards died, many of them in acts of insane violence and cruelty. Pierre Vilar says, "It would be absurd to underestimate the acts of violence on both sides which still dominate the memory of the average Spaniard [who lived through the civil war]. . . . One must bear in mind that in certain aspects the events reflect a Spanish temperament. There were priests who blessed the worst fusillades, mobs who hurled monks and nuns to their graves."[26] The Argentine educator and statesman Domingo Faustino Sarmiento wrote an apt warning in 1851:

> Terror is a sickness of the spirit which infects people, like cholera, small-pox, or scarlet fever. And after you have worked for ten years to inoculate

against it, the vaccine fails to work. Don't laugh, people of Hispanic America, when you see such degradation! Remember that you are Spanish, and that is how the Inquisition educated Spain. This sickness we carry in our blood. Be careful, then![27]

In addition to those who were killed or wounded, perhaps three hundred thousand Spaniards identified with the Republic went into exile, most of them from the professions. More than half a billion dollars in gold reserves were wiped out. (The Republican forces needed about that much foreign exchange to pay for external—mostly Russian—support of their cause. Most of the gold actually ended up in the Soviet Union.) Two hundred and fifty thousand houses were destroyed, a like amount damaged. Fifty percent of railroad rolling stock was lost. GNP dropped by 25 percent.

The carnage ended half a century ago. The vast majority of Spaniards today were born after the civil war and have no recollection of its brutality and devastation. But the older generation surely does. They were traumatized by the experience. Many of them said, "Never again." One of those was General Manuel Gutiérrez Mellado, who was to play the architect's role in the modernization of Spain's military institution. In an interview a few years ago with Nobel Prize–winner Camilo José Cela, General Gutiérrez said:

> During my years in government I have fought to assure [the civil war] was never repeated. . . . that hecatomb, that madness . . . in '36 . . . the Spaniards became intoxicated and the explosion occurred. I think we are beyond that now. I was in the Congress with people who had fought against one another [during the civil war] . . . [now] they were debating with conviction, with vehemence, but afterwards they invited one another to go out for a cup of coffee. . . . that was good.[28]

Thus, the Spanish Civil War itself may have been a principal trigger of the process of cultural change that has led to Spain's democratization.

Economic Realities Force Franco's Hand

Generalísimo Francisco Franco, leader of the victorious Nationalist forces that were supported by Nazi Germany and Fascist Italy, inherited a nation in physical, institutional, economic, and psychic shambles. As the quintessential *caudillo*, Franco ruled with an iron fist, especially during his first decade, when supporters of the Republic were hunted down, jailed, and often executed. Although his rhetoric was progressive and nationalistic, he "tried to freeze Spain into a sociopolitical mold similar to that discarded by England a century and a half ago." As the official statutes of Nationalist Spain stated: "the Chief assumes full and absolute authority. The Chief answers to God and to History."[29]

Franco's philosophy was clearly closer to Hitler's and Mussolini's than to the Allies'. But he was prudent enough to adjust Spain's foreign policy to the ebb and flow of the war. As the tide turned against the Axis, Spain became increasingly neutral, finally tilting toward the Allies in the last years of the war.

Franco's finger-to-the-wind foreign policy was accompanied by a domestic policy of autarchy—economic self-sufficiency. This policy was forced by the war's disruption of trade, but it was also probably congenial to Franco's vision of a self-contained Spain safe behind the Pyrenees. (Remember Ortega y Gasset: "The perfect Spaniard needs nothing; more than that, he needs nobody.") Autarchy meant highly protected and controlled import substitution in the industrial sector, price controls and rationing in agriculture, discouragement of foreign investment, and government control of labor-management relations. I might add that there are close parallels between Franco's autarchy and the import-substitution strategy of the Argentine economist Raul Prebisch that so dominated Latin America—and Third World—economic policy for decades after World War II.

Franco's foreign policy adjustments notwithstanding, the newly created United Nations voted a trade boycott of Spain late in 1946—clearly designed to topple Franco—that effectively deprived Spain of access to Marshall Plan aid. The consequence of the civil war and its aftereffects, and Spain's self-imposed and externally imposed economic isolation, was a period of acute deprivation worse than in many of the European countries that had been battered in World War II. The late 1940s are referred to by Spaniards as the *años de hambre*—years of hunger. Had not Argentina's dictator Juan Perón lent Franco $250 million, the consequence could have been famine.

As early as 1947, with East-West relations increasingly marked by hostility, U.S. military and foreign policy planners concluded that air and naval bases in Spain would be highly beneficial to the security interests of the West. Although the UN boycott of Spain was lifted in 1950 (Spain was finally admitted to the UN in 1955), America's NATO allies continued to treat Spain as a pariah. But that did not deter the Truman administration from beginning base-rights negotiations in 1951, having already approved limited economic aid for Spain through the Export-Import Bank in 1950. Partly to improve relations with the United States, Franco took a first step away from autarchy and interventionism when he shuffled his cabinet in 1951, installing several ministers who were disposed to some relaxation of state controls of the economy.

The Pact of Madrid was signed late in 1953, giving the United States the bases it wanted in return for sustained economic and military assistance. The bases included air force facilities at Torrejón, Zaragoza, and Moro de la Frontera; a naval base at Rota; and storage depots at Seville and El Ferrol del Caudillo, Franco's hometown. Numerous smaller installations followed. The massive base-construction program was an important stimulus to the economy, as was an economic aid program that was, for that time, substantial.

The economic aid—about a billion dollars was furnished during the first ten years—was administered by a U.S. Operations Mission that developed a wide range of contacts in Spain's public and private sectors. In addition to managing the flow of food, funds, and technical assistance, the Operations Mission also provided economic policy advice which, from the beginning, emphasized the need to open up the economy. The military aid was administered by a Joint U.S. Military Assistance Advisory Group that developed close relationships with the Spanish military at all levels. A major training program was mounted that brought thousands of Spanish soldiers, sailors, and airmen to the United States for short- and long-term studies.[30]

The American economic aid, the heavy infusion of dollars for base construction, and the modest policy liberalization undertaken by Franco resulted in fairly impressive growth during the 1950s, on the order of 5 percent annually. Substantial growth occurred in the industrial sector, more than 8 percent annually during 1950–57, but the agricultural sector remained stagnant. Unemployment consequently intensified, and a massive rural-to-urban migration started. (Fifty percent of the labor force was employed in agriculture in 1950.) Large numbers of Spaniards—ultimately 1.5 million—were to seek employment in other European countries, particularly France and Germany.[31]

In the second half of the 1950s, Spain encountered increasingly serious balance-of-payment difficulties, and inflation accelerated. (Although industrial production had increased impressively, decades of protectionism had left Spanish industry uncompetitive in most products, and Spanish exports suffered the consequences.) In 1957, for the first time since the civil war, students and workers took to the streets. Franco, who had little understanding of or interest in economics, was forced to make a cabinet change that was to have profound consequences for Spain. He named Alberto Ullastres Calvo as Minister of Trade and Mariano Navarro Rubio as Minister of Finance. Both were technocrats, and both were members of Opus Dei, a Catholic society that combines pro-capitalist, ascetic economic views akin to Calvinism with highly conservative theological views that include, for some members, self-flagellation. A few years later, Opus Dei member Laureano López Rodó, who had been appointed Technical General Secretary to the Ministry of the Presidency in 1956, was named Minister of Planning.

Simultaneous with the appointments of Ullastres and Navarro, the United States intensified its pressure on the Spanish government to make major economic policy changes, finally making it a condition for additional assistance:

> The regime hardly needed American pressures to recognize that its economic policy, much of it the by-product of outmoded syndicalist and neofascist theories, had failed to revitalize the economy. Along with the International Monetary Fund, the United States recommended that Spain dismantle state regulations that restricted trade and capital investments, devalue the peseta, curtail government spending, encourage industrial growth, and attract foreign capital. The two further urged Franco to orient Spain's economy toward greater integration with Europe's and away from its autarchic basis. These proposals squared essentially with the recommendations of the Spanish government's own economists.[32]

The stabilization plan was announced in 1959, and its effects started to be felt soon thereafter. From 1961 to 1973, the Spanish economy experienced a revolution. Growth averaged more than 7 percent annually, the highest in Europe. With population growing at about 1 percent per year, that meant a per capita increase of 6 percent—a *doubling* in twelve years. Industry, powered in important part by foreign investment, grew by more than 9 percent annually. Industrial wages increased by 7 percent annually in real terms. In 1960, there had been 10 cars for every 1,000 inhabitants; in 1975, there were 111 cars per 1,000. During the 1960s, the number of homes with a washing machine rose from 19 percent to 52 percent, and of homes with a refrigerator from 4 percent to 66 percent. The number of university students tripled, and by the early 1970s the infant mortality rate in Spain was lower than in Britain or the United States.[33]

During this fast-growth period, often referred to as the *años de desarrollo* (years of development), income distribution, which forty years ago had been comparable to the highly skewed pattern that persists to this day in Latin America, became steadily more equitable. Today income distribution in Spain is no different than that in the developed countries of the West.[34] It is true, however, that through the mid-1970s, a few of the most affluent controlled a highly dispro-portionate amount of income: "by the time Franco died, the top 4% of households accounted for 30% of total income."[35] By 1980, even that anomaly had been substantially corrected: according to World Bank statistics, the top 10 percent of Spain's households accounted for 24 percent of total household income, about the same as in most of Western Europe, Canada, Japan, and the United States. (The top 10 percent received 50.6 percent in Brazil in 1972, and 40.6 percent in Mexico in 1977.)[36]

Like other oil importers, Spain experienced an economic slow-down for several years after the first petroleum price shock, in 1973. But the economy recovered in the 1980s and is currently the fastest growing in the European Community, averaging in recent years about 5 percent annually. In 1960, the value of Spain's manufactured exports totaled $205 million; in 1987, over $24 billion. In 1959, exports and imports represented 13 percent of GDP; in 1987, almost 29 percent.[37]

Spain was an underdeveloped country in the 1950s. Today, the World Bank places it in the "high income economies" category, along with the other countries of Western Europe, New Zealand, Australia, Japan, Canada, and the United States. (Spain does have the second lowest per capita GNP of the countries in that category, however.) In 1950, Spain was a country of a few very rich, a small middle class, and many very poor. Today, it is essentially a middle-class country. The structure of the Spanish economy has been trans-formed and is now similar to that of other Western European coun-tries (see table 2.1).

The opening up of the Spanish economy, including the elimina-tion of a visa requirement for Western Europeans and Americans, and the devaluation of the peseta triggered a surge of tourism. In 1958, 3.5 million tourists visited Spain. By the end of the 1960s, the number approached 30 million. Today, the number of tourists—mostly from Western Europe and the United States—exceeds

TABLE 2.1
ECONOMIC STRUCTURE:
SPAIN AND WESTERN EUROPE

Distribution of GDP (percentage)

	Spain		Western Europe (average)
	1960	1978	1978
Agriculture	21	9	4
Industry	39	38	38
(manufacturing)	(27)	(30)	(26)
Services	40	53	58
	100	100	100

Distribution of Labor Force (percentage)

	Spain		Western Europe (average)
	1960	1978	1978
Agriculture	42	18	9
Industry	31	43	42
Services	27	39	49
	100	100	100

Source: World Bank, World Development Report (New York: Oxford University Press, 1980), p. 115.

Spain's population of about 40 million. Spaniards also visited Western Europe and the United States much more for business, work, studies, tourism. (Many of them got the message from foreign government officials that political liberalization was indispensable for closer economic ties.)

The substitution of the autarchy policy by an outward-looking economic policy in 1959 had the effect of fully opening Spain to the West for the first time in its history. The new policy has not only sparked high levels of economic growth but also marked the end of the Counter-reformation and the arrival of the Enlightenment—the symbolic leveling of the Pyrenees.

Behind the Economic Miracle

The fundamental question at this point is, Why has Spain grown so rapidly for so long? If traditional Spanish values, attitudes, and institutions are the principal explanation for Spain's economic backwardness as late as the 1950s, how has Spain's economic miracle been possible?

Spain was not totally bereft of an industrial base, even in the last century. Cotton textiles were produced in Catalunya, principally for export to Spain's New World colonies, as early as the late eighteenth century. The loss of the colonies and the small internal market set the industry back in the middle decades of the nineteenth century, but even then, Catalunya's cotton textile production made Spain the fourth largest producer of textiles, after Great Britain, France, and the United States. Continuing marketing difficulties, aggravated by the low productivity of the Catalan mills, most of which were small-scale family enterprises, led to strong pressures for protection. The result was the high tariff structure instituted in 1891 that persisted into the 1950s. Another consequence was the gradual diversification of the Catalan industrial base.

Spain's other important industrial region was the Basque provinces. The discovery of the Bessemer process of steel production in 1856 led Britain to seek ore for its rapidly expanding steel industry. Substantial deposits of a suitable red haematite ore were discovered near Bilbao on the Bay of Biscay, a good location for export to Britain. With the participation of foreign, especially British, capital and technology, steel production commenced in the Bilbao region in the 1870s. Both ore and steel were exported, mostly to Britain. Transportation was cheap because the ships returned filled with Welsh coal for the furnaces. Handsome profits were made by the Basque entrepreneurs, who, as the ore reserves declined after 1900, increasingly sought diversified investment opportunities, particularly in hydroelectricity, insurance, paper, and banking. In the last decades of the nineteenth century, the Bilbao stock exchange was Spain's most active. In 1901 alone, financing for 146 companies was floated through the exchange.

I might add that both the Catalans and the Basques have long been considered more entrepreneurial—and democratic—than Spaniards from the South. The same reputation attaches to Catalans and Basques who have migrated to Latin America. Indeed, one often hears in Central America the explanation, as yet unsubstantiated by data, that Costa Rica's unique achievements, particularly its political development, are the consequence of large numbers of Basque and Catalan immigrants. It is also interesting that the cooperative form of organizing enterprises is more developed in Catalunya and the Basque country than elsewhere in Spain.

Thus, in the middle of the twentieth century, as Spain recovered very slowly from the ravages of the civil war, an industrial base existed. But it was small and inefficient for two mutually reinforcing reasons: (1) high levels of tariff protection and Franco's autarchic policy, and (2) the small scale of plants and the tendency toward family ownership—a reflection, I believe, of the family-limited radius of trust and confidence.

The principal engines of the "miracle" that followed the outward-looking stabilization program instituted in 1959 were the surge in earnings from tourism, remittances from Spaniards working in Western Europe, and foreign investment and technology. They operated in a favorable broader environment that included the vast opportunities presented by Spain's backwardness and the economic dynamism of the world in general, Western Europe in particular.

Visitors have made Spain one of the world's major tourist attractions. Tourists find Spain fascinating because of the variety and beauty of its art and architecture, influenced by the Greek, Roman, Gothic, and Moorish civilizations; the variety of its geography; a generally benign climate; the attractions of its Mediterranean coast and islands; and a rich tradition of artisanry. Add to this the bargains resulting from the 42 percent devaluation of the peseta and an increasingly sophisticated tourism-promotion campaign by the Spanish government, and it is not difficult to understand why receipts from tourism, which amounted to $129 million in 1959, soared to more than $3 billion in 1973. By 1988, Spain received 54 million foreign visitors, who spent $16.8 billion. Tourism accounted for 10 percent of the Spanish economy.[38]

Rapid industrial growth and related growth of services were insufficient to absorb the mass emigration of agricultural workers, however. Although the emigration precipitated an increase in agricultural wages, wages in the cities were three to four times higher, and growing rapidly in real terms. But there were not enough jobs. The sharp devaluation made work in countries like France and Germany, where there were labor shortages, particularly attractive because pay was in francs or marks, which offered a highly favorable exchange rate against the peseta. By one calculation, worker remittances approximated 25 percent of Spain's earnings from tourism in 1966 and 1967.[39]

Alex Inkeles and David Smith make a compelling case that employment in industry is a highly effective means of transforming traditional values into modern ones.[40] Spain's rural population has declined from about 50 percent of the total in 1950 to less than 20 percent today. The modernizing effects on Spanish culture of that shift alone have to be profound. We should also consider the impact on the values and attitudes of those 1.5 million Spaniards, many of them rural, who migrated temporarily to Western Europe to work. Not only were they thrust into circumstances where previously un-imaginable income levels were within their reach; they were also exposed to the discipline, organization, and cooperation demanded by modern industry—and to pluralistic political and social environ-ments that were almost totally unknown in their native country.

An important dimension of the stabilization program was a policy that made it much easier for foreign companies to invest in Spain—up to 50 percent of capital without governmental approval in most sectors. Attracted principally by low wage rates, foreign investment surged, initially to produce for the domestic market, subsequently for export. The chief source of capital was the United States, but Switz-erland and West Germany were also important. Foreign capital accounted for about 20 percent of gross industrial investment during the 1960s.[41] It was concentrated in large plants in the chemical, metal, and automobile industries. By the 1970s, foreign investment accounted for 50 percent or more of the capitalization of 188 of Spain's 500 largest companies.[42]

With the foreign investment came modern technology and man-agement that served as a breeding ground for a new generation of Spanish technicians and managers, often English-speaking. John Hooper observes:

> The young businessmen recruited by the new foreign companies picked up their employers' habits and attitudes and passed them on to their counterparts in Spanish-owned firms. Soon, a new breed of *ejecutivos* began to emerge—clean-shaven, wearing button-down shirts, casual suits and sometimes a pair of black-rimmed spectacles. Their speech, liberally sprinkled with English words and phrases, is known as *ejecudinglish*. [43]

Capitalism and entrepreneurship are doubtless more congenial to the Spanish value system now than they were in 1950. I interviewed a Spanish sociologist/pollster in Madrid in 1989 who asserted that, in the 1960s, Spain experienced a surge of entrepreneurship (he called it *"McClellandismo,"* referring to David McClelland's focus on achievement and entrepreneurship in *The Achieving Society*).[44] In his view, the surge tapered off in the 1970s but reappeared in the 1980s. And indeed, home-grown entrepreneurship may have played an important role in the current resurgence of the Spanish economy. On the other hand, it is also quite possible that the extraordinarily high levels of unemployment, currently about 18 percent, reflect some persistence of the traditional Spanish indisposition toward capitalist innovation and risk taking—and work. And foreign managers often complain about the business/work attitudes of Spanish firms and employees.

Table 2.2 indicates the importance workers in different countries attach to various sources of work satisfaction.

Spanish ambivalence toward capitalism continues. Almost half of all respondents in a 1984 survey viewed capitalism as "illegitimate and inefficient," while only about 10 percent viewed it as "legitimate and efficient."[45] In a group of fifteen countries (Canada, Japan, South Africa, the United States, and eleven from Western Europe) sampled in the 1981 *World Value Survey*, the opposition of Spaniards to businesses run by their owners without participation by employees in decisions was higher than in any other country except France.[46]

One has to wonder whether the persistence of working hours that most Westerners would consider bizarre—roughly 9 A.M. to 1 P.M. and 4 P.M. to 8 P.M.—might be symbolic of the reluctance of many Spaniards to give up their traditional attitudes about business. The siesta is still practiced, and the evening meal is rarely eaten before 10 P.M. There are four rush hours in Spanish cities.

Victor Pérez Díaz, writing in 1984, observes,

The practice and the spirit of the free market have occupied, and occupy, a very limited space in the experience of the Spaniards (including, significantly, many businessmen). . . . The capitalist system has not been considered wholly legitimate in Spain for a long time. Traditional Catho-

TABLE 2.2

FACTORS IN WORK SATISFACTION

	Spain	West Germany	Italy	United States
Opportunity to use initiative	37%	63%	37%	54%
Sense of achievement	37	62	43	74
Sense of responsibility	36	54	25	59
Interest	44	71	44	72

Source: I am indebted to Ronald Inglehart for the relevant 1981 *World Value Survey* data.

lic culture has viewed the market with reserve. . . . Franco did not
legitimize capitalism. . . . On the contrary, Spanish capitalism . . . was
contaminated by Franco's own lack of legitimacy.[47]

The Spanish economic miracle of the 1960s and early 1970s was,
then, principally driven by massive external forces operating in a
highly propitious international economic environment. The lesson,
recapitulating the lesson of Brazil's economic performance for much
of this century, is that Iberian culture may be a prodigious but not
insuperable obstacle to economic development if it is exposed to
more progressive outside forces. There are some parallels between
Spain's externally driven economic surge and Argentina's Golden
Age from 1880 to 1930: high levels of foreign investment (principally
British) and European immigration combined with Argentina's vast
natural resources to produce affluence (albeit inequitably distributed
and temporary). I hasten to add that, in citing the examples of Brazil
and Argentina, I do not intend to suggest that Spain, too, will
experience economic backsliding. I think that Spain's membership
in the European Community is insurance against that.

The past three decades have almost surely witnessed movement
away from traditional Spanish/Catholic values and attitudes about
economic creativity, capital accumulation, and development, and
toward the values and attitudes typical of the West. But the indigenous entrepreneurial role so important to the economic success of
Japan, Korea, and Taiwan was clearly less significant in the case of
Spain. And the anti-entrepreneurial tradition continues to be of
concern. As Juergen B. Donges has noted: "if the overriding need
to develop entrepreneurship—to make it more of a calling, to make
it more professional and creative—is not inculcated in Spanish society, it will be very difficult to solve the economic problems we
already confront, not to mention those that might arise in the future."[48]

Spain is a case where rapid economic development contributed to
political development by attenuating the extensive poverty that
helped to polarize politics. The middle class now dominates Spain,
and it is far less susceptible to the blandishments of radical politics,
particularly after the trauma of the civil war. But economic growth
was not the only force pushing Spain toward political development.
Just as Spain's opening up to Western and Japanese investors and
tourists, and to the outflow of Spanish sojourner workers, played a
crucial role in that growth, Spain's opening up to the *ideas* of the

West played a decisive role in the historic shift from authoritarianism to pluralism.

The Transformation of the Church

The opening to the West helped to bring about important changes
in several key Spanish institutions, perhaps above all the Church,
even while Franco was still alive. "Historically, the Spanish clergy has
been among the most conservative in the world. The church that had
spearheaded the Counter-reformation was quite incapable of coming
to terms with the new ideas that flooded into Spain during the
nineteenth century and took refuge in the forlorn hope that the old
order of things could be reestablished," John Hooper observes. The
Church was, of course, one of the principal targets of the Republicans, and several thousand priests, monks, and nuns were killed
during the civil war. On the day of the victory of the Nationalists,
Franco received a telegram from Pope Pius XII that read, "Lifting
up our hearts to the Lord, we rejoice with Your Excellency in the
victory, so greatly to be desired, of Catholic Spain."[49]

The warmth of the relationship between Franco and the Church
was formalized in a concordat signed in 1953, the same year the
United States and Spain signed the bases-for-aid Pact of Madrid.
The two agreements marked the end of Spain's diplomatic isolation,
an objective long sought by Franco, and he made numerous concessions to the Vatican to achieve the concordat. Yet, little more than
a decade later, the Spanish Church had been transformed into one
of Franco's most outspoken critics.

Even before the concordat was signed, Spanish prelates, influenced by priests from other Western European countries, had
initiated an evangelizing campaign among workers and the poor, and
three organizations were created to that end: the Workers' Brother-
hoods of Catholic Action, the Catholic Workers' Youth movement,
and the Young Workers' Vanguard. Large numbers of priests moved
into the slums and quickly learned the reality of life for Spain's poor.
Hooper notes, "In the end, the urban working classes were to have
a much greater effect on the Church than the Church ever had on
the urban working classes."[50]

The this-world, social justice emphases of Pope John XXIII, confirmed by the Second Vatican Council (1962–65), further impelled
the Spanish Church to the Left. The Council's explicit emphasis on

separation of Church and state was particularly significant through its impact on Cardinal Vicente Enrique y Tarancón, who assumed control of the Spanish Church in 1971 and who was to play a key role in the transition to democracy following Franco's death.

Another factor contributing to the transformation of the Church was the involvement of priests in the expression of regional nationalism, above all in the Basque country, where many priests had sided with the Republic. By one count, Franco had sent 187 priests, most of them Basques, to prison by 1970.[51]

By the time of Franco's death, the Spanish Catholic Church had moved from the Middle Ages into the twentieth century. Its ideological composition had evolved toward that of the Church in Western European countries and the United States. Hooper cites the "Red Bishop" Iniesta's disaggregation: "a minority right wing, a minority left wing, and a majority belonging to the center."[52] The Church no longer saw itself as a major political actor and refused to adopt partisan postures. Its leadership was committed to pluralism. And its followership, swept up by the strong secularization current, no longer felt strong bonds to the Church.

From the time of the Catholic Kings of the fifteenth century through the mid-twentieth century, the observation of Americo Castro was apt: "Spanish history is essentially the history of a belief, of a religious sensibility."[53] Spain's transformation since the 1950s was in part the result of fundamental changes within the Church, making Castro's observation no longer apt. In three decades, Spain has been converted from a confessional to a secular society. Richard Gunther notes, "In 1965, over 80% of all Spaniards described themselves as 'practicing Catholics'; by 1983 only 31% described themselves as 'practicing Catholics' or 'very good Catholics.' "[54] The secularization of Spain is underscored by its legalization of divorce in 1981 and of abortion in certain circumstances in 1985.

The Path to Democracy

In 1969, Franco proclaimed as his successor Prince Juan Carlos, grandson of the last Bourbon Monarch, Alfonso XIII, who had been forced to abdicate in 1930. Franco passed over Juan Carlos's father, Don Juan, and in effect established a Francoist monarchy. His decision was based on his close knowledge of Juan Carlos, gained over many years, and his belief that the prince would carry on his policies.

"Juan Carlos enjoyed the support of an influential group of conservative Catholics within the regime. . . . The corollary of this was that the young Prince was regarded as a mere puppet of Franco by the democratic opposition."[55] In fact, Juan Carlos, who had traveled extensively and had contacts throughout Spanish society, sensed the need for change, and this sense intensified during the last years of Franco's life.

The increasingly senile Franco presided over an increasingly chaotic Spain during his last years. The campaign of violence by Basque nationalists intensified; students and workers repeatedly took to the streets; and criticism of Franco grew, particularly within opposition political groups, including the outlawed Communist Party, the Church, and a few outspoken publications, notably *Ya* (*Now*), a Catholic daily; the magazine *Cuadernos para el Diálogo* (*Notebooks for the Dialogue*); and the Opus Dei evening newspaper, *Madrid*.

The political unraveling was magnified by the first oil price shock in 1973, which brought an end to the years of high growth. When Franco died two years later, the political environment became fragmented, polarized, and violent. The coronation of King Juan Carlos, at which Cardinal Tarancón pronounced the homily, took place the day after Franco's death.

About the only common denominator Juan Carlos had to work with was a vague, generalized desire for peace and democracy, principally the product of the trauma of the civil war and the dictatorship, and the exposure to Western norms and institutions that followed the economic opening up, or *apertura*. But it was apparent to the king that Franco's last premier, Carlos Arias Navarro, whom Juan Carlos had inherited, was not the man to move Spain into the twentieth century politically. "Arias was the most cautious kind of *aperturista*. Dimly aware that the nation was clamoring for democracy yet temperamentally and ideologically committed to dictatorship, Arias was incapable of moving with any determination either forward or backward."[56]

In June 1976, Juan Carlos paid a triumphal visit to the United States, where he was assured of support, apparently very important to his democratization plans. On 1 July, he asked for and received Arias's resignation. To the disbelief, even outrage, of many, he chose the forty-three-year-old Adolfo Suárez, who had served Franco throughout his career and was widely regarded as a reactionary. The recently established liberal newspaper *El Pais*, which would become

Spain's most prestigious and important daily, ran a column headlined "WHAT A MISTAKE! WHAT AN IMMENSE MISTAKE!"[57]

The *El Pais* columnist could not have been more wrong. In a tour de force, Suárez navigated Spain through the perilous minefields laid by extremists on the Left and Right similar to the same extremist forces that had precipitated the civil war. He also had to deal with the Basque separatist terrorists. By the mid-1970s, however, the large majority of Spaniards did not identify with the extremes. In polls taken during the elections of 1977, 80 percent of Spaniards described themselves as in the area between Left-center and Right-center.[58]

Within three months of forming his government, Suárez easily passed a political reform law through the *Cortes*—what had been Franco's rubber-stamp legislative body—that guaranteed universal suffrage and established a bicameral legislature within a parliamentary system. The Socialist and Communist parties were legalized (legalization of the latter shocked most military officers) a few months later, as were labor unions and the right to strike. Against a backdrop of intensifying inflation and balance-of-payments difficulties, elections were held on 15 June 1977, the moment when Paul Preston asserts that "the Franco regime [was] laid to rest."[59] Suárez's party, the Union of the Democratic Center, won more parliamentary seats than any other party, but not a majority. Rather than form a coalition government, he negotiated in October the Pact of Monclóa in which the Communists—their leader, Santiago Carillo, himself signed the document—and Socialists agreed to ceilings on wages, credit, and government spending, which inevitably meant that labor would bear the brunt of the anti-inflation program.

Suárez's final great achievement was the ratification of a modern constitution late in 1978. Hooper says, "The new Spanish constitution is arguably the most liberal in Western Europe. Spain is defined as a parliamentary monarchy, rather than just a constitutional monarchy. There is no official religion and the armed forces are assigned a strictly limited role. The death penalty is forbidden and the voting age fixed at eighteen."[60] The basic democratic infrastructure was substantially complete. The political debate now moved from the cosmic issue of democratic transformation to the more mundane arena of economic policy, interest groups, social reform, and foreign policy. Suárez was not comfortable in the new arena.

Although his party repeated its winning performance in elections held early in 1979, Suárez was unable to sustain his leadership of the center-right forces through the second energy shock, particularly as it became increasingly apparent that his own sympathies were moving leftward. He resigned in January 1981, and it was during the interim government of Leopoldo Calvo Sotelo that, to quote Hooper, "all Spain's nightmares came true."[61] A military faction headed by Lieutenant-General Jaime Miláns del Bosch attempted a *pronunciamiento,* the most dramatic moment of which occurred when, on 23 February, a Civil Guard officer entered the Congress with a platoon of his men and kept virtually every prominent Spanish politician at gunpoint for almost twenty-four hours. The coup was suppressed principally through the courage and good sense of King Juan Carlos.

The democratization of the military was tested by the elections of November 1982, which were won by Felipe González's Socialist Party, the same PSOE (*Partido Socialista Obrero Español*—Spanish Socialist Workers' Party) that had been anathema to the military for more than four decades. To be sure, González shaped his program to reassure the military of his intentions. But the PSOE had opposed Spain's entry into NATO, which Calvo Sotelo had negotiated in 1982, and which most of the military supported. González called for a referendum on NATO, but it soon became apparent that Spain's entry into the European Economic Community depended on its membership in NATO. To the consternation of many doctrinaire Socialists, González endorsed NATO membership, which carried the referendum. Spain joined the Economic Community in 1986.

González has moved steadily toward the center since taking power. (In a conversation during my 1989 visit, one informed Spaniard who is a PSOE member described González's vision of his party as the same as the Kennedy wing of the Democratic party.) The PSOE won handily in the general elections of 1986, maintaining its majority in Congress. In the elections of 1989, held against the backdrop of the political earthquake in Eastern Europe, the PSOE fell one seat short of an absolute congressional majority. A good number of Socialists had supported the United Left, which, with 10 percent of the popular vote, more than doubled its congressional seats.

For Spain, the 1980s saw the defeat of an attempted military coup d'état; three elections, all won by the increasingly moderate PSOE; entry into NATO and the European Economic Community; and, after the pause of the 1970s and early 1980s, a revival of high rates of economic growth. Most observers believe that Spain's transformation to democracy is irreversible. Some believe that, particularly following the revolution in Eastern Europe, *capitalism* will soon cease to be a dirty word.

LESSONS OF THE SPANISH MIRACLE

What are the lessons of the Spanish miracle for lagging countries, particularly Spain's former colonies in the New World, the vast majority of whom are still searching for stable democratic institutions, dynamic economies, and social justice? Who or what were the agents that transformed Spain from an underdeveloped to a developed country, from a system of traditional values to one of modern values, in three decades?

In the broadest sense, the answer has to be the opening of Spain to the values and institutions of the West and to the world market. But that answer needs to be disaggregated.

In *Underdevelopment Is a State of Mind—The Latin American Case,* I mentioned seven agents that could bring about progressive cultural change: leadership, particularly political leadership; religious reform; educational reform; the media; certain kinds of development activities (for example, cooperatives); modern management practices; and, particularly, improved child-rearing practices. The Spanish case confirms the relevance of those factors. It also underscores an omission from the earlier list—intellectuals.

Several Spanish intellectuals early in this century perceived and analyzed the Spanish reality, in the tradition of Cervantes. Such writers as Ortega y Gasset, de Madariaga, and Díaz-Plaja understood how Spanish culture stood in the way of progress, and they crusaded for cultural change. Theirs was the role of pathologist, and their impact was profound.

I've already discussed two other major forces for change: the traumatic impact of the civil war and the modernization of the Catholic Church, including the progressive and constructive role played by Cardinal Tarancón. Religious reform has also meant secularization for Spain, but this may well have had positive consequences with respect to the rigor of the ethical system: José Maria Martín Patino observes, "With the abandonment of religious practice [that is, church attendance] has come a 'clandestinization' of religion, that is, a tendency to understand Christianity as moral rectitude and social and political commitment."[62] We are reminded of Weber's comment about Protestantism: "The God of Calvinism demanded of his believers not single good works, but a life of good works combined into a unified system."[63]

Clearly, political leadership has been a key factor. King Juan Carlos, contrary to what Franco expected of him and indeed groomed him for, has turned out to be a committed democrat, a skillful and courageous leader, and a good judge of people. His choice of Adolfo Suárez to manage the transition to democracy was widely criticized, but it probably could not have been better. The king put down the 1981 *pronunciamiento* virtually singlehandedly.

Suárez guided the transition through a minefield that included intransigent military and civilian supporters of Franco and highly volatile elements on the Left. But, as Gunther observes, "Spanish political elites interacted with one another in such a fashion as to stabilize and depolarize the political atmosphere . . . their behavior was markedly different from that of the founders of the Second Republic."[64] The process was enormously facilitated by, among others, the Communist Party leader Santiago Carrillo who, anticipating the transformation of Communist parties in the Soviet Union and Eastern Europe by fifteen years, committed himself to the give and take of pluralism. Felipe González, in his decade in power as of this writing, has weaned the Socialist Workers' Party from its early extremism to a position in the mainstream of Western social-democratic parties.

While civilian control of the military is not as firmly established as it is in other countries of the West, much progress has been made. Lieutenant General Manuel Gutiérrez Mellado, whom Suárez named as Deputy Prime Minister and Minister of Defense in 1976, was the principal architect of military reform. Like his friend, General Manuel Díez Alegría, before him, Gutiérrez Mellado was labeled a liberal by Franco's old guard. His reaction:

> I don't mind being called a liberal if that means that I admit to not being utterly right all of the time, that I am ready to discuss things with whomever wishes to discuss things, that I prefer there should be no more fratricidal wars, that I want Spain to belong to all Spaniards . . . and that I think one has to look to new and brighter horizons, not restricting oneself with transient ideas and institutions that have been outdated by the reality of a young, restless, vibrant Spain which aspires to a better and juster world.[65]

Gutiérrez Mellado's reforms redefined the limits of political activity by the military, significantly reduced military jurisdiction, and modernized the pay system. He also reorganized the command structure along the lines of that of the United States and other Western democracies, creating a joint chiefs of staff in the line of command between the three services and the Minister of Defense. He also had a lot to do with the naming of a civilian as his successor.

I have already mentioned the constructive role played by the newspapers *Ya* and *Madrid* and by the magazine *Cuadernos para el Diálogo,* in Franco's last years, and of the newspaper *El Pais* after his death. Since his death, the media has become a major growth industry, one that has profoundly influenced values and attitudes. The left-of-center *El Pais* has become Spain's most important and prestigious newspaper. Two weekly newsmagazines are very popular: *Cambio 16* and *Tiempo,* the latter's circulation enhanced by a liberal sprinkling of nude photographs. The Spaniards rank second in Europe, after Great Britain, in time spent watching television.[66] More than 90 percent of Spanish homes have color TV sets. Until 1990, all television was state-controlled. The advent of privately owned television networks will surely intensify Spain's love affair with the tube.

I have also mentioned the impact of foreign managers and modern management techniques on Spanish executives. As in Latin America,[67] traditional Hispanic authoritarianism has tended to suffocate initiative, risk taking, and innovation in both private and public enterprises. The more egalitarian, participatory modern management style introduced by the numerous foreign companies that have invested in Spain during the past thirty years is not the only source of change. MBA programs are now common in Spanish universities, and many Spaniards have attended such programs in other Western countries.

It is clear that a sweeping economic policy reform was the most immediate trigger of the process that has transformed Spain. Many Spanish technocrats realized that the economic *apertura* and stabilization were prerequisites to sustained and rapid growth. But it is not clear that Franco would have followed their advice had it not been for the long-standing efforts of the U.S. aid program to encourage the opening up, culminating, at the crucial moment, in the conditioning of further assistance on execution of the stabilization program. The International Monetary Fund also played a highly constructive role.

We should also take note of some effective micropolicies and programs subsequently initiated by Spanish governments. Two examples: (1) a policy to encourage home ownership, which has resulted in 70 percent of Spanish families owning their own dwellings (and, I might add, an enhanced appreciation of private property and decreased susceptibility to extremist solutions); and (2) an effective program of taxpayer compliance that has made important inroads on the Iberian (and Latin American) tradition of tax evasion. Robert Graham reports that there were 300,000 income tax payers in 1970, over 6 million in 1982.[68]

While I have found no studies on the subject, I think it is reasonable to assume that Spanish child-rearing practices have changed significantly in recent decades. The legalization of divorce and abortion in certain cases has brought a revolution in relationships between the sexes in Spain, which has resulted in far greater equality for women. Girls of the new generation are likely to see themselves as more autonomous and mobile. And mothers are less likely to encourage the *machismo* in boys that is a principal root of male *soberbia*.

A VISIT TO SPAIN AND
TO BANFIELD'S "MONTEGRANO"

My first visit to Spain in the fall of 1989 afforded me the opportunity to discuss the Spanish miracle with a number of Spaniards and foreigners living in Spain. Some of the documentation in this chapter derives from those conversations. But I also had an opportunity, admittedly anecdotal, to develop some small sense of the way Spaniards of different classes relate to one another and of what day-to-day life is like, in both large cities and small towns. I of course carried with me the impressions of the thirteen years I lived in Latin America and could not help but compare.

What struck me most was the civility and openness of human relationships, far more akin, for example, to France than to Latin America. That doubtless reflects the social leveling symbolized by the vastly more equitable pattern of income distribution. But it also must reflect, I believe, a strengthened sense of community, egalitarianism, and tolerance, all of which have characterized the conduct of politics at the national level since Franco's death. It is not only the political leaders whose values and attitudes have been transformed.

After leaving Spain, I made what was for me a pilgrimage to the mountain village of Chiaromonte, in southern Italy. Chiaromonte is the "Montegrano" of Edward Banfield's seminal book, *The Moral Basis of a Backward Society.* When Banfield and his wife, Laura, who is of Italian descent, spent nine months there in 1954–55, Chiaromonte's inhabitants were dirt-poor and illiterate; the village was bereft of institutions, riven by family rivalries, virtually without hope—in Banfield's view, all largely because of a traditional peasant value and attitude system that confined identification and trust to the family and viewed all outside the family as competitive, even hostile. Banfield concluded his book in a pessimistic frame of mind with respect to the chances for progress in Chiaromonte.

What I found in that brief visit was dramatic change. Almost everyone was literate. Half were high school graduates. All families had television. Sixty percent had telephones. Sixty percent had automobiles. Several agricultural cooperatives had been formed. Families are now much smaller, averaging two children. A highway was built in the 1970s that cut travel time to Naples in half (from six hours to three). People now travel much more, and many attend school elsewhere. Many Chiaromontese have migrated to Northern Italy and other European countries to work, and a fair number of them have returned.

Chiaromonte is no longer Montegrano, although I have no doubt that a residue of traditional values can be found there. Chiaromonte has been opened up, by education, by road, by television, by newspapers and magazines, to the progressive values and institutions of modern Italy and Western Europe. Left to its own devices, the town would no doubt today be essentially what it was when the Banfields lived there. But its isolation has been broken down. Chiaromonte, which coincidentally was part of a Spanish colony between the mid-fifteenth and early eighteenth centuries, is today an apt metaphor for the Spanish miracle.

3

Taiwan and Korea
The Entrepreneurial Power of Confucianism

I visited Costa Rica in 1988 and was told the following story by a firsthand witness: The government of the Republic of China ("Taiwan") sent a team of rice experts to Costa Rica a few years ago to set up a demonstration rice farm. After a year, the farm was operating smoothly, with yields vastly above typical Costa Rican yields. A group of Costa Rican farmers was invited to visit the farm and was duly impressed by its efficiency and productivity. One of them asked a Taiwanese how many hours a day he worked. The Chinese responded, "Twelve." The Costa Rican smiled and said, "¡Asi cualquiera!" ("Oh, anyone could do that!")

In 1945, Taiwan and Korea were liberated from the crumbling Japanese empire. Both were extremely poor in terms of human well-being as well as natural resource endowment. Both soon confronted major threats to their security: Taiwan, from a newly Communist mainland China; Korea, from a Soviet- and Chinese-supported assault by the North Koreans on the South. Both received substantial economic and military support from the United States.

Nearly fifty years later, Taiwan and Korea are on the verge of joining the ranks of the developed countries. Since 1960, they have sustained growth rates in the vicinity of 9 percent annually, as have their fellow "dragons," Hong Kong and Singapore. Their exports, which were inconsequential in the 1950s, have grown explosively, to the point where they are among the dozen most important exporting countries in the world. Moreover, their astonishing growth has been accompanied by a substantial degree of social justice and movement, albeit slow, toward democratic institutions.

Sound long-range economic policies emphasizing the world market have had a lot to do with the success of Taiwan and Korea. But those policies would not have gone as far had it not been for the blossoming of a robust entrepreneurial drive in both countries. That entrepreneurial drive is, I believe, rooted in some of the key tenets of Confucianism, as indeed are the effective economic policies of these two countries.

The Confucian Value System

Confucianism is not the only source of Sinic values and attitudes, but it is certainly the main one.[1] Confucius (the name is the Latinized version of K'ung-fu-tzu), who lived about five hundred years before Christ, was a secular thinker and educator whose philosophical concerns were similar to Plato's. Confucius dedicated himself to the building of the good society in this life, and, as the Asian expert Edwin Reischauer notes, "This lack of concern with the other-worldly . . . led in time to a strong agnostic strain in the Confucian tradition."[2] Confucianism assumes that human nature is basically good, and that the good, ethical life can be assured by order, harmony, moderation, good manners, and his formulation of the Golden Rule: "Do not do unto others what you would not have others do unto you."

The Confucian system* is built on five relationships: father/ teacher and son (filial piety is the most important of all virtues), ruler and subject, husband and wife, older brother and younger brother, and friend and friend. Three of the five concern the family, which is the building block of society and is organized on authoritarian principles. Reischauer observes, "this authoritarian family pattern was applied to the whole of society. . . . The role of the emperor and his officials was merely that of the father writ large."[3] While the first four relationships are those of superior to subordinate, responsibilities run in both directions for all five. If both participants in the relationship respected their responsibilities, peace and harmony would be assured. If the ruler were wise, virtuous, and responsible, the society would follow his lead. If the ruler strayed from righteousness, he relinquished his entitlement to lead.

The traditional Confucian society was aristocratic, authoritarian, and static. Hierarchy was a dominant feature, and the five basic relationships tended to keep people in their places. But Confucius also placed heavy emphasis on education as an engine of progress.

*Confucius was the principal but far from the only architect of the system. Most prominent among his many disciples through the ages was Meng-tzu (Latinized as Mencius), who lived some two hundred years later.

The goal was the achievement of a level of knowledge—principally knowledge of classical Chinese literature—that would qualify a person for the most important human activity: governing. Merit thus formed the basis for selecting those who governed, and merit was determined by testing the scholarly achievements of those who would aspire to govern. Thus, social mobility was possible, and there are many examples in Chinese history of talented people rising from the lower strata to leadership. (Merit and testing, of course, continue to be emphasized in the selection of future leaders in Taiwan, Korea, and Japan. And in all three countries today, the public administration and teaching professions have substantially higher prestige than in the United States.)

Confucius ranked agriculture as the second highest calling, after government/education. Crafts followed agriculture, and at the bottom of the scale was commerce, which, because of its association with profit, was viewed as somewhat illicit.

Confucius's focus on the family reinforced China's tradition of extended familism and ancestor worship. Reischauer notes, "The Chinese kinship group was extensive in scope and was conceived as reaching out in each direction to the fifth generation. This meant that an individual's ancestors back to his great-great-grandparents, his descendents down to his great-great-grandchildren, and his contemporaries to his third cousins (descendants of his great-great-grandparents) were all acknowledged members of his family nexus."[4] This tradition is the root of the clan, which has played so important a role in Chinese history.

The desire to please ancestors has been a very practical concern for the Chinese: if the ancestors were displeased, they might return as spirits to wreak their displeasure on their living relatives.[5] Ancestor worship was thus a spur to achievement and accumulation of wealth, and a reinforcement of the Confucian emphasis on education. During our 1990 trip to East Asia, my wife observed that, for the Chinese, today's child is tomorrow's ancestor. The orientation of the Chinese is very much in the future, as well as in the past. "In this sense, Eastasia has always been 'otherworldly,' if 'the other world' is taken to mean the world of the future for one's associates and descendants."[6]

Confucian values ebbed and flowed in China and elsewhere in East Asia in the centuries that followed. But the other popular systems of thought, Taoism and Buddhism foremost among them, were also of the other world—the world of gods, spirits, and life after death—and it was possible to adhere to them and Confucianism at the same time. Taoism was, in part, an individualistic protest against the hierarchical communitarianism and snobbery of Confucianism. Taoism consequently held special appeal for the common people. It has left its imprint on East Asian culture as the source of the philosophical/religious emphasis on frugality, as Weber points out,[7] but also in its emphasis on restraint and inaction—"Do nothing and nothing will not be done," which Reischauer translates as "everything will be achieved spontaneously."[8] But it was also mystical and spiritist, and these dimensions of Taoism were tolerated by the Confucian mandarins.

Buddhism reached China a hundred or so years before Christ. Its focus on salvation filled a void in Chinese thought that led to its dominance from the fourth to the eighth centuries. It reinforced the asceticism of Taoism and coexisted comfortably with Confucianism. (Buddhism also reached Japan during this period and was a dominant element of Japanese religion and philosophy until it was supplanted by the Confucianist emphasis of the Tokugawas in the seventeenth century.)

But against the sweep of Chinese—and Korean—history, it is clear that Confucianism has most profoundly influenced the value system. Reischauer concludes, "Moderation and balance are perhaps the major reasons for the eventual triumph of Confucianism in China."[9] Moderation and balance surely characterize the recent economic—if not political—history of Taiwan and Korea.

Confucianism, Pluralism, and Social Equity

In the political sphere, Confucianism is principally a force for authoritarianism, hierarchy, and orthodoxy, and East Asian history is similar in many respects to the history of Iberian and Ibero-American countries. There are, for example, analogies to be made between the political evolution of Taiwan and Korea since the 1950s and that of Mexico.

In March 1990, I attended a lecture in Seoul by Professor Gari Ledyard, a historian at Columbia University and an expert on Korea, who argued persuasively that the difficulties Korea has experienced in constructing a modern pluralistic political system are largely the consequence of Confucian values and practices. He stressed that, in the Confucian system, power is unitary, flowing from the leader, whose unitary power is reinforced by the legal and administrative system; people have their place, and harmony depends on people knowing their place; the individual is subordinated to the group; peace and harmony depend on consensus (correspondingly, dissent and voting are disruptive of consensus, peace, and harmony).[10] Ledyard also noted that, in both China and Korea, cities were formed not on the basis of economic/marketing activity, as in the West and Japan, but as bureaucratic centers. Thus, economic pluralism, whose early emergence played so prominent a role in the subsequent evolution of political pluralism in the West, is but a few decades old in Korea. Professor Ledyard concluded, "Most Koreans think that Confucianism is old-fashioned [but] inside their psyche there is such a heavy residue of Confucianism that they are not conscious of it." In the discussion period following the lecture, I observed that almost everything he said about Korea applied with equal force to Taiwan; he agreed.

The conservative, even reactionary nature of Confucian politics is underscored by Lucian Pye in a paper analyzing the cultural currents behind the 1989 Tiananmen massacre:

> [of Chinese political culture] Any conflict arouses hate, and it becomes almost impossible to disagree politically without becoming disagreeable.
>
> . . . in Chinese political culture the ultimate sin is selfishness, and hence the Chinese abhorrence of individualism. . . . Every issue has to be dressed up as being in the collective interest. There is no room for respecting individual rights.
>
> . . . there are few political cultures in which there is greater sensitivity to matters of status and gradations of hierarchy.[11]

With respect to social justice, Confucianism cuts both ways, as it does in economic development. In theory, its rigid hierarchical structure operates in the context of the golden rule, and superiors are bound to treat inferiors with respect and decency. Pye observes, "the most basic principle of Confucianism . . . holds that a ruler should always be benevolent and kind to the people."[12] Compensating somewhat for the importance of people knowing their place is the emphasis on merit (in contrast to "connections") as the basis for advancement. High respect for education also implies social mobility.

Taiwan has achieved a highly equitable pattern of income distribution by any standards, and Korea's is close to that of many advanced democracies. Sinic familism/clannism notwithstanding, the radius of trust and identification in Taiwan and Korea substantially exceeds, in my judgment, what one finds in most Iberian societies. The racial/ethnic/linguistic homogeneity of both East Asian countries (and Japan) obviously contributes to national identity. But while the ruler-subject relationship comes after filial piety in the Confucian scheme of things, it is in many respects similar—the ruler is a father figure. Respect for the ruler, the symbol of community as well as nationhood, is something that all Chinese and Koreans (and Japanese) learn, along with their ABCs (or ideographs). But they also learn some respect for their fellow citizens through the fifth (and only nonauthoritarian) Confucian relationship: friend to friend.[13]

TAIWAN: HISTORICAL OVERVIEW

In 1960, after a decade of GNP growth in excess of 7 percent annually, resource-poor Taiwan's per capita GNP was approximately the same as El Salvador's and Nicaragua's and substantially below that of Mexico, Cuba, and Brazil. Taiwan's adult literacy rate in 1960 was 54 percent, comparable to the Central American average (exempting Costa Rica) and below Mexico's, Cuba's, and Brazil's (although higher than that in most Asian countries). Life expectancy in Taiwan in 1960 was sixty-four years, comparable to such countries as Panama, Costa Rica, Cuba, and Argentina.[14]

In 1987, Taiwan's per capita GNP, at about $5,000,[15] was more than twice as great as any Latin American country's except oil-rich Venezuela, whose per capita GNP was $3,230 that year.[16] Illiteracy fell below 10 percent, and life expectancy was well in excess of seventy years. Furthermore, income distribution, which was comparable to highly skewed Latin American norms in 1960, is today comparable to the most equitable patterns of the developed countries of the West and Japan.

Progress toward democratic political institutions has been much slower, but with the passing of Chiang Kai-shek, and as a consequence of the reforms of his son, Chiang Ching-kuo, the political system has opened up substantially.

Taiwan's transformation has occurred in roughly the same time frame as Spain's. But, while external forces have had important effects on Taiwan's economic performance, the principal engine for the Taiwanese miracle, unlike the Spanish one, appears to have come from within.

Europeans and East Asians Vie for Domination

With about twenty million people living on an island about the size of Massachusetts and Connecticut combined, Taiwan is among the most densely populated countries in the world: more than 1,400 persons per square mile compared, for example, with Belgium and the Netherlands at about 800 per square mile, and Haiti, the most densely populated in the Western Hemisphere, with about 550 per square mile.

The island is mountainous and virtually without navigable rivers. About a quarter of the land is arable. Minerals are rare, and Taiwan is dependent on external sources for oil. Some two hundred thousand aborigines, believed to be of southeast Asian/Malay origin, preserve their languages and customs in Taiwan today.[17] But the vast majority of the population is of Chinese extraction. A trickle of Chinese immigration probably started before A.D. 1000, but the Chinese numbered only in the tens of thousands when the Dutch established a trading station there in 1624. Before that, the island was best known as a pirates' lair. (The Portuguese had already named the island Formosa—"The Beautiful.") A Spanish trading station followed a few years later, but the Dutch expelled the Spaniards in 1641 and effectively took control of the island. The Dutch, in turn, were ousted in 1662 by the Ming Chinese leader Cheng Ch'eng-kung, known to the Dutch as Koxinga. As the Manchus took over the mainland, Taiwan became the last bastion of the Ming Dynasty. The Manchus, now referred to as the Ch'ing Dynasty, conquered the island in 1683 and made it part of Fukien Province. During the next two centuries, Taiwan experienced an influx of Chinese settlers, who brought mainland China's mode of agricultural production to the island. Sugar was the principal export, although surpluses of rice and tea were also exported.

Japanese pirates had been using bases on Taiwan for centuries when, in 1871, fifty-odd shipwrecked Ryukuan sailors were massacred by Taiwanese aborigines. Both China and Japan claimed the Ryukyus, of which Okinawa is the best known, but the Ryukyuans' ties to Japan were stronger. Three years later, Japan's Meiji leaders sent a punitive expedition to Taiwan that overwhelmed the Chinese defenders and secured for the Japanese undisputed control of the Ryukyus as well as a sizable indemnity from the Chinese.

In 1895, some twenty-five years after the new Meiji rulers of Japan embarked on their astonishingly successful program of modernization (see chapter 4), Japan routed China in warfare and acquired both Taiwan, with about three million inhabitants, and the Pescadores Islands between Taiwan and the mainland. Taiwan remained a Japanese colony for fifty years, until the American defeat of Japan in 1945.

Japan sought both to gain economically from, and to extend its own culture to, its colonies. The Japanese were more purposeful than the European colonial powers: "Year by year, the Japanese census taker, the health inspector, the teacher, and, most ubiquitously, the policeman went earnestly, humorlessly, and sometimes mercilessly about their tasks of order, improvement, regimentation, and those activities we may collectively call modernizing."[18]

The first order of business was the suppression of the widespread banditry that had been common in Taiwan for so long. With peace consolidated, the Japanese turned to the promotion of agriculture as their top priority. Land tenure was studied and regularized, and the land of nonfarming landlords was purchased with bonds for distribution to those working the land, a reform that was repeated with great success half a century later under American auspices. The farmer associations that have played such a constructive role in Taiwanese agriculture in recent decades had initially been promoted by the Japanese. Except for state-owned sugar mills, which accounted for about 50 percent of industrial production in the 1930s, and other agro-industries, industrialization was deemphasized. The Japanese also invested in infrastructure—roads, irrigation, communications systems—and education, although advanced education was largely confined to agriculture and medicine.

Lewis H. Gann summarizes the economic consequences of Japan's colonization of Taiwan as follows:

> The Japanese . . . built railways, harbors, roads, schools, agricultural research stations, clinics. Government investment played an important part in capital formation. Taiwan had traditionally formed part of China's settlement frontier; much of the island had been developed during the late seventeenth and eighteenth centuries by emigrants from the mainland who had built up a market-oriented agricultural system from the inception of Taiwan's modern economy. The Japanese found favorable conditions when they attempted to modernize traditional sys-

tems of property rights, to assist cultivators by irrigation works, and to mobilize savings to finance domestic investments. The agricultural growth rate rapidly expanded, and Taiwan became a major producer of sugar and rice. Agricultural development . . . gave a boost to agricultural processing industries like sugar refining. . . . Private consumption rose in striking fashion . . . capital formation proceeded apace, as did the development of an indigenous working class and the expansion of an indigenous bourgeoisie with a stake in both farming and industry.[19]

Samuel Ho adds an important point: the principal export commodities were produced by small farmers, not on plantations. "Consequently, the peasant sector was increasingly brought into contact with the rest of the economy. . . . Because postcolonial Taiwan inherited a more integrated economy, it had a considerable head start, in comparison to other ex-colonies, in its efforts to industrialize."[20] On the other hand, as Ho notes, the Japanese suppressed the emergence of an entrepreneurial class.

In part because of traditional Japanese respect for Chinese culture, the Japanese treated the Taiwanese generally better than the Koreans, whose homeland formally became a Japanese colony in 1910, following the Russo-Japanese War. Dwight Perkins observes, "Taiwan did much better [than Korea] with a per capita GNP of nearly four hundred dollars (in 1981 prices) in the 1930s and with the people of Taiwan the main beneficiaries, but Taiwan's economy was still largely agricultural."[21] There was some anti-Japanese activity, particularly on the part of students, but to this day the Taiwanese are less negative in their view of Japan than are the Koreans.*

The Japanese Depart; Mao Threatens

With the defeat of the Japanese in 1945, Taiwan reverted to Chinese rule. The island was in bad shape as a result of bombings during the war and the departure of Japanese managers and technicians following Japan's capitulation. Chaos in China, as the Nationalists confronted both the vast problems of reconstruction and growing Com-

---

*During my 1990 trip to East Asia, one interlocutor suggested that another reason that Japan treated Taiwan better than Korea was that the Japanese Navy was responsible for Taiwan, the Army for Korea.

munist power, aggravated Taiwan's problems. One consequence was
an accelerating inflation that reached 3,500 percent in 1949.

The final defeat of Chiang Kai-shek's forces by the Communists
in 1949 completed the migration of about two million Nationalist
Chinese, about a quarter of them military, from the mainland to
Taiwan. The composition of the emigrants was in some respects
similar to the large numbers of Cubans who left their homeland for
the United States following Fidel Castro's victory: they were highly
educated (about one-half of the Chinese had at least a high school
education), including large numbers of managers, engineers, and
other professionals. The arrival of the mainlanders, who soon took
control of the island, antagonized the natives, who were three times
as numerous. Thousands of the natives had been massacred by the
mainlanders during a 1947 uprising. The vast majority of the Taiwanese were, to be sure, Chinese, but they spoke a different dialect
from most of the newcomers and in any event resented their intrusion and hegemony. On the other hand, the managerial/technical
gap caused by the departure of the Japanese was substantially filled
by the trained newcomers.

The cold war arrived in full force with the coming of Chiang
Kai-shek and his followers. With the outbreak of the Korean War
in 1950, the attention of the United States was partially diverted
from Europe to the apparently monolithic threat of Sino-Soviet
aggression in East Asia. Taiwan was a natural geographic link in an
East Asian defensive chain, along with Korea, Japan, the Indo-
chinese states, and the Philippines. With Mao's Chinese People's
Republic threatening Chiang's Republic of China over the control
of Taiwan, the United States began air and sea patrols in what was
then referred to as the Straits of Formosa. The U.S. military presence
was accompanied by a massive program of military and economic
assistance.

From 1949 until 1965, when economic assistance was terminated,
the United States provided Taiwan with grants and loans, including
food, totaling more than $1.4 billion.[22] Much of this assistance
expanded Taiwan's capacity to import, at the same time generating
New Taiwan Dollars for internal investment. Together with an additional $920 million of economic aid to support Taiwan's defense
effort, this assistance eased the country's balance-of-payments pressures and alleviated pressure on a budget swollen by defense require-
ments—and Chiang's overriding preoccupation with the threat from
the mainland. Substantial quantities of military hardware were also

provided, initially as grants, then as loans. (Since the mid-1970s, Taiwan has purchased defense equipment outright from the United States.)

In the early 1950s, U.S. aid played an important role in stabilizing an economy that had been prey to soaring inflation. It contributed to higher levels of investment—Samuel Ho estimates that U.S. aid financed almost 40 percent of gross domestic capital formation in the 1950s[23]—as the Taiwanese worked to increase their own savings. It had particularly important benefits in the agricultural sector, especially through the Joint Commission on Rural Reconstruction (JCRR), which helped Taiwanese farmers achieve significant increases in productivity and income, building on the farmer associations promoted by the Japanese. Taiwan's experience with community development was copied in Latin America and Africa, although with decidedly mixed results.

The aid program also enabled thousands of Taiwanese to study in the United States, most of them at the graduate level. Today, U.S.-educated Taiwanese abound in key public and private-sector institutions. As one example, of the forty-eight professional staff members of the prestigious Chung Hua Institute for Economic Research, twenty-eight have advanced degrees from American universities, almost all of them Ph.D.'s. In the 1989 cabinet, twelve of the twenty-one ministers had studied in the United States.[24]

But the huge aid program also gave the United States influence in economic policy matters, and, as in the case of Spain during the same years, U.S. advice served as a foundation for future dynamic growth. The United States supported the highly successful Taiwanese land reform program that not only rationalized production but also gave the former landlords capital for investment in industry;[25] opposed Chiang's Socialist proclivities and helped nurture the private sector; and served as a counterbalance to Chiang's efforts to expand the defense budget. Like Franco, Chiang was committed to an import substitution, autarchic economic policy, but in a country with a domestic market half the size of Spain's. As evidence accumulated that the policy of autarchy was running into the inevitable constraint of a small domestic market, American advisers pressed for an opening up of the economy that would reduce protection, expand exports, and encourage foreign investment. With the United States using aid as leverage, Chiang shifted to more open policies in 1959, the same year that Franco, also under pressure from the United States, shifted the course of Spain's economic policy in the same direction. Within a few years, the economies of both countries were booming.

Samuel Ho summarizes the impact of U.S. aid as follows:

> U.S. aid permitted a higher rate of growth; but beyond its effects on growth, aid also influenced the type of economy and society that developed in Taiwan. Politically, it made possible the survival of the Nationalist government and allowed it to remain in power in Taiwan. Economically and socially, it was helpful to restore stability and facilitated the development of a viable private sector and a growing middle class. Indeed, in the 1950's and the 1960's there was hardly an aspect of Taiwan's political, economic, and social life that was not in some way influenced by the presence of U.S. economic and military aid, albeit not always beneficially.[26]

Shirley Kuo, an economist who did graduate work at MIT and who is today governor of the Central Bank, adds, "U.S. aid was really an indispensable . . . factor in the economic development of Taiwan. However . . . [it was] . . . a 'necessary but not sufficient' factor. That U.S. aid could have helped bring such tremendous achievements in Taiwan was greatly due to the diligent and economical character of the Chinese, political stability, and the efficient policies implemented by the government."[27]

The Takeoff

Through the 1950s, Taiwan's net domestic saving averaged about 5 percent of national income annually, and U.S. aid allowed Taiwan to exceed the savings target that Walt Rostow establishes as a precondition for "take-off"[28]—net domestic savings at a level of 10 percent. Thereafter, savings increased rapidly as foreign aid declined, in part a response to government policies that promoted savings. In 1965, when aid was terminated, the net domestic savings rate had reached 16.5 percent. The rate increased steadily thereafter, exceeding 30 percent for the first time in 1972 and remaining above 30 percent in most subsequent years.[29]

The rapid increases in agricultural productivity in the 1950s, due especially to the land reform and the JCRR programs, expanded rural incomes, domestic food consumption, and export earnings. Industrial expansion in the 1950s and early 1960s was dominated by food processing. But the 1959 policy reforms, which increased incentives for exports, led to rapid diversification of the export sector. At first, textile and leather products surged, reflecting their predominant labor component. As management, marketing, and labor skills and productivity—and wages—improved, more emphasis was placed on capital-intensive products: petrochemicals, metals, machinery, and electronics.

Table 3.1 shows that, as in Spain (see table 2.1, page 65), industry rapidly supplanted agriculture in Taiwan both in contribution to national production and as a source of employment.

For most of the 1950s, public-sector industries, principally agroindustries inherited from the Japanese, accounted for the bulk of industrial production. Private-sector industries reached parity with the public sector in 1958, and by 1987, the private sector accounted for more than 85 percent of Taiwan's industrial production. Small- and medium-scale enterprises, the vast majority family-owned, have accounted for more than 98 percent of firms since at least the early 1960s. Its very small number of large enterprises distinguishes Taiwan from Korea and Japan,[30] but in all three countries, government has played an active role not only in policy but also in stimulating the growth of specific industries.

At the same time, Taiwan's inequitable income distribution has been transformed into one of the most equitable patterns in the world, almost identical to Japan's. In 1953, the top 20 percent accounted for 61 percent of national income, the lowest 20 percent for 3 percent. In 1986, the top 20 percent accounted for 38 percent, the bottom 20 percent for 8 percent.[31] As in Spain, the shift from an agricultural to an industrial economy has been an engine of equity. Also contributing to the dramatic improvement in income distribution, as well as the surge in productivity, has been a comparable

TABLE 3.1

TAIWAN'S ECONOMIC STRUCTURE

| | Percentage of Production | | | | Percentage of Employment | | | |
	1952	1963	1974	1985	1952	1961	1971	1987
Agriculture	35.9	26.7	14.5	7.0	56.1	49.8	35.1	15.3
Industry	18.0	28.2	41.2	44.8	16.9	20.9	29.9	42.7
Services	46.1	45.1	44.3	48.2	27.0	29.3	35.0	42.0

Source: Left side of table from Chi-ming Hou, "Strategy for Economic Development in Taiwan and Implications for Developing Economies"; right side from Shirley Kuo, "The Achievement of Growth with Equity"; both in Conference on Economic Development Experiences of Taiwan and Its New Role in an Emerging Asia-Pacific Area (Taipei: Academia Sinica, 1988), pp. 57, 77.

improvement in education. The literacy rate now exceeds 90 percent. And the percentages of secondary- and postsecondary-age Taiwanese youngsters actually in school compare with those of the industrialized countries.

The Taiwanese economy has grown with phenomenal speed. The average annual growth of GNP during the 1960s was 9.9 percent, during the 1970s 9.4 percent, and during the 1980s about 8 percent. During the same decades, exports grew at the annual rate of 23 percent, 13 percent, and 13 percent, respectively. Taiwan, which typically ran a small negative trade balance with the United States during the 1950s and 1960s, has since built up massive surpluses—about $16 billion in 1987. Taiwan's foreign exchange reserves currently approximate $75 billion.[32]

Real GNP has multiplied almost twenty times since 1952. The oil price shocks of 1973 and 1979 affected Taiwan (and Korea—both are wholly dependent on outside sources) at least as adversely as Argentina and Brazil, both of which have substantial petroleum deposits. But the prudence that has characterized Taiwanese and Korean economic policy since the 1950s permitted these two East Asian "dragons" to take these shocks, which staggered Argentina and Brazil, in stride.[33]

If the World Bank were still publishing data on Taiwan (it isn't, because mainland China, now a World Bank member, has insisted on Taiwan's exclusion), the island would almost surely appear in the list of high-income economies in the next few years.

Political Evolution Under the Chiangs

While Chiang Kai-shek focused his energies on the security problem, economic policy fell under the influence of a group of technocrats, mostly U.S.-trained, who, over the years, evolved into world-class professionals. Their basic orientation was toward the promotion and facilitation of rapid growth and the limiting of government involvement in production. The environment, including relative political stability and continuity, was optimal for private entrepreneurship, which has been dominated since the late 1940s by native Taiwanese. Many former landowners acquired liquidity for investment by selling the bonds they had received for land reform compensation. Driven by those aspects of Confucianism that in large part explain the striking success of the Chinese outside China, but with further impetus probably imparted by the native Taiwanese desire to show the mainlanders (and perhaps the Japanese) that they were just as good as they,[34] family manufacturing enterprises sprang up with astonishing speed and success, particularly after the 1959 opening up of economic policy.

Chiang ruled the political sphere with an iron hand, employing a network of security police unconstrained by due process. His short-term goal was to defend Taiwan from attack by the mainland Chinese. His long-term goal was to return to the mainland and overthrow the Communists. Like the dynastic Chinese emperors, he assumed an inherent right to power for himself and his Kuomintang party. Native Taiwanese aspirations for a greater say in politics were suppressed, often by force. As in many Latin American right-wing dictatorships, "democracy" was equated with "communism." In 1967, for example, the prominent writer and social critic Bo Yang, an early and influential voice for democratization, was imprisoned for nine years and tortured as a Communist agent.

But time and the dynamic economy were working against Chiang's autocratic presumption. As the years passed, economic pluralism produced not only unprecedentedly high growth rates but also an increasingly affluent, educated, cosmopolitan, and upwardly mobile middle class that communicated easily with the government professionals responsible for economic policy. Time was also running out for Chiang—he died in 1975 at the age of eighty-eight.

He was succeeded by his son, Chiang Ching-kuo, who had held high-level political and internal security posts from 1950 to 1965 in which he became known as a hard-liner. He was named defense minister, vice-premier, premier, and finally, three years after his father's death, president. In the words of Selig Harrison, "Adapting with surprising ease to the role of politician, Chiang [Ching-kuo] shed the hard-line image. . . . He developed a folksy political style; a baseball cap and turtleneck sweater became his trademark. Above all, he recognized the need to make political concessions to a rising middle class and Taiwan-born majority that resents domination by the Kuomintang . . . in-group of post-1945 mainland immigrants."[35]

An important element in Chiang Ching-kuo's strategy of liberalization was his selection as vice president in 1984 of Lee Teng-hui, a Taiwanese, Cornell University–trained agricultural economist. Lee assumed the presidency when Chiang Ching-kuo died in 1988 with two years of the term remaining. The opposition Democratic Progressive party for the first time won seats in the Taiwanese legislature

(21 of the 101 contested) in elections held in December 1989. (An additional 189 seats, most held by octogenarians representing mainland districts, were not up for election.) Following several violent demonstrations against the elderly incumbents of the noncontested seats, President Lee, unopposed, was reelected by the legislature in March 1990.

Taiwan is not yet a full-fledged democracy, but, in circumstances similar to those of Korea, it has taken several important steps in that direction. Moreover, the highly educated and affluent Taiwanese people, accustomed to economic pluralism and mindful of recent events in Eastern Europe and mainland China, are likely to insist that the final steps be taken.

KOREA: HISTORICAL OVERVIEW

Korea is a mountainous peninsula extending southeast from Manchuria. Slightly larger than the state of Minnesota, although with nothing like that state's arable land, it has a population of approximately sixty-five million, roughly two-thirds in the south, one-third in the north.

The first inhabitants of Korea were North Asian tribespeople of Mongoloid stock.[36] Their primitive culture was first affected by Chinese culture, particularly its agriculture and use of metals, in the third or fourth century B.C. It was at this time that the first state, Choson, emerged, in northwestern Korea. That name would be used for the entire country on several subsequent occasions, including during the Japanese occupation from 1910 to 1945, when Korea was referred to as Chosen.

The Han Dynasty Chinese colonized most of north and central Korea in the first century B.C., and China's colonial presence continued for about four hundred years. With China itself under attack by northern tribes, the Chinese presence in Korea was displaced by three Korean kingdoms: Koguryo, Paekche, and Silla, the first two of which were profoundly influenced from the outset by Chinese culture, including Confucianism. Within a century, Silla, too, adopted major elements of Sinic culture. T'ang Dynasty China attempted to reestablish colonial hegemony over Korea in the seventh century A.D. but failed, and Korea was unified under Silla leadership toward the end of that century.

What followed was "a wholesale borrowing of [T'ang Dynasty] Chinese culture and institutions," with Chinese Buddhism rather than Confucianism initially dominant. Reischauer observes, "the Koreans showed little interest in [Confucianism] during this period. For one thing, Confucianism was too closely associated with the examination system to have much appeal for the aristocratic Silla leaders. . . . [Nonetheless] Silla was remade into a little T'ang."[37] A century later, with Silla in decline, the examination system—using testing to measure merit—was adopted.

Silla's hegemony was followed by the Koryo (from which Korea gets its name) Dynasty, which lasted from 918 to 1392. Although the examination system was in use, commoners were rarely given access to it. Mahayana Buddhism reached its peak of popularity and influence during this time.

The Mongols conquered Koryo in 1258 and effectively controlled it for a century. The Koryo Dynasty was further weakened by repeated attacks by Japanese pirates. With the collapse of the Mongol empire in the mid-fourteenth century, the Koryo Dynasty was overthrown by a general, Y. Yi Song-gye. The Yi Dynasty, founded in 1392, was to endure for more than five hundred years. "Until the last few years of this period, Korea was in close tributary relationship with her great neighbor, and Chinese cultural influences were overwhelming. Yi Korea became a far more perfect replica of Ming China than Silla ever had been of the T'ang. In fact, Korea during this period of its history seemed at times even more Confucian and traditionally Chinese than China itself."[38]

Quite a different social structure evolved in Korea, mostly as the result of a sweeping land confiscation and redistribution carried out by Yi in 1390. The beneficiaries of the redistribution formed a landed aristocracy, the *yangbans*, who also controlled the bureaucracy. While the examination system was in use, in reality only *yangban* families had access to it, reminding us of the elitism of the Silla period. Reischauer observes:

> The examination system in Korea displayed many of the same virtues and faults that it had in China. It produced a bureaucracy chosen in terms of personal merit more than inheritance, though the class base [the *yangbans*] was much narrower in Korea than in China. It made government service the great ideal of the upper class, though, as in China, high government office was recognized as the surest means to personal enrichment. It placed men of intellectual inclination and philosophical training in charge of the mechanisms of government but at the same time exces-

sively emphasized the scholarly and literary skills and antiquarian and historical interests.[39]

The five hundred years of the Yi Dynasty were, however, marked by factionalism and strife that weakened Korea's ability to defend itself. The Japanese leader, Hideyoshi, invaded Korea in 1592, after the Koreans balked at joining Japan in an attack on China. With help from the Chinese and the fortuitous death of Hideyoshi in 1598 (the Tokugawa shoguns followed him), Korea succeeded in reestablishing its sovereignty, but the destructiveness of the fighting left Korea in chaos.

Japan Supplants China

The influence of the West was first felt in Korea through Roman Catholic missionaries who arrived in the second half of the eighteenth century. The Korean authorities viewed Christianity as a threat and attempted to suppress it, and Christians were persecuted throughout the nineteenth century. But the Western religion continued to spread. Religious intrusion from the West was followed by the nineteenth-century commercial and military intrusion that was the catalyst to profound change throughout East Asia. The Koreans, whose rigid class system had produced extreme poverty for the masses, were more aggressively isolationist than the Chinese in dealing with the West, and Reischauer suggests why: "they adopted Confucian ritual forms with a literalness that far surpassed the Chinese. This literal and sometimes blind acceptance of Chinese ideas naturally proved stultifying to intellectual development. It took even greater courage to be an innovator or iconoclast in Korea than in China itself."[40]

While China was immobile and Korea isolationist in the face of the threat from the West in the nineteenth century, Japan responded very differently indeed, as we shall see in chapter 4. The Meiji Restoration converted Japan from a traditional, isolated East Asian society into a world power in less than forty years. Following a show of Japanese naval force in 1876, Korea opened two additional ports to trade with Japan (Pusan had served as an entrepôt since a 1609 treaty), and the Japanese presence in Korea increased substantially. The Japanese and Chinese competition for influence in Korea led to the Sino-Japanese War (1894–95), in which Japan over-whelmed China and, among other things, acquired Taiwan as a colony.

The subsequent competitors for Korea were Japan and Russia. That competition ended in 1905 when the Japanese navy sent a Russian fleet to the bottom of the Straits of Tsushima. After years of bloody resistance by the Koreans, Japan formally annexed Korea in 1910 and renamed it Chosen. As I have noted, Japan was far harsher in its administration of Korea than of Taiwan, especially because the Japanese had greater respect for the Chinese, whose civilization had made an indelible impression on them starting in the sixth century B.C., than for the Koreans, whom they had temporarily conquered at the end of the sixteenth century. Intensifying Korean nationalism, fanned by Christian missionaries—mostly Protestant and mostly American—also contributed to the harshness of Japanese administration.

But while the Japanese abused the Koreans (they killed thousands during demonstrations for independence in 1919), they also invested more heavily in Korea than in Taiwan, particularly in infrastructure and industry. By 1940, Korea had the best railroad system in East Asia after Japan, as well as advanced highway, electricity, and com-munications systems. The public sector was the principal promoter of industrialization, which was focused in the north. But the colonial authorities coordinated closely with the *zaibatsu* (industrial con-glomerates) in a pattern of government–private sector cooperation that has been the hallmark of both Japan's and Korea's—and, to a degree, Taiwan's—industrial surge since World War II. (In Korea, a conglomerate is called a *chaebol*.)

Agriculture was modernized, but the Japanese took control of much of the land; the vast majority of Koreans farmed as tenants. Japanese and Korean landlords were the principal beneficiaries of increased agricultural production, but so were Japanese consumers: "By the 1930's half the rice crop was being exported to feed Japan, but the per capita consumption of rice in Korea had reportedly dropped 45 per cent."[41] As in Taiwan, the Japanese extended and modernized the education system, while confining the curriculum to skills that supported Japanese interests. The influence of the Japa-nese educational model, as with government-business collaboration, is still felt in South Korea today.

Dwight Perkins summarizes the economic impact of Japanese rule as follows: "a sustained rise in per capita GNP over three decades was accompanied by a fall in the standard of living of most Koreans. Japanese businesses and Japanese and Korean landlords reaped most of the benefits."[42] Japan's political legacy was reinforced authoritarianism, intensified nationalism, and disruptive factionalism, the latter including a vigorous Communist cadre.

The Japanese Depart; the Americans Arrive

Korea was in chaos as World War II ended. Within a few months, seventy thousand Japanese managers (roughly one-tenth of the total Japanese population of Korea), the backbone of colonial administration, had returned to Japan, leaving a massive vacuum. Troops of the Soviet Union, which shares a small border with Korea, arrived on the scene a few days before V-J Day. American troops arrived three weeks later. The 38th parallel became the line of demarcation between them. What followed was typical of the first cold war skirmishes. American hopes for a unified Korea notwithstanding, the Russians quickly linked up with Korean Communists in the north and established a typical Soviet-style government headed by Kim Il-sung. The U.S.-educated and Christian—but autocratic—Syngman Rhee headed a party that won elections in mid-1948, and he was installed as president of the new Republic of Korea. Within a year, Soviet and U.S. troops had withdrawn, and the stage was set for North Korea's attack on the South.

North Korea was substantially stronger than South Korea, in part because it possessed most of the industrial capacity built up by the Japanese, in part because of extensive military aid from the Soviets. The United States returned in force to defend the South, rolled back the North Korean troops, was in turn set back by the massive intervention of the Chinese, and settled for a stalemate near the 38th parallel. Casualties were very high: 900,000 Chinese, 520,000 North Koreans, 300,000 South Koreans, 142,000 Americans.[43]

Following the 1953 armistice, the United States shifted its attention to the reconstruction and development of South Korea, although U.S. military forces remain there to this day. Rhee ruled the country until 1960, and his obsession with security, like Chiang Kai-shek's in Taiwan, led not only to a large military budget but also to intimidation and worse of his political opponents. U.S. aid played a crucial role in keeping the economy afloat, but in the face of inflationary pressures, little more than stabilization could be achieved with Rhee's inward-looking economic policy, essentially the same kind of policy that impeded growth in both Spain and Taiwan. It was during this period that Confucianism was viewed by some Americans as an obstacle to progress, and indeed, in terms of the political authoritarianism implicit in Confucianism and the way that authoritarianism was wielded by Rhee, no doubt it was.

The Takeoff

A popular uprising, led by students, precipitated Rhee's resignation in 1960. Elections were held, but the Democratic Party's leader, Chang Myon, was unable to get things under control. The military stepped in during May 1961, and General Park Chung Hee became president. Edward S. Mason observes, "Rhee was very little an administrator and very much a politician as contrasted with Park, who had shown himself to be a very effective administrator but to whom politics and politicians were anathema."[44] Park's Democratic Republican Party won elections in 1963 that set the stage for major economic stabilization programs in that year and in 1966, policies that emphasized the external market and both domestic and foreign investment, although with limits on the latter. The new policies, in part stimulated by the announcement that the United States intended to terminate economic assistance in the near future,[45] triggered the explosive, export-driven growth of the Korean economy for at least the next two decades, much as the reforms of 1959 triggered the Spanish and Taiwanese economic miracles.

Korea's economy responded rapidly to the new policies. Growth from the end of the Korean War to 1962 had averaged about 4 percent annually. From 1962 to 1987, it averaged about 9 percent. (Growth exceeded 12 percent annually during 1986–88.) During those twenty-five years, real GNP increased almost nine times, and real per capita GNP almost quintupled. From 1965 to 1980, exports increased at the phenomenal rate of 27 percent annually, while industrial production increased by 17 percent annually. In 1955, Korea was among the poorest countries in the world. Today, the World Bank lists it as an upper-middle-income country with a standard of living roughly comparable to Portugal's (but with a more dynamic economy). The change in the structure of the Korean economy is comparable to that of Spain and Taiwan (although income distribution is somewhat less equitable in Korea). See table 3.2.

TABLE 3.2
STRUCTURE OF PRODUCTION AND LABOR FORCE

	Percentage of GDP			Percentage of Labor Force		
	1960	1978	1987	1960	1965	1980
Agriculture	40	24	11	66	55	36
Industry	19	36	43	9	15	27
Services	41	40	46	25	30	37

Source: World Bank, World Development Report 1980 and 1989 (New York: Oxford University Press).

In 1960, 72 percent of Korea's population lived in rural areas; in 1987, the figure had dropped to 31 percent.

The growth of education in Korea since World War II has, as in Taiwan, been among the most rapid in the world, partly as a consequence of government policy but also clearly reflecting the high priority the Korean people attach to education (as evidenced, for example, by the high proportion of educational costs financed by Korean families). At least a quarter of the population was literate when the Japanese departed. Today, not only is literacy well in excess of 90 percent but the proportions of youngsters of primary, secondary, and postsecondary age who are actually in school are comparable to those of the developed countries of the West, Japan, and Taiwan. As in Taiwan, Korea's technocrats and other professionals are now world-class. Thousands have studied in the United States.

As in Spain and Taiwan, improvement of the rural standard of living has principally been the consequence of rapid industrialization, although it was also facilitated by the sweeping land reform initiated by the U.S. military government in the late 1940s. With 60 percent of the land owned by either Japanese or Koreans who were judged to have collaborated with the Japanese, the reform was relatively easy to implement and highly confiscatory. The result was both a vastly more equitable pattern of landholding and improved farm family income that neutralized the Communist's only viable issue.

But industrial investment, increasingly self-financed, and export were the principal engines of growth. In the mid-1950s, Korea was still a predominantly agricultural and mining (principally iron and tungsten) country. Raw materials accounted for 95 percent of exports in 1954. By 1965, 61 percent of exports were manufactured, principally fabric, clothing, and wood products. As in the case of

Taiwan, the government played an active role in guiding and promoting investment and exports. For example, the decision to go into shipbuilding, now a highly important component of Korea's economy, was forced on the private sector by President Park. Rapid export-led growth shifted industrial production away from employment-intensive products (for example, textiles) to capital-intensive products (for example, automobiles). But the industrialization process was unlike Taiwan's in one important respect: it was led by large conglomerate industries (the *chaebol*), such as Samsung, Hyundai, and Daewoo, rather than by family enterprises. In this respect, Korea's economic miracle is more like Japan's than Taiwan's.

In the 1950s, most investment was financed by U.S. aid programs. In the early 1960s, gross domestic savings approximated 3 percent of GNP. Stimulated by growth and government policies, and by the decline in aid, the rate exceeded 15 percent late in the same decade and is today well above 30 percent, once again comparable to the experience of Taiwan.[46]

Many Koreans feel incredulous about the scope of their achievement and anxious about their country's future, particularly should the world economy sour. Exports and imports represent almost 60 percent of Korean GNP, among the highest in the world (the figure for the United States is about 18 percent). Their anxiety intensified when growth dropped below 7 percent in 1989, still highly respectable by world standards but following three years when annual growth exceeded 12 percent. But it is difficult to foresee circumstances, short of acute worldwide recession, in which a country that has developed so much entrepreneurial, technical, and public policy talent will not continue to progress, albeit more slowly than at the astonishing rates of recent years.

Moving Toward Pluralism

In Korea . . . the imposition of a high degree of centralism on a homogeneous society has resulted in a vortex, a powerful, upward sucking force active throughout the culture. This force is such as to detach particles from any integrative groups that the society might tend to build—social classes, political parties, and other intermediary groups—thus eroding group consolidation and forming a general atomized upward mobility. The updraft also tends to hinder such developments as definition of function, legal boundaries, formal procedures, and specialization. This vortex appears to account in part for Korea's unnatural retardation in these areas at the same time that she is developed in personal and family culture, education, political consciousness, and even urbanization.[47]

This characterization of Korean politics by Gregory Henderson as a vortex rushing through a vacuum, to the top, with no intermediating institutions, describes well the country's political evolution after World War II, particularly its difficulties in achieving democratic pluralism.

Elections were again held in 1967, and President Park Chung Hee was reelected by a narrow margin.* By the terms of the constitution that he had promoted, this should have been his last term. But two years later, Park proposed a constitutional amendment, subsequently endorsed in a referendum, that would permit him a third term. In the 1971 election, he narrowly defeated Kim Dae Jung, a young congressman, but his Democratic Republican party failed to win the two-thirds congressional majority he wanted for freedom of action. Park seized the opportunity presented by bellicose North Korean gestures to declare first a national emergency and then martial law.

This was followed by the promulgation of a new constitution that placed virtually all power in Park's hands. The government arranged the kidnapping of Kim Dae Jung, who was saved by the intervention of the United States. Park's concern with security understandably intensified when North Korea tried to assassinate him in 1974. Demonstrations against Park, often led by students, increased in frequency and intensity, in part reflecting the rapid growth of an educated, politically aware middle class. Some demonstrators identified Park with the United States and attacked U.S. cultural centers.

In an increasingly chaotic political environment, Park was assassinated by his Director of Central Intelligence late in 1979. General Chun Doo Hwan took power two months later, dashing the chances of liberalization. Many Koreans returned to the streets, above all in the neglected (by both Rhee and Park) province of South Cholla, the home of Kim Dae Jung. On 18 May 1980, students in the city of Kwangju were joined by the populace in demonstrations approaching insurrection, which provoked a violent response from the army. Somewhere between two hundred and two thousand demonstrators were killed, and, since the troops were under the overall (but not operational) command of an American general, the United States

---

*Some observers believe that there was so much manipulation of elections prior to the presidential elections of 16 December 1987 that it is inaccurate to use the word *elections* without adding quotation marks.

was blamed by some either for provoking the massacre or for not putting an end to it. Neither allegation was justifiable, but the Kwangju massacre is to this day a rallying point for anti-Americanism in Korea.*

Chun was "elected" by indirect vote later in 1980. His authoritarian government was under continuing pressure, particularly from demonstrators, to open up the political process. National assembly elections were held early in 1985, and Chun's Democratic Justice party narrowly defeated the New Korea Democratic party of Kim Dae Jung, who had been under house arrest and was prohibited from running for office, and Kim Yong Sam. The opposition insisted on direct elections for president, but Chun resisted. The pressure, including that of the U.S. government, became so intense, however, that General Roh Tae Woo, Chun's hand-picked successor, reversed the latter's stand and committed himself to a generalized liberalization of political activity and to open direct elections in which Kim Dae Jung could participate.

Four major candidates ran in the elections of December 1987, which the *New York Times* described as "South Korea's first experiment with a freely elected democracy":[48] Roh Tae Woo, Kim Dae Jung, Kim Yong Sam (who had split with Kim Dae Jung), and newcomer Kim Jong Pil. Roh won with 36 percent of the vote; Kim Yong Sam, with 27 percent, narrowly beat Kim Dae Jung. An activist National Assembly was installed. Early in 1990, President Roh made the stunning announcement that Kim Yong Sam and Kim Jong Pil had joined his government, leaving only Kim Dae Jung in opposition. Korea, whose evolution from authoritarianism to democratic pluralism had, like Taiwan's, been slow and painful, had advanced to the point where some observers were talking about the irreversibility of the movement toward full democracy,

*At the request of the United States Information Service, I spoke to Korean professors and students in Kwangju and Pusan in March 1990 on the subject of dependency theory—the view that the poverty of the underdeveloped countries is explainable by imperialistic exploitation by the developed countries, above all the United States. The two lengthy sessions were strikingly similar in tone and content to discussions I have had with professors and students in Mexico, Central America, and South America on the same subject. The irony, of course, is that Korea has been one of the world's foremost examples of how an open, outward-looking economy—tantamount to the "dependency" model—can produce rapid growth. Many of the Korean participants had studied in the United States, where they had learned, from American professors, dependency theory, which was until quite recently the conventional wisdom for many U.S. social scientists.

widespread student demonstrations in the spring of 1991 notwithstanding.

As in the case of Taiwan, dynamic economic pluralism appeared to be dragging Korea toward political pluralism.

THE COMMON DENOMINATOR: CULTURE

The post–World War II histories of Taiwan and Korea track each other closely. The departure of the Japanese left both former colonies in chaos. Both confronted a military threat from Communist compatriots. Both received substantial military and economic aid—and advice—from the United States. Both executed effective agrarian reform programs (it is noteworthy that no agrarian reform programs in Latin America have been comparably successful). Education has received a high priority in both countries, and educational levels are comparable to those in advanced countries. Both chose economic policies that depended heavily on private-sector production for export, but the governments of both played an activist role. Both have achieved inordinately high levels of domestic savings and have experienced extremely high growth rates sustained over decades, the oil price shocks notwithstanding. Policy continuity has been assured by autocratic leaders who have governed both countries for most of the postwar period, but both appear to be evolving toward democratic pluralism in recent years.

As for the differences, per capita GNP is higher in Taiwan by about $2,000, reflecting, in part, the higher standard of living of the Taiwanese at the end of World War II. Income distribution is more equitable in Taiwan, although Korea's income distribution is far from the extremes of inequality common in Latin America and elsewhere in the Third World. Government has played a somewhat more active and direct role in promoting production and export in Korea than in Taiwan, and Korea has controlled foreign investment more tightly. Big conglomerates, largely unknown in Taiwan (but of great importance in Japan), have been a key factor in Korea's economic miracle.

There are also oft-commented national differences in personality and style. Lucian Pye notes that the Chinese tend to be conservative, judicious, and reserved, while the Koreans are characterized by "a bold, risk-taking style of action." He attributes this in part to differences in child rearing: filial piety has been a more powerful force in the Chinese household, and "pressures [for achievement] were secondary to those involved in being a dutiful son. . . . In Korea the parents' responsibility to protect the children's interests was explicitly recognized, so that socialization was more than just training in dutifulness. . . . The home provided a sanctuary from which the young could go out to do battle and assume high risks, knowing they could always retreat to their homes without shame."[49] By contrast, in the Chinese family, "[s]elf-expression or the strivings for autonomous behavior on the part of children are discouraged or suppressed as nothing more than selfishness."[50]

On balance, the similarities between Taiwan and Korea far outweigh their differences. Moreover, there are striking parallels between their postwar performance and that of Japan, Hong Kong, and Singapore. Those parallels are also relevant to the historic success of the Chinese in Thailand, Malaysia, Indonesia, and the Philippines; of the Japanese in Brazil; and of the Chinese, Japanese, and Koreans in the United States (see chapter 5).

I know of no one who will disagree that culture is a factor in East Asian achievement. The problem, as the University of California political scientist Robert Scalapino observes, is how to "determine that mix of culture, scale, timing, leadership, and policy that shapes a given society at a given period."[31] If, however, in that mix, culture plays the principal role or, to use Ronald Inglehart's words, if "culture is an essential causal element that helps shape society,"[52] we are getting close to a scholarly taboo—"cultural determinism"—which, in Scalapino's words, "is no more acceptable than economic determinism or a form of political determinism currently in vogue which I would label 'policy determinism.' "[53]

Nor do I know of anyone who will argue the case for cultural determinism as forcefully as Marx did the case for economic determinism. In my earlier book, I cited some of the numerous factors other than culture that influence how societies develop: resource endowment, geography, leadership, government policies, international economic forces, the vagaries of history, sheer luck.[54] But in analyzing the course of Latin America's evolution over the centuries, I concluded that culture is the *principal* factor explaining its disappointing performance. If that constitutes cultural determinism, so be it. The erosion of the credibility of the Marxist thesis to disintegration at the end of the twentieth century in no way invalidates the Weberian thesis. In my own view, the demise of Marx, along with the striking progress of East Asia and its contrast with persistent underdevelopment in Latin America and Africa, strengthens Weber's credibility.

In his 1988 lectures at Harvard, Scalapino observed that "China, Japan, and Korea . . . shared a respect for education, for the family as the critical nucleus of society and repository of values, and for a pervasive work ethic—all of which could support developmental goals under certain conditions. . . . by the same token, each of the four so-called Small Dragons—South Korea, Hong Kong, Taiwan, and Singapore—have drawn deeply upon the benefits available from the Sinic culture which they share."[55] But he did not attempt to weight the causative cultural and other factors in those fascinating lectures.

The Harvard economist Dwight Perkins, who has specialized in East Asia, has attempted a mathematical analysis aimed at isolating the significance of culture. The analysis separates out of high East Asian growth rates the components of growth attributable to quantitative increase of labor, quantitative increase of capital, and the residual, which he labels the "productivity growth rate." Productivity is a function of the amount of capital available to the worker as well as the skill, efficiency, and working hours of the worker. In Perkins's analysis, the capital contribution to productivity is factored out (it appears in the quantitative increase of capital), and what is left in the residual is strongly influenced by such factors as education, motivation, organization, management, and technology.[56]

Perkins concludes that "capital and labor growth rates . . . account for about half of the 9 to 10 percent national product growth rates achieved for sustained periods in East Asia from the 1950s to the 1970s. The other half was accounted for by increases in productivity."[57] That does not mean that "culture" can claim 50 percent of the causation of the East Asian miracles. Even with capital and labor growth factored out, there are noncultural dimensions to the education, motivation, organization, management, and particularly technology components of productivity. On the other hand, there are important cultural dimensions to the growth of capital (the propensity to save, which, as we have seen, is inordinately high in Sinic cultures) and the growth of employment (which reflects the propensity for entrepreneurship).

The bottom line of Perkins's calculation with respect to the importance of culture is probably unquantifiable with any precision. But it is quite possible that values and attitudes have contributed more to growth than any other single factor, such as policy, the world economic environment, and surely geography/natural resource endowment. This conclusion gathers strength when one considers the wide variety of policy (for example, Brazil), economic (for example, the United States), and geographical/resource (for example, Hong Kong) environments in which East Asians have excelled. We might also add that prudent policies—and leadership—can be interpreted as reflecting culture at least in part. There are, after all, some parallels between the success of individual Taiwanese and Korean enterprises and the success of the two national economies.

This short review of Taiwanese and Korean history pinpoints several noncultural factors as contributors to the rapid growth of these two countries in recent decades: the infrastructure endowment from the Japanese colonial period, the pressure of an external threat, U.S. aid and advice, and political stability and continuity (I will argue that the last mentioned has important cultural roots). But there have been other countries—Egypt and Pakistan come to mind—where these same factors have been substantially in place without producing high rates of growth with equity.

I appreciate that, with the exception of Perkins's analysis, the evidence of the significance of culture is circumstantial and inferential. But I believe that the patterns of achievement and success of the East Asians in so many different settings are so strikingly similar that most readers will conclude that if culture isn't the most important single factor, as I suspect it is, it is surely *one* of the most important.

Weber on Chinese Culture

Max Weber's *Confucianism and Taoism* was published in German *(Konfuzianismus and Taoismus)* in 1920. It was first published in English as *The Religion of China* in 1951.[58] In it, Weber analyzes the impact of Confucianism and Taoism on the capacity of the Chinese to achieve dynamic capitalism, particularly in contrast to the Protestant ethic and, especially, Calvinism. The subsequent success of the overseas Chinese (and the Koreans) has been cited as evidence of a fundamental flaw in Weber's analysis.*

*The post–World War II economic success of Italy and Spain has also been cited as evidence of a fundamental flaw in Weber's belief that Catholicism provides an

In noting the absence of modern capitalist development in China between the middle of the seventeenth century and the end of the nineteenth, Weber points to the power of the literati elite—the mandarins—as a force against innovation: "each and every innovation could endanger the interests of the individual official with regard to the perquisites of his office." Yet he gives full recognition to "the quite extraordinary degree of development and intensity of the money-making urge of the Chinese," and adds, "Material well-being has never in any civilized land been so emphatically represented as the ultimate goal as it has been in China."[59]

In stressing the absence of capitalist accumulation and investment, he notes that, whereas the rural population of Western Europe declined as capitalism spread, and farm size there increased through consolidation, in China, the rural population expanded rapidly while farm size shrank. The resulting predominance of small farms reinforced both traditional rice agriculture and the traditional peasant world view. The failure to modernize the rural sector was an important consequence of the mandarins' resistance to tax and administrative reforms that threatened their interests.

Weber also cites the absence of an effective legal system: "the best known of [the imperial] edicts constituted codifications of ethical, not legal, norms, and were distinguished by their literary scholarship." Subjective and often irrational decisions by the emperor or the mandarins discouraged investment. Weber further observes that, in contrast with Protestant ethic Puritanism, which "impersonalized everything . . . in China, all communal activity remained enclosed in and conditioned by purely personal relations." He concludes:

> The limitation of viewing things in an objective manner imposed by the ascendancy of personal relations has . . . had considerable significance for economic attitudes as an obstacle to objective rationalization. . . . it had a tendency to bind the individual over and over again in his inmost feelings to the members of his kinship group and those with whom he had kinship-like relations. . . . The great achievement of the ethical religions, and in particular of the ethical, ascetic sects of Protestantism,

---

unpropitious value setting for economic dynamism. Readers of chapter 2 will appreciate how external factors and Spain's secularization leave Weber's views, at least in the case of Spain, substantially intact. Similar factors of outside stimulation and secularization have operated in Italy since the end of World War II. Its rapid recent growth notwithstanding, Italy remains at the lower end of the range, as measured by per capita GNP, of European Community countries.

was to break down kinship bonds and confirm the superiority of community based on faith and an ethical way of life over community based on blood ties. . . . In economic terms this meant confidence in business matters being founded on ethical attributes of each individual as proved in his objective work at his calling.[60]

But it is in another dimension of the Confucian value system that Weber encounters the principal obstacle to the development of rational enterprise capitalism. The Confucian values riches but sees them as the natural consequence and perquisite of the mandarin's role—or of luck or corrupt behavior. The other way of making money—producing, buying, and selling—is, in the Confucian view, *infra dig.* (This looking down the Confucian nose at artisans and tradespeople has its analogue in the traditional attitudes of landed gentry toward the "working classes" in other cultures, including traditional Iberia and Hispanic America.) Weber put it this way:

For Confucius all real economic vocational work was the Philistine task of professionals. The specialist . . . could, for the Confucian, never be elevated to a position of really positive honour, whatever his value in terms of social utility. The reason for this—and this was crucial—was that "the superior man" (the Confucian gentleman) was not a "tool," i.e. he was in the self-perfection of his adaptation to the world an ultimate goal in himself; he was not . . . a means to impersonal goals of any kind whatsoever. *This central statement of the Confucian ethic was a rejection of specialization of profession, of a modern professional bureaucracy and of vocational education; above all . . . it constituted a rejection of economic training in the pursuit of profit.* [61] [Italics added.]

The mandarins were not only snobbish but intrusive. The historian John K. Fairbank observes, "Merchants were dominated by officials, on whom they depended for protection, or else they became semi-officials themselves, showing the spirit of monopolistic tax-gatherers rather than of risk-takers in productive enterprise. The classical doctrines of the state gave little thought to economic growth and stressed the frugal use of agrarian taxes rather than the creation of new wealth."[62]

The mandarin administration created a two-tiered society: the literati and the others. The mandarin structure extended down to district (but not village) level. Aloofness of local administrators was assured not only by virtue of their self-assessed intellectual and moral "superiority" but also by such standing policies as moving administrators every three years and prohibiting their assignment to their hometowns. Those people governed by the literati generally had no use for them and ignored them as much as possible in pursuing their own interests. For this second tier, the masses, frugality was "a form of hoarding, ultimately to be compared with the peasant accumulating his savings in his stocking. Saving was undertaken in order to guarantee funeral expenses and the good name of the family, and in addition for the sake of the honour and delight of possession as such, as is the case everywhere where the attitude towards wealth has not yet been broken down by asceticism."[63] That translates into accumulation of wealth without investment. (Iberian—and Latin American—mercantilism could be similarly characterized.)

Weber believed that Confucianism propagated passive attitudes about accumulation of wealth. Since accumulation of wealth was, in the Calvinist doctrine, the evidence of God's grace, a key difference between Confucianism and Calvinism is the latter's stress on striving for success (what Pye refers to as "psychic anxiety" leading to "desire for achievement").[64]

The Cross-currents of Confucianism

Weber's analysis highlights the powerful cross-currents that characterize the traditional Chinese value system. The dualism is apparent from a shift I often heard mentioned during my 1990 visit to Korea: in the 1950s, Americans cited Confucianism as a major impediment to progress; in the 1980s and 1990s, many see Confucianism as the principal engine of progress.

With respect to economic development, the Confucian emphasis on education, merit, hard work, and discipline, combined with the achievement-motivating tradition of ancestor worship and Tao emphasis on frugality, constitutes a potent, albeit largely latent, formula for growth comparable in its potential to Weber's view of Calvinism. This potentially explosive mixture was suppressed by the low prestige the Confucianists attached to economic activity; by the limits placed on such activity by the Confucian emphasis on the family/clan above the broader society; by the relative rigidity of Confucian hierarchy and authoritarianism (the merit system serving as the principal path for social mobility); by the burden of filial piety (Lucian Pye observes, "For the Chinese the rules of Confucian filial piety make loyalty the supreme value, even to the point of hobbling merit and effectiveness");[65] and above all, by the extraordinary influence of the literati bureaucrats in the shaping of national policies, which almost always reflects their interest in preserving their privileged position as well as their disdain for economic activity.

But the latent positive forces as well as the stultifying forces have been perpetuated. When the Chinese have emigrated—a process of self-selection of achievers, as John Kenneth Galbraith has pointed out in *The Nature of Mass Poverty* [66]—they have almost always found themselves in circumstances where the stultifying forces have been diluted: economic activity has been more prestigious in most of the societies to which they have migrated (as indeed it has become in Taiwan and Korea); in an alien setting, the family/clan became a particularly valuable institution for self-help, especially since most emigrants were natives of southern China, where the clan structure was most highly developed;[67] the weight of filial piety was often removed by geographic separation; and the Confucian (and Marxist/Maoist)[68] unification of politics and economics, which underlay the disproportionate and suffocating influence on economic matters by the mandarins, did not confront the Chinese overseas.

With the suppressing forces of traditional Chinese culture diminished, the explosive potential of the positive forces has been substantially realized not only in Taiwan and Korea but also by the Chinese in Hong Kong, Singapore, Thailand, Indonesia, Malaysia, the Philippines, Indochina, and elsewhere, including the United States, as we shall see in chapter 5. (Japan's spectacular performance has been driven in part, as we shall see in chapter 4, by some of the same Confucian ideas, although they operate in a distinctive setting.)

Thus, it seems to me that the answer to what Edward Mason describes as "the perplexing question why the Confucian culture, which assigns so low a value to business activity, has accommodated itself to the rise of so many successful entrepreneurs"[69] lies in the conflicting currents of Confucianism itself. Neutralize the forces that suppress entrepreneurship, above all bureaucratic suffocation, but also promote entrepreneurship's prestige, and you have a critical mass of achievement motivation that approximates that of Weber's Calvinists. As Ambrose Y. C. King observes in explaining the extraordinary levels of entrepreneural activity in Hong Kong, "unlike Imperial China, the most promising road to social eminence in Hong Kong is not by becoming officials and scholars, but through gaining wealth in the business world."[70]

If there is any doubt about what happens to Chinese entrepreneurship in the absence of an overbearing bureaucracy, it should be dispelled by the performance of the Chinese economy after Deng Xiaoping's economic liberalization of 1978: growth had averaged 10 percent annually until the Beijing Spring in 1989. Deng's reforms, by the way, also document the cross-cutting nature of Confucian values: one of his objectives in 1977 in reinstituting the examination system (an eminently Confucian concept) that was discontinued (as elitist) by Mao early in the Cultural Revolution was to combat the familism/clannism (eminently Confucian) that had evolved as the basis for personnel decisions.[71]

To be sure, as I have already noted, other, noncultural factors also contributed to the Taiwan and Korea miracles, for example, the security threat from a neighbor, substantial aid (although in Korea's case, this was a mixed blessing) and generally good advice from the United States, sound policies, and continuity of policy. But I believe that culture may be more important than any other single factor. For one thing, as Stephan Haggard notes, sound policies do not appear from out of the blue,[72] and good policies in part reflect the Confucian tradition. But particularly compelling is the performance of overseas Chinese in countries where policies have not always been sound or purposefully executed (for example, Thailand and Indonesia, until recently, and the Philippines), as well as their superior performance in good policy settings (as in contemporary Thailand and Indonesia).

Weber's analysis of the impact of Chinese culture on economic growth identifies both positive and negative forces. Where both forces have been preserved—as in China itself, at least until Deng's reforms—the result has been entirely consistent with his observations about the suffocating effects of mandarinism. That Chinese have migrated to settings where the negative forces have been suppressed or diluted, often under Western influence, and done very well, as have the Koreans with pro-growth leadership (and also with some Western influence), would not, I think, have come as a surprise to Weber.[73]

CONTRASTS:
EAST ASIA AND LATIN AMERICA

There are both parallels and divergences between the cultures of Confucian East Asia and Ibero-Catholic Latin America. With respect to the radius of identification and trust, the Chinese (and Taiwanese) and Koreans are family- or clan-focused, as in Iberian culture, but that focus extends to nonfamily members through the fifth Confucian relationship (friend to friend) and to the broader community and nation through the first Confucian relationship (ruler to subject). These broader identifications are substantially stronger than those of traditional Iberian culture, which is reflected in the income distribution patterns of Taiwan and Korea, which are so much more equitable than the typical Latin American pattern (and than Spain's, until recent decades). The radius of trust in Taiwan and Korea is probably not as far-reaching as it is in the Protestant (and perhaps secularized Catholic) countries of the West, where a universal ethical code tends to override familism. One indicator of this difference: most enterprises in Korea and particularly Taiwan are family-owned.

The five Confucian relationships largely circumscribe the East Asian ethical code, while Catholicism is the principal source of the Iberian ethical system. The former is more exigent than the latter, although the familism common to both cultures (and enshrined in three of the five Confucian relationships) is a force for a double ethical standard—rigorous within the family, flexible and self-serving outside.

Authoritarianism is deeply rooted in four of the five Confucian relationships, and it has been the hallmark of the political histories of Korea and China. The authoritarian traditions of East Asia and Latin America are both strong, and both regions have had difficulties in constructing democratic pluralist institutions.

But unlike Iberian culture, Sinic culture also stresses values—education, work, discipline, merit, frugality—that, if not squelched by bureaucracy, are powerful engines of economic growth and economic pluralism. Progress toward political pluralism in both Taiwan and Korea has been driven by the attitudes and educational levels engendered by dynamic economic pluralism, and by the achievement of relatively equitable patterns of land and income distribution.

Moreover, both countries have been profoundly influenced by the United States and its value system, principally through large aid programs related to security concerns, a U.S. military presence (still substantial in the case of Korea), the many Taiwanese and Koreans who have studied in the United States, and extensive business relationships. There are some parallels with the Spanish miracle in several of these respects.

THE GENIUS OF CONFUCIUS

In this chapter we have noted the contemporary vitality and relevance of the ideas of Confucius and his disciples. Yet he lived 2,500 years ago. By modern standards, his precepts concerning authority, hierarchy, and order are both reactionary and obsolete. But his views on education, merit, discipline, and work, coupled with the Taoist tradition of frugality, have been an important driving force in the immense achievements in human progress in East Asia during the past forty years. It is well worth remembering that Confucianism was also the principal force behind a Chinese civilization that in most respects, including human well-being, outpaced Europe until the Enlightenment. Among Chinese inventions were paper, printing, the wheelbarrow, gunpowder, porcelain, the use of coal, and the water mill.

The persistence of the Confucian ethos through more than two millennia is a compelling reminder of the power of culture, as well as an eloquent tribute to its creator.

4

The Japanese Miracle
The Meiji Restoration Shows the Way

[S]ocialization within the Japanese culture causes its members to internalize and perpetuate a culture pattern that demands much from succeeding generations in standards of performance. To become ethnically Japanese by growing up in a Japanese family, whether in Japan, the United States, or Brazil, is to become motivated in such a way that energy is mobilized and directed toward the actualization of long-range goals. A strong need for accomplishment in some form, be it traditional or modern, artistic or economic, motivates Japanese generally.
— George A. DeVos, *Socialization for Achievement* (1973)

[T]he Japanese capacity for saving and investment was to prove unique in the modern world. Wide familiarity with long-range economic investment, the goal-oriented nature of the society, and a tradition of frugality and pride in simple living may account for this phenomenon. In any case, no other people in the past century have, without government compulsion, consistently saved and invested so high a percentage of the national income.
— Edwin O. Reischauer, *East Asia: The Modern Transformation* (1960)

The Meiji Restoration was a cultural revolution carried out in order to create a modern state.
— Kuwabara Takeo, in *Meiji Ishin: Restoration and Revolution* (1985)

The world is well aware of Japan's astonishing transformation from the devastation and militarism of World War II to economic dynamism and affluence within democratic norms, all during just a few decades. The enlightened policies of the American occupation clearly contributed to this extraordinary achievement. But the Americans had pursued comparably enlightened occupation policies in Nicaragua, Haiti, and the Dominican Republic earlier in this century with little enduring benefit for those countries. Nor did the American presence in the Philippines for almost half a century result in anything like the spectacular Japanese success.

The principal reason for the Japanese "miracle" is the Japanese themselves. A look at the Meiji Restoration, a comparably dramatic transformation that occurred in Japan during the second half of the nineteenth century—a transformation in which the United States also played a role—should dispel any doubt that the roots of Japan's performance since World War II reside in Japanese soil, above all, Japanese values and attitudes. Those values and attitudes were shaped in part by Confucianism, which continues to influence Japanese culture profoundly as we approach the end of the twentieth century.

HISTORICAL OVERVIEW

The West Arrives in East Asia

As late as the fifteenth century, China surpassed the West in most aspects of human achievement and progress, and Japan, profoundly influenced by Chinese culture, was not far behind. Four centuries later, in the wake of the Enlightenment and the Industrial Revolution, the West had overtaken China and Japan in virtually all the factors that constitute national power: military technology and strength; industrial and commercial technology and dynamism; institutional vitality; infrastructure and communications; educated and skilled human resources; and national cohesiveness.

The Ch'ing (Manchu) Dynasty in China and the Tokugawa shoguns in Japan, both of whom had come to power in the seventeenth century, had each pursued essentially isolationist policies, but for different reasons. The Chinese, secure in their high self-esteem and low regard for foreigners, were convinced that they had little to learn from the "barbarians." The Japanese, far less secure, perceived foreigners (other than the Chinese, from whom they had taken so much, starting in the sixth century), particularly Christian foreigners (there were some 300,000 Japanese converts to Catholicism by the early seventeenth century),[1] as a threat to Japanese culture and security.

In the first decades of the nineteenth century, both the Ch'ings, in their Confucian/mandarin unitary empire, and the Tokugawas heading "a largely feudal state . . . [with] a highly developed status structure and committed to Confucian norms,"[2] were experiencing dynastic fatigue—the cyclical erosion of vitality and unity common throughout East Asian history. One indicator of deterioration in China was the increasingly widespread use of opium. As many as ten million Chinese, including many government officials, may have been addicted to the drug by the early 1830s.[3] The principal source of opium was British India, and the importance of that trade to the British led to confrontation with China, as it attempted to arrest the flow, and eventually to the Opium War of 1839–42. Superior British military technology prevailed, and in the first of the "unequal treaties," China ceded Hong Kong to Britain, opened five ports to trade, and granted "extraterritoriality" to British subjects, who thenceforth operated in China under British, not Chinese, law.

Trade concessions and extraterritoriality were soon extended to other Western countries, including the United States. The British and the French forced the full opening of China to trade through military action in the late 1850s. Shanghai, with much of its municipal administration and system of justice in the hands of Western countries, principally Britain, became a symbol of Ch'ing China's impotence, further underscored by repeated peasant rebellions during the second half of the nineteenth century; by the crushing defeat of China by Japan in the Sino-Japanese War of 1894–95; by the West's suppression of the xenophobic Boxer Rebellion in 1900; and by the collapse of the Ch'ing Dynasty in 1911.

The reaction of the Japanese to the intrusion of the West in the nineteenth century contrasts strikingly with Chinese complacency and impotence. That intrusion combined in a mutually reinforcing chemistry with the steady erosion of Tokugawa power to produce the Meiji Restoration—and what may well be the most sweeping, most rapid national development experience in history. Against the backdrop of the Meiji achievements, Japan's astonishing success in the second half of the twentieth century should come as no surprise.

The Tokugawa Shogunate

In 1603, Tokugawa Ieyasu* proclaimed himself shogun—military governor or overlord—ending a period of more than a hundred years of civil strife among feudal lords, or *daimyo*. He succeeded in pacifying and uniting Japan first by military skill and power, then by "devis[ing] mechanisms for maintaining an advantage over his recently defeated peers; and ensur[ing] that his retainers would remain agents of his own and his family's will rather than pursue ambitions of their own."[4]

Tokugawa Ieyasu increasingly viewed the presence of Spanish and Portuguese Catholic missionaries as a threat both to his control and to Japan's integrity. Many of the daimyo, particularly on Kyushu, and several hundred thousand lesser Japanese had converted to Catholicism, placing in doubt their loyalty to the emperor, who was, after all, supposed to be descended from the gods. Tokugawa consequently pursued a policy of persecution against the missionaries and their followers that culminated in a brutal suppression of Catholic clergy and lay people by his successor, Hidetada, comparable in its use of torture and execution, ironically, to the Inquisition conducted by the Catholic Church in Spain at the same time. Thereafter, except for a trickle of trade through Nagasaki, Japan was hermetically sealed for two and a half centuries.

One of the most effective Tokugawa devices to assure tranquillity was *sankin-kotai*, a system requiring the daimyo to spend alternate years in the Tokugawa capital of Edo (which was to be renamed Tokyo by the Meiji leaders). When a daimyo returned to his domain, his wife and children had to remain in Edo, essentially as hostages. The capital thus became a dynamic crossroads, attracting large numbers of other Japanese to feed, clothe, educate, and entertain the semiresident nobility and their entourages, as well as the shogunate's bureaucracy, the *Bakufu*. Edo also became a center for cross-fertilization of ideas.

Japan's experience with feudalism paralleled Europe's in many respects. While the Tokugawas succeeded in establishing centralized control over Japan through the Bakufu, their feudalist system nur-

---

*Tokugawa was the prototype for Toronaga, who became shogun, in James Clavell's enormously popular novel's *Shogun*. One of Tokugawa's advisers was Will Adams, an English pilot of a Dutch ship, who was the prototype for the novel's protagonist, Blackthorne.

tured a degree of decentralization, even a limited kind of pluralism, in sharp contrast to China's bureaucratic centralism. Feudalism fostered the evolution of towns, artisans, merchants, and guilds, as it did in Europe. The growing towns placed pressure on agriculture, both by attracting low-paid agricultural workers to higher-paid urban jobs and by increasing the demand for farm products. These pressures, in turn, increased the leverage of those who stayed to work the farms and created incentives for increased production and productivity.

Japanese feudalism diverged from European feudalism in at least two respects: a disproportionately large number of Japanese were *samurai*, or military-caste feudal retainers—as many as two million of the total population of some thirty million in the mid-nineteenth century; and the system did a better job of educating its people: 40 percent of boys and 10 percent of girls had attended schools in 1868.[5]

Nathan Rosenberg and L. E. Birdzell, Jr., note that "Western European and probably Japanese feudalism seem to have contained the seeds of social arrangements suited to sustained economic growth." They go on to observe, "The most striking political effect of Western and Japanese feudalism was to create a plurality of power centers, each combining major or minor military strength with the economic base necessary to its support."[6] In Japan's case, this pluralism was a central factor in the demise of the Tokugawas—and feudalism—in 1868. By then, most of Europe had already experienced two centuries or more of postfeudal nationalistic capitalism and, in a few cases, most prominently Britain, substantial progress toward liberal democracy.

"Troubles at Home; Dangers from Abroad"

Japan made significant economic progress during the peaceful centuries of Tokugawa rule. Consistent with the Confucian value system, agriculture was the most esteemed productive activity, second in prestige only to government or military service. The taxation system was based on agriculture, which expanded notwithstanding the tax burden, although not as rapidly as industry, commerce, and finance. Largely ignored by the daimyo, prosperous Japanese peasants increasingly invested in highly profitable commercial and industrial enterprises instead of investing in more land. Industry and commerce, initially the least prestigious professions, flourished, in part because of low tax burdens and the growth of cities. The use of money and credit expanded, as did the sophistication and reach of financial institutions.

But by the middle of the nineteenth century, three key feudal groups—the shogunate itself, the daimyo, and the samurai—were in acute economic distress. Their financial well-being was tied to the taxes on agriculture, which grew relatively slowly. Because of the financial burdens of *sankin-kotai* visits to Edo, a rising standard of living accompanied by rising expectations, and inflation, pressures to spend were intensifying. One way for the daimyo to cut expenses was to reduce stipends to the samurai, which intensified the latter's problems without solving those of the former. The Bakufu resorted to "forced loans" and the creation of revenue-producing monopolies to cover its chronic deficits. Many daimyo fell deeply in debt to merchants and bankers; many samurai at the lower end of the complex rank structure descended into poverty.

Tax pressures also reduced many farmers to poverty. Rural unrest intensified: nearly four hundred incidents of large-scale violence were recorded between 1813 and 1868,[7] some involving significant numbers of not only peasants but also others in economic distress, including lower-level samurai and village headmen. It is perhaps an exaggeration to conclude that Tokugawa feudalism was in crisis in the mid-nineteenth century, but it was surely in trouble.

It was not Europe but the United States that was to present the "dangers from abroad" that combined with "troubles at home" to topple the Tokugawas.[8] American interest in Japan stemmed principally from the whaling operations of New Englanders near Japan and the trading voyages to China of American clipper ships. Provisioning and sanctuary from typhoons were the main attractions of having access to Japanese ports, but, like the Europeans in China, the Americans were also seeking trade opportunities.

Although several American ships had docked in Japanese ports beginning as early as the late eighteenth century—and had, I might add, been treated with uniform hostility and rudeness, consistent with Tokugawa xenophobia—it was not until Commodore Matthew Perry steamed into Edo Bay in 1853 that the dangers from abroad became real. Perry's squadron, two steam frigates and two sloops, was vastly superior in firepower, speed, and maneuverability to anything the Japanese possessed, and it was capable of both leveling Edo and bringing it to its knees by blockade (most of the city's food supply arrived by sea).

Perry in effect delivered an ultimatum to the shogun, exceeding his instructions: either open your ports or we attack. He pledged to return the following year to receive the response of the Japanese, who were both traumatized and intimidated. A Japanese observer noted:

The military class had during a long peace neglected military arts; they had given themselves up to pleasure and luxury, and there were very few who had put on armour for many years. So that they were greatly alarmed at the prospect that war might break out at a moment's notice, and began to run hither and thither in search of arms. The city of Edo and the surrounding villages were in a great tumult; in anticipation of the war which seemed imminent, the people carried their valuables and furniture in all directions to conceal them in the house of some friend living farther off.[9]

The ultimatum prompted the shogun's chief adviser, Abe Masahiro, to seek the advice of all the daimyo for the first time in 250 years of Tokugawa rule. They could reach no consensus. Many concluded that early hostilities would result in defeat for Japan; a minority supported concessions to the Americans. When Perry returned early in 1854, this time with eight ships that constituted 25 percent of America's naval strength, Abe agreed to open two ports. Other concessions followed, particularly as a result of the skillful diplomacy of the American consul, Townsend Harris. By 1860, Japan was substantially open to trade.

The Bakufu's concessions alienated a majority of the daimyo and accelerated the unraveling of Tokugawa power. Fighting broke out between those domains who supported the Bakufu and those who wanted to do away with the shogunate. The rallying cry of the latter was *sonno-joi*— "Honor the emperor, expel the barbarian." Choshu, an important domain at the southern tip of Honshu, confronted the central government and was ultimately joined by a former foe, Satsuma, at the southern tip of Kyushu. Both domains had resisted the Western encroachment and had fired on Western ships, with disastrous consequences. The policies of both were guided by young, nationalistic, and talented samurai bureaucrats, particularly Kido Koin of Choshu and Okubo Toshimichi of Satsuma. Their vision was of a dynamic, modern Japan unified under the emperor, whose importance had dwindled to insignificance during the 250 years of Tokugawa rule. *Sonno-joi* was replaced by *fukoku-kyohei*— "Enrich the country, strengthen the army."

On 3 January 1868, the forces of Choshu and Satsuma, supported by troops from the domains of Echizen and Nagoya, ousted the last Tokugawa shogun, Keiki. Marius Jansen notes, "The . . . coup d'état was . . . a product of a fierce competition for leadership in the cause of reconstruction and modernization; there was virtually universal agreement that some new structure of governmental decision-making was necessary."[10] The Emperor Mutsuhito, fourteen years old, became the first emperor of the *Meiji Ishin*. *Meiji* means "Enlightened Rule"; Nagai Michio notes that "[a] literal translation of *ishin* might be 'renewal,' 'evolution,' or 'innovation,' but at least two other English expressions have been widely used . . . 'restoration' [applied to the role of the emperor] . . . and . . . 'revolution.' "[11] Indeed, the Meiji Restoration has been compared to the American, French, Russian, and Chinese revolutions.[12]

The Meiji Revolution

During its first decade, the Meiji government was guided principally by Kido Koin and Okubo Toshimichi, whose "breadth of understanding and openness of mind show what remarkable men had been propelled to national leadership by the turmoil of the preceding two decades." Like most of their colleagues, they were pragmatists and utilitarians. Their philosophy was "a natural and easy blend of the Confucian concept of the perfectibility of society through proper ethico-political organization and leadership, and Western confidence in science as leading to unlimited progress."[13]

Early in 1868, Kido established two key goals: to "promote men of talent on every side, [the government] devoting itself fully to the welfare of the people," and to place Japan on "an equal footing with other countries of the world."[14] The Charter Oath of April 1868 set the tone:

1. An assembly widely convoked shall be established and all matters of state shall be decided by public discussion.
2. All classes high and low shall unite in vigorously promoting the economy and welfare of the nation.
3. All civil and military officials and the common people as well

     shall be allowed to fulfill their aspirations, so that there may
     be no discontent among them.
4. Base customs of former times [that is, an isolationist foreign
     policy] shall be abandoned and all actions shall conform to
     the principles of international justice.
5. Knowledge shall be sought throughout the world and thus
     shall be strengthened the foundation of the Imperial
     polity.[15]

The first operational priority of the Meiji government was the dismantling of the feudal structure and the reinforcement of the central government. The former was accomplished in three major steps: in 1869, the daimyo were retitled imperial governors, and land registers were centralized; in 1871, the domains were converted to prefectures and the tax system was unified; in 1876, income payments to the imperial governors were discontinued and they were paid off, handsomely, with bonds. Stipends to samurai were terminated in the same year, but their compensation, also in bonds, left them with a fraction of their earlier income.

By 1871, the central government had been reorganized along typical Western lines into ministries (of, for example, finance, war, foreign affairs, justice, industry, education) that were principally responsible for the conduct of government affairs. An appointed bicameral legislature had also been created. Military conscription was introduced in 1873, the first major institutional step toward the militarism that would characterize Japanese governments for decades to come. With the collapse of the feudal hierarchy, social mobility increased dramatically. In a period of just a few years, a rigid caste system had been dismantled and replaced by a virtually classless system based on merit.

The longer-term foundation of the Meiji program was education, and the education system was designed to produce both effective workers and effective citizens. Some Japanese had interested themselves in Western learning starting in the mid-eighteenth century. Under the Meiji government, Western learning—indeed, all things Western—became an obsession. Late in 1871, 107 Japanese, led by Kido and Okubo themselves, started off on a tour that was to include eight months each in America and Europe. The impact of their visits was profound. Kido, writing from America in 1872, "confessed that he had not previously realized how far ahead of Japan the Western world was in matters of civilization and enlightenment: 'Our present civilization is not true civilization, our present enlightenment is not true enlightenment.' Only education in 'true schools' could close the gap."[16]

One shortcut was to invite foreign experts to Japan. Dr. David Murray of Rutgers College served as a key adviser to the Ministry of Education for six years, starting in 1873. The United States Commissioner of Agriculture, Horace Capron, advised the Japanese in the early 1870s on the development of Hokkaido, the northernmost large island. The president of the Massachusetts Agricultural College, William S. Clark, became the first head of the Sapporo Agricultural College, which ultimately became Hokkaido University. (Clark uttered the immortalized words, "Boys, be ambitious for Christ!"—the last two of which have since fallen into disuse.) German physicians were the dominant influence in medical sciences. Aids to navigation were installed under the guidance of an Englishman. Professor E. S. Morse of Harvard was the founder of Japanese studies in zoology, anthropology, archaeology, and sociology. Reischauer notes that "[b]y 1879 the Ministry of Industry employed 130 foreigners whose salaries accounted for nearly three-fifths of the ministry's fixed expenditures."[17]

Foreign missionaries, especially Americans, also made a major contribution to education. For example, missionaries founded schools in Tokyo in 1874, 1883, and 1886, which evolved into universities. Japanese Christians played a major role in promoting university education for women. In 1872, sixteen months of schooling became compulsory for both boys and girls. (Compulsory education had been instituted in England in 1870, in France in 1882, in the United States in 1918, and in Germany in 1919.) The term was subsequently increased to three, then six, years. Beyond primary school were middle academic and technical schools, academic and technical high schools, women's high schools (women were not expected to go beyond this level), and the state universities, of which the University of Tokyo, founded in 1869, is Japan's best known and most prestigious.

Initially, the curriculum was influenced by French and American educational concepts; consistent with the American pattern, administration of the schools was decentralized. A major shift occurred in the 1880s that symbolized a turning away from the West and a reaffirmation of Japanese culture. The Meiji leadership opted for "[a] highly centralized, strictly controlled education system . . . more in keeping with the Confucian concept of the close relationship between education, morality, and government; and better adapted to building a strong and prosperous state than the decentralized and freer American system."[18] The 1890 Imperial Rescript on Education captures the profoundly Confucian quality of the prevailing educational philosophy:

> Our Imperial Ancestors have founded our Empire on a basis broad and everlasting, and have deeply and firmly implanted virtue; Our subjects ever united in loyalty and filial piety have from generation to generation illustrated the beauty thereof. This is the glory of the fundamental character of Our Empire, and herein also lies the source of Our education. Ye, Our subjects, be filial to your parents, affectionate to your brothers and sisters; as husbands and wives be harmonious, as friends true; bear yourselves in modesty and moderation; extend your benevolence to all; pursue learning and cultivate arts, and thereby develop intellectual faculties and perfect moral powers; furthermore advance public good and promote common interests; always respect the Constitution and observe the laws; should emergency arise, offer yourselves courageously to the State; and thus guard and maintain the prosperity of Our Imperial Throne coeval with heaven and earth. So Shall ye not only be Our good and faithful subjects, but render illustrious the best traditions of your forefathers.[19]

In a period of less than two generations, and without foreign aid programs, the Japanese transformed their country from one of substantial illiteracy, comparable to that of many poor countries today, to virtually full literacy. The extraordinary success of the Meiji education program is apparent from table 4.1.

TABLE 4.1

PERCENTAGE OF
ELEMENTARY SCHOOL–AGE
CHILDREN ENROLLED

	Male	Female	Total
1873	39.9	15.1	28.1
1880	58.7	21.9	41.1
1895	76.7	43.9	61.2
1905	97.7	93.3	95.6

Source: Hara Hiroko and Managawa Mieko, "Japanese Childhood Since 1600," English manuscript version of a chapter in Zur Sozialgeschichte der Kindheit, ed. Jochen Martin and August Nitschke (Freiburg/Munchen: Verlag Karl Alber, 1985), p. 176.

The First Economic Miracle

The Meiji leaders saw industrialization as crucial to the strengthening of the nation's military capability, and it received a high priority. A start had been made on weapons production under the shogunate, particularly in the Satsuma domain, and on shipbuilding, at yards constructed in Nagasaki and Yokosuka. The Meiji government managed these facilities and built several additional ones. What would become one of the finest railroad systems in the world was born in 1872 with the inauguration of a nineteen-mile stretch between Tokyo and Yokohama. A line was opened between Kobe and Osaka in 1874 and extended to Kyoto in 1877. By 1880, most major cities were connected by telegraph lines.

But heavy industry and communications did not help a "dangerous imbalance that had developed in its trade."[20] Basically starting from scratch, the government, through the Ministry of Industries, built or promoted mining, machine tool, glass, and textile enterprises, the last mentioned of special importance as a means of reducing imports. Foreigners were paid to advise Japanese industries on new technologies, and many Japanese studied engineering and related disciplines in Europe and the United States.

The promotional role of government, as described by Reischauer, will sound very familiar to those who have studied today's intimate relationship between the Ministry of International Trade and Industry (MITI) and the private sector:

> In their eagerness to see Japan grow economically, [the government leaders] cajoled reluctant businessmen into new and still risky fields of activity; they helped them assemble the necessary capital, sometimes by putting pressure on other businessmen, sometimes by providing government subsidies of a type that would now be considered examples of corruption; they helped enterprising younger men to advance at the expense of their more conservative elders; and they forced weak companies to merge into stronger units."[21]

Government dominated industrial development in the early Meiji years, either by direct ownership and management of large plants or through its promotional role. But the principal engine of growth was not government but a vast pool of energetic, innovative, and thrifty entrepreneurs. In the later Tokugawa years, the Confucian stigma to business in general but commerce in particular began to dissipate as the wealth and power of businesspeople increased. The process was accelerated by the Meiji emphasis on national power and the crucial role played by the productive sectors in that quest.

The merchants/financiers, who were so influential in the later Tokugawa years as the Bakufu, the daimyo, and the samurai went deeper into debt, expanded their activities and founded several *zaibatsu* conglomerates, including Mitsui and Sumitomo. Many samurai put their military training, particularly management know-how, to good use as entrepreneurs. With the discontinuation of their stipends in 1876, many had no choice but to find work, but they did have the advantage of the capital represented by their severance bonds. It was an ex-samurai, Iwasaki Yataro, who founded Mitsubishi. Interestingly, the peasant sector was an even more important source of entrepreneurs than the samurai. Farming was substantially on a commercial footing in the late Tokugawa years, and many farmers achieved levels of affluence and business savvy that permitted them to diversify into commerce and industry. Some went on to establish *zaibatsu*.

The Meiji modernization program and the heavy financial obligations involved in liquidating the feudal structure, as well as the cost of suppressing daimyo rebellions, precipitated a fiscal crisis in the late 1870s. As inflation accelerated, some Meiji leaders proposed to float a loan in London. But the government consensus called for a program of retrenchment instead, and it was guided by the talented Matsukata Masayoshi, first as Home Minister (1880), then as Minister of Finance (1881–92). A major feature of the austerity program was the sale of the government's industrial enterprises to the private sector—what we today call "privatization." There were no buyers until the government dropped the prices substantially, and many insiders, both friends of government officials and government officials themselves, then benefited handsomely. Many of the beneficiaries expanded their holdings into *zaibatsu*. The government finally divested itself of all its industries except armaments and naval shipbuilding, communications, and public services.

With Matsukata guiding policy, the economy recovered rapidly from retrenchment, and a prolonged period of stability and rapid growth ensued. Although Japan has never produced significant amounts of cotton—as is true of so many other raw materials used in Japanese production to this day—cotton spinning expanded rapidly, as did railroad construction. Japan was still importing 90 percent of its cotton yarn in the early 1880s. By 1897, Japan had become a

net exporter. From 1883 to 1890, railroad mileage increased from
244 to 1,449. Growth in a wide range of other industries, including
mining, cement, chinaware, and electricity, was comparably impressive. Further impetus was imparted by the military victories over
China in 1895, the Chinese indemnification for which covered all
of Japan's costs in waging the war and included the ceding of Taiwan
to Japan; and over Russia in 1905, which led to Japan's annexation
of Korea in 1910.

In a span of less than forty years, Japan had transformed itself from
a traditional, essentially agricultural, feudal society into a world
power.

The Seeds of Contemporary Japanese Democracy

Western influence extended beyond education and industrialization
to political philosophy. The Japanese historian Taguchi Ukichi observes: "We study physics, psychology, economics and the other
sciences not because the West discovered them but because they are
the universal truth. We seek to establish constitutional government
in our country not because it is a Western form of government, but
because it conforms with man's own nature."[22] Kido returned from
his trip to the United States and Europe convinced that constitutional government should be Japan's goal.

The first political grouping, the Society of Patriots, was formed in
1873 at the initiative of Itagaki Taisuke, a prominent samurai of the
Tosa region, with active support of disgruntled samurai and in the
wake of intense debates over policy toward Korea (see page 98).
Among its objectives was an elected legislature. Two years later,
discussions among Itagaki, Kido, and Okubo led to the creation of
a Supreme Court, designed to assure independence of the judiciary,
and a Chamber of Elders that was assigned the task of drafting a
constitution (an effort that foundered a few years later). Conferences
of prefectural governors were held in 1875, 1878, and 1880, the
second producing an agreement on the election, by male taxpayers,
of prefectural assemblies.

Itagaki was dissatisfied with the execution of his agreements with
Kido and Okubo, and he revived his Society of Patriots with a call
for a liberal democratic government. The response was massive,
particularly from intellectuals, who dominated a burgeoning journal-

ism (by 1875, over a hundred periodicals were being published), and prosperous peasants, who constituted the principal taxpaying group. At a convention in 1880, the party adopted a new name: the League for Establishing a National Assembly. A year later, the name was changed again, to the Liberty (or Liberal) party. Other parties soon sprang up in support of constitutionalism.

The government responded to these challenges by suppressing dissent through libel laws aimed at throttling press criticism of government and through a law limiting public gatherings. Repression reached an extreme when a decree authorized the government to expel from Tokyo anyone judged to threaten public tranquillity.

But as opposition intensified, the government also committed itself to a constitution, with a national assembly, by 1890 and assigned Ito Hirobumi, former Minister of Industries, to the task. Ito led a group to Europe in 1882, spending most of his time in Germany and Austria, where he found Bismarck's political theories particularly congenial. Upon his return, and in anticipation of the constitution, he eliminated the headless Council of State and replaced it with a cabinet formed of the departmental ministers, naming himself its prime minister. As decisions on the constitution approached, he relinquished the prime minister's job in favor of the presidency of the Privy Council, which was created in 1888 to approve the constitution.

The constitution was promulgated early in 1889 as "the gift of the emperor." While it contained an equivalent of the bill of rights, the wording about its application was ambiguous (for instance: "except in cases provided for in the law" or "within limits not prejudicial to peace and order").[23] A bicameral legislature, the Diet, was established: a House of Representatives and a House of Peers, composed mostly of nobility, which was to serve as a conservative check on the lower house. Members of the House of Representatives would be elected by adult males who paid sufficiently high taxes—less than 2 percent of the population was eligible to vote.

The Diet was far from a debating society. Its approval was required for all laws, although the emperor could temporarily dismiss it. The constitution also contained a provision that assured continuation of appropriations at the prior year's level if the Diet failed to pass a budget.

But the Meiji constitution contained flaws that inevitably undermined the consolidation of democracy:

[It] left quite vague the degree of control the Diet could exercise over the administrative processes of government through its functions of voting budgets and approving laws. It left even more ambiguous the degree of control the cabinet and Diet could exercise over the army and navy through control of the purse strings. Worst of all, it assumed clear moral leadership on the part of the emperor . . . but it failed to create a situation where emperors could give this leadership and did not provide organs which could perform this role in the place of the emperors.[24]

These weaknesses debilitated government, particularly after the passing of the gifted Meiji generation, and facilitated the rise of militarism in the 1930s. For much of the first half of the twentieth century, the forces of freedom and authoritarianism would vie with each other, as they did in the first decades of the Meiji Restoration. The authoritarian currents, which nurtured an aggressive national-ism, prevailed, with catastrophic consequences for Japan and the rest of the world. But the democratic currents were not destroyed: "In nineteenth-century terms, the progress of Meiji Japan toward de-mocracy was a significant and surprising success, for it was the first demonstration that elements of democracy could be transplanted and live in a society with neither native democratic heritage nor a strong belief in democratic ideals." And in measuring the extraordi-nary achievements of the Meiji leaders, we must be mindful that their principal goal was to strengthen their nation rapidly so that it would never again be brought to its knees by threats of force:

The success of the Meiji leaders was probably greater and more rapid than even they had expected. In a mere half century, they built a powerful modern nation out of a feudally fragmented and technologically back-ward country, thereby winning the national security and equality they longed for. In terms of their own objectives, their achievements consti-tute the national Cinderella story of modern times.[25]

The Contrast Between Japan and China

Why did Japan drive itself to modernity, and equality with the West, while Ch'ing China gradually disintegrated? The Chinese psyche, obsessed with the idea that China—the Middle Kingdom—had a monopoly on virtue, wisdom, and refinement, could not come to grips with the superiority of the West. The Chinese, inhabiting the second largest country in the world in terms of area, had for centuries relied on a centralized administration that isolated itself from the grass roots. There was thus neither a sense of urgency to mobilize the nation against the intrusions of the West nor the administrative capacity to pull it off; instead there was complacency and disintegration.

Several factors may help to explain the dramatically contrasting Japanese response. Unlike the Chinese, who had a history of first being invaded and then absorbing the intruders into Chinese culture, the main Japanese islands had never been successfully invaded. The Mongols, under Kublai Khan, tried in the thirteenth century but were repelled by a combination of Japanese grit and a typhoon, since referred to as the Divine Wind, or *kamikaze*, that decimated the Mongol fleet. Thus, Perry's demonstrably realizable ultimatum was particularly shattering.

Nor were the Japanese irrevocably anchored to their culture. They had already experienced a cultural revolution by beneficially borrowing Buddhism, Confucianism, governmental organization, financial institutions, the writing system, art, and music from the Chinese during the sixth through the ninth centuries A.D.: "By the early seventh century, the volume of borrowing had become so great as to mark the start of a new age in Japanese history."[26] To this day, the Japanese are particularly respectful of China.

By the eleventh century, the centralized Chinese-style governance of Japan had eroded, and feudal institutions had begun to root. The feudal period reached its peak under the Tokugawas and, as already noted, helped to create the preconditions for modern capitalism, particularly decentralization and the rudiments of a market system, much as had Europe's experience with feudalism.

But beyond these historic factors lies a traditional system of Japanese values and attitudes that not only helps explain the spectacular response to the intrusion of the West in the second half of the nineteenth century but also has a lot to do with the spectacular performance of the Japanese economy since Japan's shattering defeat in World War II. The Meiji Restoration—or, more accurately, Revolution—was an expression of a national commitment to progress that had been conceptualized and articulated by a gifted group of leaders. It revived a Confucian view of the role and importance of the state—as what Ronald Dore has labeled "coordinator and animator of development"[27]—that has been a hallmark of Japanese development ever since. But the Meiji Revolution was brought about principally by the Japanese people, and it reflected their own drive for achievement, progress, and dignity. Japan's post–World War II leadership pales by comparison with the architects of the *Meiji Ishin,* but the contemporary economic performance of the Japanese people is highly evocative of their performance a century ago.

JAPANESE CULTURE

A comprehensive analysis of Japanese culture is beyond the scope of this chapter, nor do I have the knowledge or experience to do it justice. It is also unnecessary for the purposes of this book to enter the hot debate over the relationship between Japan and the United States, or the comparably hot debate between those who see Japan as a model and the revisionists who see only the warts. What is beyond debate are three salient facts: Japan has experienced more rapid economic development than any other country in the world during the past 125 years; it has achieved a high degree of social equity and harmony (World Bank statistics show Japan as the most equitable of all advanced countries with respect to income distribution);[28] and a democratic system imposed on it by the United States has taken root. It is also beyond debate, as we shall see in the next chapter, that the Japanese who have migrated to America have done extremely well: Japanese-Americans and Jewish-Americans are the two highest-achieving ethnic groups. The pattern of Japanese success is the same in Brazil, as we saw in chapter 1.

I do not know how this Japanese achievement can be explained except as essentially a cultural phenomenon. Historical factors (such as the contact with China, the feudal experience) and geographic factors (such as insularity, leading to racial, linguistic, and cultural homogeneity; a temperate climate) are clearly relevant and have, it must be noted, also had important influences on the evolution of Japanese culture. But historical and geographic factors leave a vast explanatory gap that only culture can fill.

A discussion of the four basic cultural factors I have used in other contexts may be helpful here, as a means of both better understanding at least some important aspects of Japanese culture that have influenced its development and facilitating comparisons with other countries. I am fully aware that what follows implies an unrealistically static model. As Ronald Inglehart points out, Japan, like other advanced industrial countries, is experiencing a shift to postindustrial, postmaterialist values, and "[c]ultural differences [among countries] are relatively enduring, but not immutable."[29] There is no doubt that Japan is changing—but the traditional culture is still very much alive.

The Radius of Identification and Trust

At the beginning of *The Moral Basis of a Backward Society*, Edward Banfield describes his astonishment at the virtually total absence of organizations in "Montegrano," the southern Italian village he studied in 1954 and 1955, and contrasts this vacuum with the organizational beehive of St. George, Utah, a Mormon community where he had also done research. The "why?" of that vacuum focused his attention on the value system of the inhabitants of Montegrano, most of whose radius of identification and trust did not extend beyond the nuclear family. He labels that system "amoral familism."

In 1935 and 1936, John F. Embree undertook anthropological research in Suye Mura, a comparably small and remote village on the island of Kyushu. He describes a very different condition: Suye Mura abounds with organizations, including those based on like age groups, credit mobilization, women's socializing, women who practice Buddhism, archery, flower arranging, music, horse riding, and agriculture.[30] Suye Mura is much more like St. George than it is like Montegrano. (Coincidentally, James Fallows expresses the view that the American group that most resembles the Japanese is the Mormons.)[31] George DeVos, specifically citing the parallels with Banfield's work, reaches the same conclusion about the village of Niiike, on Honshu, which he studied in 1954, the same year that Banfield started his project.[32]

The Japanese style of child rearing, strongly rooted in Confucianism, emphasizes the child's membership in a group—initially the family—and tends to suppress individualism: "The social philosophy of Confucianism tended to deemphasize the individual as an end in himself and to emphasize instead the network of . . . obligations and responsibilities that the individual assumed as a member of his family and of his community."[33] The prolonged, intimate, and accepting relationship between mother and child (Japanese parents generally do not "discipline" their children)[34] reinforces the intellectual message of group membership and inculcates the need for acceptance of self-indulgence by others—*amae*—that the Japanese psychiatrist Takeo Doi believes is at the foundation of the Japanese psyche.[35]

Emotionally, according to Doi, the Japanese as an adult strives to recreate the maternal-child *amae* relationship in nonfamily contexts, particularly at work, a phenomenon that contributes to the vaunted communitarian approach to work and decision making that has come to symbolize Japan's preeminence in modern management.[36] In Doi's formulation, the family is the innermost of three concentric circles; the nonfamily group, often the enterprise, is the next circle; and beyond that is a much wider circle without emotional content, the only common denominator being Japaneseness. People in that outer circle, called *tanin*, are recognized as compatriots, which does not guarantee against discourteous treatment but makes anything stronger than that unlikely.

The Meiji experience documents a powerful current of nationalism, repeatedly confirmed in subsequent events. Jared Taylor observes of the Japanese, "Their sense of separateness gives them a reassuring sense of community while it isolates them psychologically from the other nations of the world."[37] It is clear that the Japanese radius of identification and trust extends to the national boundaries, although the area of intense identification is much smaller. This pattern is dramatically different from, for example, Brazil, where the radius of identification and trust does not extend far beyond the family. Reflecting this cultural contrast, Brazil has one of the worst income distribution patterns in the world, Japan perhaps the most equitable pattern among the industrialized democracies.[38]

There is an obvious link between identification and trust, and the data gathered by Ronald Inglehart in *Culture Shift in Advanced Industrial Society* bear this out in Japan's case: 42 percent of Japanese respondents said that "most people can be trusted," slightly higher than respondents in the United States, well below those in the countries of northern Europe, but well ahead of Spain, West Germany, Italy, and France. Argentina is at the bottom with 21 percent.[39]

George DeVos explains: "Economic development in Japan depended not only on individuals ready to take chances but also on the cooperative, concerted efforts of many persons imbued with a relatively high sense of mutual trust and social responsibility."[40] Corroboration can be found in the existence of large numbers of nonfamily enterprises, most prominent among them the *zaibatsu* conglomerates, and the extensive and highly successful system of agricultural cooperatives.

The Rigor of the Ethical System

The Japanese ethical system profoundly reflects the ideas of Confucius and his disciples. Evoking Mencius but citing scholars and statesmen of recent times, Ruth Benedict writes, "Human nature in Japan, they say, is naturally good and to be trusted. It does not need to fight an evil half of itself." Thus, "[t]he Japanese have no need of overall ethical commandments."[41] Moreover, Japanese culture is highly of this world, secular, and the traditional religions of Shintoism and Buddhism have little impact on ethics.

In Benedict's view, written forty-five years ago but still insightful and relevant, the operative ethical code derives from the pattern of reciprocal obligations, or *on,* of the Confucian relationships, above all those to the parents and to the ruler, but also to the teacher and to those who have done favors or have extended kindnesses. These obligations are discharged in the first instance by the duty (*gimu*) one owes without limit to the emperor, the law, and Japan (*chu*); to one's parents and ancestors (and "by implication, to descendants"), known as *ko*; and to one's work (*nimmu*). A lesser hierarchy of obligations (*giri*) that are time-limited and calculated to equal the *on* received, operates with respect to duties to an employer, other family members, and people who have done one favors. Finally, there is the duty one owes to one's good name, which extends from respect for Japanese proprieties (such as courtesy and moderation) to "one's duty to admit no (professional) failure or ignorance," and as far as "one's duty to 'clear' one's reputation of insult or imputation of failure, i.e., the duty of feuding or vendetta."[42]

It is important to keep in mind that all five relationships involve reciprocity, as Confucius stressed. For example, if the ruler is not benevolent and responsible, he loses his legitimacy and his followers no longer owe him duty. The sense of responsibility that superiors must feel for subordinates is akin to the noblesse oblige that motivates acts of philanthropy and charity by the affluent in the West, and helps explain the high degree of social equity achieved by the Japanese (and the Taiwanese and, to a lesser degree, the Koreans).

Benedict characterizes Japanese culture as one in which behavior is driven by "shame," fear of negative reaction by others, rather than by "guilt," deriving from a set of internalized principles and conscience, as in the West. This aspect of her analysis has been frequently criticized, and I find myself in agreement with her critics.[43]

DeVos makes the point, indeed consistent with Benedict's own analysis of *on, gimu,* and *giri,* that socialization of Japanese children involves the inculcation of a deep sense of obligation, above all to parents, that drives the child's need for achievement.[44] Failure induces a sense of shame in most human beings, but in the case of the Japanese, it also produces an acute sense of guilt for letting down one's parents—and ancestors.

It seems to me that the *on-*based ethical code basically serves the Japanese well among themselves and is related to the high degree of social justice and relatively high degree of trust, in business and elsewhere, Japan has achieved and benefited from. The contrast between contract negotiation in Japan, where lawyers are often not ▬▬nt, and in the "litigious," to use Richard Lamm's word, United States underscores the point. Japan's cohesiveness is, of course, also a function of homogeneity and a radius of identification that extends, however diluted, beyond the inner circles, to the nation as a whole.

When it comes to relationships with foreigners, however, the equation changes. It is a rare foreigner who lives in Japan, even for many years, who feels accepted, and this applies to foreign spouses of Japanese people and even to foreigners of Japanese extraction. The foreigner—the *gaijin,* if Caucasian—is viewed almost as if of a slightly different, inferior species. Jared Taylor cites the words of a prominent Japanese radio commentator: "the Japanese don't consider foreigners to be human beings."[45]

I talked to Takeo Doi about the question of Japanese ethics in dealing with foreigners during my visit to Japan in March 1990. His observation: if the foreigner can be useful to the Japanese, he or she will be extended the courtesies normal to relationships with group associates who *are* Japanese. If the foreigner is just another *gaijin,* that person is beyond the reach of the Japanese ethical system. I have to confess that when I heard Dr. Doi say that, the Bataan death march came to mind.

The United States occupation left a deep imprint on Japan through imposed policies, above all, democratization, but also through lesser initiatives, including land reform. The American presence and the subsequent blossoming of Japan into a world economic power have expanded Japan's exposure to the universal value systems of the West. And, as I have already noted, Japan, like Western Europe, Australia, Canada, and the United States, has experienced a shift toward nonmaterialistic postindustrial values. Nonetheless, the ethical system Benedict describes is still very much alive and relevant to Japan's phenomenal development since World War II.

The Exercising of Authority

Japan's reputation as an authoritarian society seems at odds with the heavy emphasis on the group in Japanese culture. Yet the reputation is clearly well-founded: unbridled authoritarianism characterized the conduct of the daimyo and lesser samurai prior to the Tokugawa period, constrained only by the loyalty and obedience owed by subordinates to superiors. The daimyo owed that vassal allegiance to the Tokugawa shogunate once it was established, in 1603. The unrestrained nature of the exercising of authority in those earlier periods is suggested by the right of any samurai to lop off the head of any nonsamurai if the whim moved him.

While Japanese feudalism implied some decentralization, particularly by contrast with the Chinese system, the degree of political pluralism was extremely limited. It was, for example, only in the last years of the Tokugawa period that the Bakufu, facing its demise, saw fit to consult extensively with the daimyo. Most of the Meiji leaders were uncomfortable with the idea of pluralism and constitutional checks and balances, and the constitution of 1889 was more Bismarckian than Madisonian. Its flaws nurtured the rise of militarism and a revival of unfettered authoritarianism that led to the catastrophe of World War II.

The United States imposed democracy on Japan during the occupation. (The exquisite irony of this imposition was the highly authoritarian personality of the American responsible for the task of democratizing Japan, General Douglas MacArthur.) The ostensibly alien system took root impressively, and we are reminded, by contrast, of the frustration American policy makers have experienced in their efforts, particularly since 1961, to promote democracy in Latin America. But we must remember the democratic currents that surfaced during the Meiji years and that played an important role in Japanese politics into the 1930s. Those currents were forced underground during the militarism of the 1930s and 1940s, but they endured and are now mainstream.

Japanese history during the past 150 years demonstrates two conflicting value systems to which the Japanese have adapted. One, based on four of the five Confucian relationships (father/teacher to son, ruler to subject, husband to wife, older brother to younger brother), is vertical, essentially authoritarian, symbolized by filial piety but also involving a two-way street in which loyalty and obedience are exchanged for benevolence and affection. The other is implicit in the fifth Confucian relationship, friend to friend, and is essentially nonauthoritarian. The intensity of the former has dissipated over the years, a process that has been propelled in part by the Meiji shift from inherited status to merit as the basis of status (another Confucian emphasis). Moreover, as George DeVos points out, authoritarianism in the family, particularly by contrast with the Chinese family, is very diluted: "Decisions are often collective efforts 'on behalf of' the family or company head."[46]

But hierarchy is still profoundly important in Japan, and a highly complex rank structure operates throughout the society. On the other hand, the vertical relationships coexist with and are modulated by the reciprocal responsibilities on which superior/ subordinate relationships depend, the strong group emphasis of Japanese culture, and a decision-making style that emphasizes consensus.

Lucian Pye summarizes these vertical and horizontal cross-currents nicely:

> the Japanese must learn early to balance their vertical ties with superiors . . . against their horizontal ties with peers, who for their part define the boundaries of the group, organization, or company that will become the basis for the individual's identity.[47] The security of the individual thus involves having the combination of a nurturing authority figure and a collectivity to which loyalty is owed in return for the self esteem it provides. . . . the great paradox about power in Japan is that although the culture was profoundly shaped by a warrior-samurai tradition, and although the country has carried out imperial conquests and . . . is considered to be a dynamic economic force, the Japanese have never embraced the idea of leadership as decisive executive power . . . the essence of Japanese decision-making has been the operation of consensus-building.[48]

The contrast between the diluted authoritarianism of contemporary Japan and traditionally unbridled Iberian authoritarianism is extreme. Indeed, the individualistic substance and style of the West, and particularly the United States, is probably closer to—although still a far cry from—the winner-take-all brand of Iberian authoritarianism than is Japanese authoritarianism.

Work, Innovation, Saving, and Profit

In Jared Taylor's words, "The single most important ingredient in Japan's success is the Japanese attitude toward work."[49] I see no fundamental difference between the values and attitudes toward work of the Taiwanese and Koreans, on the one hand, and the Japanese, on the other. The future-oriented Confucian ethos appears to be the driving force in all three:

- Progress for the individual and the family is not only an expectation but an obligation to one's parents, one's ancestors, and one's future family members.
- Hard work is intrinsically good, and it will be rewarded.
- Education is the principal way of assuring progress.
- Moderation and frugality lead to harmony, security, and progress.

This ethos permeates the entirety of Japanese society, including rural areas. In George DeVos's study of the values and attitudes of Niiike in 1954 through psychological testing, he concludes that, "embedded in rural (as well as urban) culture is a strong emphasis on values of hard work, achievement, and educational advancement which rivals the force of these values in socially and professionally mobile middle-class Americans. . . . It is as if some Oriental Horatio Alger were one of the deities of the local shrine." One of his broader conclusions is particularly worth noting:

> The emphasis on effort and perseverance, and the manner in which this is reflected in hard work, suggest a puritanlike ethic for Niiike as a whole. As an aspect of the rapid industrialization of Japan, this Japanese ethic recalls the role of the Protestant ethic in the industrialization of Europe. In Niiike one must toil diligently, but not for God's salvation; success in hard work proves that one is dutiful toward one's parents and loves them. There is no transmutation of feelings toward one's parents into a personal relationship with a transcendental deity, but there is instead a respectful idealization of a father image, and a loving devotion to a mother who deserves eternal gratitude.[50]

Hard work, perseverance, and self-denial are not the only expressions of this kind of motivation highly favorable to national development (reinforced, of course, by the emphasis on merit). Another expression is the quest for excellence that characterizes Japanese performance throughout the breadth of human activity—in the grace and beauty of the tea ceremony, the conscientious efforts of the streetsweeper, the on-time record of the famous "bullet" trains.

Japanese culture affects innovation both positively and negatively, but on balance it is clearly positive. The emphasis on work, education, and achievement all promote it. So does an aspect of the Japanese family ethos, quite different from the Chinese, that Lucian Pye illuminates. In China, the laws of inheritance resulted in equal distribution of assets (usually land) among male offspring. This combined with the more authoritarian paternalism of the Chinese family to bind it firmly together. In the Japanese case, primogeniture was the norm, and "younger sons could compensate for their subordinate status by striking out on their own and then, if successful, becoming a *gozenso*, or the founder of a new family line."[51] Many major enterprises, including Mitsubishi, have been founded by *gozenso*.

The strong group emphasis and suppression of individualism characteristic of Japan have probably cut two ways with respect to innovation. They have reined in the kind of individual creativity that results in major discoveries and inventions, and many Japanese scientists have left Japan, particularly for the United States, because of those constraints (as well as the generally lower quality of Japanese universities). Many feel frustrated by a promotion system based on seniority rather than performance. On the other hand, it is apparent from the extraordinary success the Japanese have achieved in adapting and improving the inventions of others (such as television, the microchip, photographic equipment, and automobiles) that Japanese consensus decision making can be very effective and innovative indeed. As mentioned, the communitarian approach to management has advocates around the world, even in the Harvard Business School.

The group orientation of the Japanese distinguishes them from other East Asians, including the Taiwanese, who have largely kept their businesses within the family, and the Koreans, who tend to be the most individualistic of the three, but who, like the Japanese, have benefited from intimate working relations between government and industry. But these are nuances in an otherwise essentially Confucian pattern of high value attaching to work, saving, education, thrift, and merit.

Child Rearing in Japan

Mary White has observed, "The central human relationship in Japanese culture is between mother and child."[52] As in all societies, the Japanese acquire their value and attitude systems principally through the process of child rearing. Japan's extraordinary achievements warrant examining that process.

Japanese child rearing is in many respects the reverse of American child rearing. Whereas American parents train their children to restrain "instinctive" behavior that the parents judge as bad, antisocial, or irresponsible, Japanese parents start with the assumption that children are innately good and should be indulged. That indulgence, at the core of *amae*, is communicated in part by the close physical proximity of the child to the mother, who until a few decades ago typically carried the child on her back until he or she was several years old. The indulgence is also communicated through the practice of children sleeping with their parents until the age of five or six years, and by the absence of direct discipline.

Ruth Benedict notes that freedom for the Japanese plots as a "U-curve, with maximum freedom and indulgence allowed to babies and the old. Restrictions are slowly increased after babyhood till having one's own way reaches a low just before and after marriage. This low line continues many years during the prime of life, but the arc ascends again until after the age of sixty men and women are almost as unhampered by shame as little children are. In the United States we stand this curve upside down."[53] Others have characterized the contrasting child-rearing patterns as, in the United States, a process of weaning an inherently dependent being away from its dependence and, in Japan, of building a sense of dependency in an inherently independent being.[54]

Hara Hiroko and Minagawa Mieko assert, "The Japanese seem to believe that too much scolding and prohibition of children's wants before they 'understand what adults say' hinders the development of their basic trust in other people, thereby making it difficult to acquire an ability in adulthood to maintain smooth and harmonious relations with coworkers, friends, and business acquaintances."[55] This may well explain a phenomenon noted by an American who has lived in Japan for many years, who told me he never met a bashful Japanese kid.

The parent, in most cases the mother in this society where mothering remains the principal female role, often attempts to influence the child's behavior by the use of shame or guilt. "A mother will say to her boy baby when he cries, 'You're not a girl,' or 'You're a man.' Or she will say, 'Look at that baby. He doesn't cry.' When another baby is brought to visit, she will fondle the visitor in her own child's presence and say, 'I'm going to adopt this baby. I want such a nice, good child. You don't act your age.' "[56] Lucian Pye adds, "The Japanese mother seems constantly to use the technique of professing 'hurt feelings' as a means of disciplining her children."[57]

David McClelland concludes that a desire to achieve can be inculcated in a child by a parent, particularly the mother, who establishes goals for her children that make them extend themselves, but not to the point of failure and frustration.[58] When they succeed, expression of strong parental satisfaction reinforces the process. The Japanese mother—the legendary *kyoiku mama* ("education mom")—is prototypical of the kind of child rearer that McClelland believes will produce high achievers. She operates in a society where the idea of honor and merit is highly developed, and where merit is symbolized by the transcendentally important nationwide test for university entrance that virtually predetermines for life a person's status. The mother's worth, in both her own eyes and those of others, as well as the worth of her family for generations back* and forward, is determined to a large extent by the achievements of her children. Moreover, the key role of the mother and the strongly permissive nature of Japanese child rearing minimize the likelihood of the domineering kind of child rearing, often associated with a strong paternal role, that tends to suppress achievement motivation.

But Japanese child rearing diverges sharply from the McClelland model in one respect: it inculcates a need for affiliation with others simultaneously with a need for achievement. "In contemporary Japan children from the age of three are entitled to enroll in nursery schools and kindergartens. . . . Parents believe that they should send their children to some kind of pre-school educational institution in order to provide them with opportunities to make friends and have

---

*As in other East Asian societies, some Japanese believe that recently deceased family members can, if they are unhappy, return to cause their living family members problems. When Korean Airlines Flight 747 was shot down by the Russians, some Japanese who had relatives among the victims chartered boats and dropped blankets, whiskey, and other supplies into the water for them.

group experiences. There is concern that otherwise the child might become selfish and overindulged."[59]

In McClelland's view, emphasis on affiliation undermines the individualism and self-expression necessary for achievement. DeVos makes a cogent case that, at least in the Japanese cultural context, the group identification that Japanese children learn early in their lives has a net positive impact on the development of achievement motivation and skills.[60]

That combination of affiliation and achievement that characterizes Japanese child rearing is also the fundamental formula for Japan's extraordinary success as a nation—both in the second half of the nineteenth century and in the second half of the twentieth.

PART II

THE FORTUNES OF ETHNIC GROUPS IN AMERICA

5

The Chinese, the Japanese, and the Koreans

Jewish and Japanese children . . . march off to school with enthusiasm. Mexican and Negro children are much less interested. Some sort of cultural factor works here.
—Joan W. Moore, *Mexican Americans* (1970)

The failure of children to pursue their education is not a product of social disorganization but of the fact that the values of the parents were not the standard American values, and they gave no support to education.
—Nathan Glazer and Daniel Patrick Moynihan, *Beyond the Melting Pot* (1963)

The economic miracles of Taiwan, Korea, and Japan were made by people imbued with the Confucian values of work, education, and merit, and the Taoist value of frugality. That geography, natural resource endowment, the world economic environment, and other factors were less important than culture in explaining success is apparent from the performance of the Chinese, Koreans, and Japanese outside their homelands, in settings as different as the United States (all three), Thailand and the Philippines (the Chinese), and Brazil (the Japanese)—to say nothing of the poor resource endowment of Taiwan, Korea, and Japan. The people who have migrated from these countries have brought their values with them, and their achievements have been uniformly impressive. (The case of the Chinese in China is a special one, discussed in chapter 3.)

Significant numbers of Chinese, Japanese, and Korean people have migrated to the United States. In this chapter, we shall see that the experience of these "Confucian-Americans" parallels the experience of their homelands. Beyond adapting to American culture and making it work for them, many of these Asian-Americans have imparted pro-work, pro-education, pro-merit values to the melting pot at a time when those values are much in need of revival.

But before examining the experience of East Asians in America, I want to review briefly the American immigration experience, with particular attention to the impact of immigration on the United States today.

THE IMMIGRANTS

In the United States, as the aphorism goes, we are all immigrants. And that, of course, is true even for those who were here first, the American Indians, who had, by the most widely accepted theory, immigrated from Asia across the Bering Strait some thousands of years before the arrival of the first European explorers.

The Spanish were the first Europeans to settle permanently on what would become the United States mainland—in St. Augustine, Florida, in 1565. Juan Ponce de León, after whom the Puerto Rican city of Ponce is named, had established the first permanent Spanish settlement in Puerto Rico in 1508. But it was the English, with their early-seventeenth-century settlements in Massachusetts and Virginia, who shaped the cultural and institutional foundations of the new nation. The origin and evolution of those foundations, which were substantially adopted by other early European settlers—including the Dutch, Swedes, French, and Germans—are traced in chapter 8.

Black slaves from Africa formed the first major non-European immigration movement—involuntary, to be sure—into the United States. The flow began in the seventeenth century, and by the time the British and Americans legislated against the slave trade in 1808 (Virginia had abolished it in 1778), about 400,000 Africans had been shipped to the American colonies. About ten million had been forced onto ships bound for the New World. Perhaps a million died in the pestilential holds of ships en route; the rest found their way to other colonies of the British, French, Spanish, and Portuguese. Interestingly, notwithstanding the fact that only about 4 percent of the slaves reached the United States and its predecessor colonies, by 1825 the United States accounted for more than one-third of all slaves in the hemisphere, more than any other country. Thomas Sowell notes, "the United States was the only country in which the slave population reproduced itself and grew by natural increase. In the rest of the hemisphere, the death rate was so high and the birthrate so low that continuous replacements were imported from Africa."[1]

The Irish were among the poorest people in Europe, and they were heavily dependent on potatoes. In 1845, Ireland's potato crop was decimated by blight. A million people are estimated to have died of starvation.[2] Another result of the blight was the first of the postindependence voluntary migrations en masse to the United States that continue to this day. The Irish were followed by millions of Germans, Scandinavians, British, Italians, Poles, and Jews, and hundreds of thousands of Canadians, Mexicans, and Chinese, until the first sweeping immigration control law was passed in 1924. It attempted both to stem the immigration flow and to freeze the ethnic proportions of the United States by use of national quotas. The 1924 law was blatantly racist: "Oriental" immigrants were totally excluded. But that was not the first such action taken by the United States. Chinese immigration had been banned in 1882, and Japanese immigration was limited "voluntarily" by the Japanese government in 1908.

Hitler's rise to power generated strong pressures for liberalizing the 1924 act, but, while efforts were made during the 1930s to accommodate Jews within the German quota, it was not until the horror of the Holocaust became apparent—by which time it was too late for most of its victims—that quotas were significantly relaxed. Special arrangements were made in 1956 for refugees from the Hungarian Revolution; in 1959 and thereafter for refugees from the Cuban Revolution; and after the Vietnam War for Vietnamese refugees.

National quotas were eliminated in the Immigration and Naturalization Act of 1965, the principal goals of which were to reunite families and assure that immigration was consistent with work force needs. The reverse of this second goal is, of course, the protection of American workers from an influx of competing foreign workers.

The 1965 legislation combined with historical events and currents to stimulate new waves of immigration into the United States. The communications revolution, faster and cheaper transportation, and the revolution of rising expectations triggered a vastly increased flow of immigrants, legal and illegal, from Latin America—above all, Mexico, from which substantial immigration had already been stimulated by the *bracero* (seasonal or temporary worker) program—and the Caribbean. The Vietnam War drove hundreds of thousands of Southeast Asians, many of them overseas Chinese, from their homelands. Large numbers of Koreans, Chinese, Filipinos, and Indians have immigrated during the past few decades. Tens of thousands of Africans, most of them young, have escaped from poverty and political turbulence to the United States. Many from the Middle East—Arabs, Iranians, Afghans—have done the same. The latest heirs to the Sephardic–German–Eastern European Jewish immigrant tradition are the Soviet *refuseniks*. The proliferation of small ethnic restaurants—Chinese, Japanese, Thai, Korean, Indian, Ethiopian, Latin American, Middle Eastern—in large American cities is testimony to the new diversity that immigration is bringing to America.

But with that diversity has come concern that immigration is out of control. Millions of immigrants, particularly those from Latin America, are here illegally. They place additional burdens on public services, including education. At the lowest income levels, they compete with legal immigrants and, at least in times of rising unemployment, with U.S. citizens.[3] In the 1990 census, they may well influence the apportionment of congressional seats among the states. The ethnic composition of the southwestern states is changing rapidly, and some projections show California and Texas with Hispanic pluralities in the early decades of the next century.

These kinds of concerns led to passage of the Immigration Reform and Control Act (IRCA) of 1986. It established a formula for amnesty and regularization of illegal immigrants who had lived in the United States since 1982 or had worked in perishable agriculture for at least ninety days prior to the passage of the Act; imposed sanctions on employers who knowingly hired illegal immigrants; and called for a stepped-up program of border surveillance and enforcement. Early evaluations indicate that IRCA has had some success in reducing the flow of illegal aliens, but not as much as had been hoped for by its proponents.[4] About three million illegal aliens have applied for regularized status, vastly more than had been expected.

Further immigration legislation was enacted in 1990 that will increase the flow of legal immigrants by 40 percent and modestly expand (from about 4 percent to about 9 percent) the number of immigrants who receive papers based on the needs of the United States for their skills. The vast majority of new immigrants will enter on the basis of family relationships, as has been the case for the past twenty-five years. The result of this continuing emphasis, coupled with substantial continuing illegal immigration, has been a deterioration in the education and skills of immigrants. George Borjas concludes that "the United States is losing the international competition for skilled workers to other host countries such as Australia and Canada."[5]

Give Me Your Poor?

We are a society imbued with Emma Lazarus's words on the Statue of Liberty: "Give me your tired, your poor, your huddled masses yearning to breathe free." When the statue was dedicated, 106 years ago, some sixty million people lived in the United States. The frontier was still open, and an open immigration policy clearly suited our needs.

Today, our population is more than four times greater. The frontier is long gone, and population growth is a principal contributor to pressure on the environment. Immigration is a major source of population growth. High levels of immigration have supersaturated the melting pot and contribute to what Richard Estrada calls "tribalism," and what Arthur Schlesinger, Jr., has labeled "the disuniting of America."[6]

As popular awareness of America's economic plight intensifies, people are asking, Why? Why the lowest per capita income growth of all developed countries? Why the lowest labor productivity growth? Why the lowest rate of net national investment? Why the trade imbalance? Why the runaway fiscal deficits? Why the drop in real income of nonsupervisory workers? Why ten million unemployed? Why the sudden crisis in state and local finance?

There is obviously no one answer, although it is tempting—and not without substance—to blame a generalized erosion of traditional American values: the work ethic, entrepreneurship, education, austerity, excellence. It is also tempting—and not without substance—to blame the Reagan-Bush economic policies that, at great expense, have created a surface prosperity on top of a weakening foundation.

But the fact is that all those "lowest" indicators cover the period from 1950 to the present. Interestingly, during all these years, the United States has had the *highest* population growth of the developed countries. Immigration, legal and illegal, has been a major contributor to that growth. Since 1950, twenty million people have immigrated legally. No one knows how many have entered illegally. Estimates range from five million to eight million. In the wake of the liberalizing legislation of 1990, upward of one million immigrants are now entering annually.

In *The Competitive Advantage of Nations,* the Harvard economist Michael E. Porter stresses the contribution *skilled* immigrants can make to "the principal economic goal of a nation—a high and rising standard of living" through the entrepreneurship and innovation that drive high and increasing levels of productivity. But he goes on to note that large-scale immigration of the unskilled may retard the process.[7]

American immigration policy has emphasized political concerns—for example, Cuba, Vietnam—and family relationships, not skills, and has turned a blind eye to the vast flow of illegal immigrants, most of whom are unskilled and uneducated. The result, as Borjas concludes, has been that "the skill composition of the immigrant flow . . . has deteriorated significantly in the past two or three decades."[8]

The loss of competitive advantage of many American products in recent decades is mainly the consequence of the slow growth of labor productivity. That is partly the result of low levels of research, development, and investment in the United States compared with our principal competitors, Japan and Germany. But it is also the consequence of a labor force relatively unskilled by comparison with Japan's and Germany's, a labor force whose real income has been *declining* while the incomes of Japanese and German workers have been increasing. American wages are no longer the highest in the world.

In fact, the United States now emphasizes relatively cheap labor—a good part of it available because of immigration from Third World countries—much as Third World countries do. Aside from the retreat from the objective of a high and rising standard of living implicit in it, cheap labor encourages investors to use labor-intensive means of production, and that means slow or no technological advance and further slippage in our competitive position. Porter notes, "The ability to compete *despite* paying higher wages would seem to represent a far more desirable national target."[9]

Thus, the heavy flow of unskilled immigrants has braked labor productivity, technological advance, and per capita income and has contributed to the drop in the real income of nonsupervisory workers. The declining competitiveness of many American products has contributed to the slow growth until recently of exports and the rapid growth of imports. The resulting slow overall growth of the American economy has meant lower federal, state, and local revenues.

Certainly, immigration is but one of several causes of our economic malaise. But it is not an insignificant one.

Some researchers, Borjas among them, have concluded that immigrants—legal and illegal—do not compete with native Americans, although they do compete with other immigrants, including citizens. More recent studies conclude that immigrants do indeed compete with natives, above all at a time of relatively high unemployment.[10]

The argument goes that immigrants, particularly illegal immigrants, accept wages and working conditions that citizens, even poor citizens, wouldn't. The obvious implication is that employers would have to pay more and provide better working conditions if there were not an ample supply of immigrants—not a very good argument for expanding immigration. In fact, there are cases, for example, building maintenance workers in Los Angeles, where native Americans, mostly black, have been displaced by immigrants, mostly Mexican. Moreover, immigrants may well compete with poorer citizens for low-cost housing—which means higher rentals—and public services, including education.

As we shall see in chapter 6, several researchers have also studied the extent to which immigrants are a burden on public budgets, requiring, for example, welfare, social services, subsidized housing, and education. Two principal conclusions emerge: what most immigrants pay in taxes does not cover the costs of the services they receive, particularly when education is included; and the downward trend in immigrant skills has been accompanied by an upward trend in their use of public assistance.

The problem of refugee/immigrant demand for services has been particularly acute in Massachusetts, where the Dukakis administration adopted a policy of ensuring the availability of all state services to refugees, and both the state and the city of Boston provided many services to immigrants without reference to the legality of their status. Massachusetts consequently became a magnet for immigrants: between 1980 and 1990, the Hispanic population more than doubled, from 141,000 to 288,000, while the Asian population almost tripled, from 49,000 to 143,000. The treatment of immigrants did not become a really hot issue until the sharp downturn in the state's economy and the resulting budget crisis. Now there can be no question that immigrants compete with needy citizens (and legal resident aliens) for drastically reduced public services.

Congress passed the 1990 legislation, which will bring total immigration, legal and illegal, to over one million annually, in the face of repeated polls showing that an overwhelming majority of Americans—including 74 percent of Hispanic-Americans and 78 percent of black Americans in a 1990 Roper poll—oppose increased immigration. In addition, two-thirds support reducing legal immigration, and 91 percent support an all-out program to stop illegal immigration.[11] Meanwhile, the executive branch has allowed the flow of refugees across the border to double since 1987—to over 140,000 annually.

More than 70 percent of the legal newcomers will enter because they are related to naturalized citizens, resident aliens, and former illegal immigrants who qualified for the amnesty provisions of the 1986 immigration act. As many as three million immigrant workers will enter the United States legally and illegally during the next five years. But the large majority of them will come without the skills we need to upgrade the labor force, the wage structure, and the competitiveness of our products.

The Haitian boat people are a case in point. Almost all have risked their lives in leaky vessels to reach the United States. Those activists who insisted that the boat people were refugees from Duvalier's political persecution now have to explain why the flow increased during the eight months when President Jean-Bertrand Aristide, the landslide populist winner of the 1990 elections, was in office. What principally motivated the boat people, hundreds of thousands of other Haitian immigrants, and indeed the vast majority of all immigrants is economic opportunity and social services that vastly exceed what their homeland offers. (Haiti's per capita GNP is about $400.)

A 1985 study of recent Haitian immigrants in Florida revealed the following: average length of education was 4.6 years; 4.9 percent were high school graduates, 81.8 percent had limited or no English; 92.8 percent had limited or no knowledge of the United States; 63 percent were unemployed; almost all who were employed worked at low-skill jobs; 29.2 percent were receiving welfare aid.[12]

High levels of immigration, legal and illegal, have not produced the positive economic results that advocates like Ben Wattenberg and Julian Simon expected. For four decades, we have accepted vastly more immigrants than any other advanced country. During those four decades—surely a long enough period to test Wattenberg and Simon's theories—the performance of the U.S. economy has been among the worst of the advanced countries, roughly comparable to Great Britain's. Many other factors also explain the decline of American competitiveness, but the low-skill immigration of recent decades has surely not been helpful, except to the labor-intensive businesses that have profited from the supply of cheap, docile labor—leaving the community at large to pick up the social costs.

Other proponents of large-scale immigration are motivated by humanitarian concerns, the adverse impact on American citizens notwithstanding. I'm reminded of a comment made about her own country by the Australian sociologist Katherine Betts in *Ideology and Immigration*: "Humanitarianism became the chief goal of immigration for some people and immigration itself came to be seen as a form of international aid . . . the relatively poor in this country pay a disproportionate share of the cost of the conscience of the rich."[13]

Our immigration policies should be based on the needs of our own society, particularly economic revival and raising the standard of living of our poorer citizens, not on the failures of other nations to meet the needs of their poor. That means a significant reduction in legal immigration, redoubled programs to control illegal immigration, and an upgrading of the skills of those immigrants we accept. These measures won't solve America's economic problems, but they will certainly help.

Policy Implications

Even with the enactment of the Immigration Reform and Control Act of 1986 and the Immigration Act of 1990, immigration to the United States continues to be largely controlled by the individual decisions of literally millions of people in countries where economic opportunity, social mobility, and political freedom are often severely limited. The large majority of those who enter legally do so under family preference provisions of the law. Large numbers continue to enter the United States illegally each year, most of them from Latin America, most of those from Mexico. The United States is one of the few advanced countries in the world that does not effectively control immigration. France was similarly unpreoccupied with illegal immigration until the 1990–91 recession when, as unemployment approached 10 percent, the Socialist government imposed rigorous new immigration regulations.

We should be working toward a policy based on U.S. national interests, one that leaves the decisions about who enters the United States in the hands of the U.S. authorities rather than in the hands of individual citizens of other countries, one that emphasizes our obligations to our own society and *its* citizens, particularly those in need.

I appreciate the complexity and expense that control of our lengthy borders implies. But I believe it is possible to devise an effective and humane control system if we decide it's important enough. As a hypothetical example, if adequate surveillance of the border with Mexico required one person every 220 yards (eight people per mile), the total force would be 16,000 people, surely a manageable number. But the fact is that the problem of surveillance is much smaller, since 95 percent of the border is desert that deters crossing by all but the hardiest and most daring. Modern remote-sensing technology should in any event simplify the task. We should not be deterred by fatuous comparisons with the Berlin Wall, whose role was to keep dissatisfied citizens in, not dissatisfied foreigners out.

We should be working toward a policy that meshes the needs of our society with the educational and professional experience of immigrants, rather than one that emphasizes family relationships. We should also be moving more aggressively to deport those who are here illegally and have not qualified under the amnesty provisions of the 1986 act.

Deportation is painful for Americans to contemplate except at moments of high unemployment. In most cases, the deportee returns to extreme poverty and hopelessness. But it is a fact, apparent at a time of fiscal crisis at all levels of government, that illegal immigrants absorb resources that could be used for citizens in need. As already noted, illegal immigrants contribute to public revenues in various ways, but the net of contributions by and expenditures for illegal immigrants is likely to be a deficit.

That is a short-run argument for tighter immigration controls. In the long run, we have to concern ourselves with preservation of the values and institutions of our society, the size of our national population, and the environment.

The Melting Pot

Does the concept of a melting pot work? Sometimes completely; in most cases substantially; in a few cases only marginally. The basic, although far from unvarying, pattern is for the first generation to be substantially tied to old-country ways, including language, and to live in urban or rural surroundings predominantly of the same ethnic group. The second generation retains some of the Old World ethnic characteristics, often including language, but is more American than

ethnic and may live in more mixed surroundings. The third generation is substantially American, knows only a few words of the old-
country language, and is more likely to intermarry. With the generation after intermarriage, the operation of the melting pot is
substantially complete, although those who have "melted" may be
quick to identify themselves with the ethnicities of their great-grand-
parents.

In practice, the melting pot often works less efficiently, particularly when the members of an ethnic group isolate themselves—or
are isolated by others—from the cultural mainstream. There are still,
for example, Irish, Italian, and Polish neighborhoods in many large
American cities, neighborhoods in which generation after generation
grow up and live and in which the old-country language—and some
of its values—may be perpetuated. People tend to stay in these
neighborhoods by choice; many leave to live in mixed neighborhoods. Moreover, the neighborhood itself tends to melt somewhat:
the children are exposed to mainstream culture in the schools and
on television; visits are paid to and by relatives who have moved to
the suburbs; gentrification sometimes affects the neighborhood; and
the "voluntary" ethnic neighborhoods receive mainstream visitors—
for example, for their ethnic restaurants.

But there are other neighborhoods, often labeled "ghettos," where
ethnic groups live more by necessity than choice. The groups that
have lived in these circumstances have often been nonwhite—in
particular, black and Chinese—and have historically been subjected
to the intense prejudice based on race that is found in all multiracial
societies. The ghettos have tended to be far more sealed off from the
cultural mainstream, an isolation also experienced by Indians on
reservations. I will argue in the next two chapters that traditional
Iberian culture in the case of Hispanics and slavery culture in the case
of unacculturated blacks are important roots of the ghetto problem
that manifests itself in high unemployment, low income, drug use,
high crime rates, adolescent pregnancy, high welfare dependence,
and other social ills. Indicative of the momentum of culture in
isolation is the fact that ghetto language, be it Spanish or the black
English dialect that derives from slavery, tends to persist through
more generations than does the old-country language of the ethnic
neighborhoods.

THE MINEFIELD OF COMPARATIVE
PERFORMANCE

Of particular interest about ethnic groups in America for the purposes of this book are their relative levels of progress and achievement. If it is true that values and attitudes go a long way toward explaining why some countries do better than others, then people from those countries that do better should do better as immigrants in the United States. By "doing better," I have in mind three indicators that usually correlate with one another: level of education, kind of employment (basically white collar versus blue collar), and family income.

Comparative analysis of ethnic/racial* group performance, particularly when the analysis is focused on values and attitudes, is a minefield. It is emotionally charged. It collides with the taboo on value judgments dictated by cultural relativism—"all cultures are of equal value and fulfill roughly the same functions everywhere"[14]— which permeates so much thinking today, particularly in the academic world. People confuse comparative cultural analysis with racism, which it most assuredly is not, since genetic endowment does not change (at least not in the time spans we are concerned with), while values and attitudes can change dramatically in just a few decades—witness contemporary Spain.

There is also a hot debate over the worth of values that stress upward mobility and achievement. By some, those values are regarded as the root of many of the world's ills: inequality, war, environmental degradation, greed, consumerism, erosion of the family. And the relationship between discrimination—the denial of opportunity on the grounds of color, religion, or ethnicity/national origin—and ethnic group performance is a highly controversial subject, particularly for blacks.

I personally am uncomfortable with the white-collar/blue-collar hierarchy because of the implications of superiority that attach to the former, in the view of some rendering the latter less dignified, less important, less worthy. That kind of snobbery is repugnant to me, yet movement from blue-collar to white-collar jobs is clearly central

---

*For the sake of convenience, I use the word *ethnic* hereinafter to cover ethnic groups, whose identity derives from nationality, as well as groups whose identity derives from race (for example, blacks, American Indians).

to the idea of social mobility and progress, which is an important part of what America is about.[15] On the other hand, even in a "postindustrial" society, professionalism in blue-collar jobs can be of overriding importance, as the Japanese surge in automobiles, electronic products, cameras, and so on has demonstrated. And a successful blue-collar career can now lead to the material benefits of the upper middle class, a condition not assured by a white-collar job, particularly at a time when a good part of the employment created by the American economy is lower-paying service jobs. (I argue in chapter 8 that one of the facets of traditional American culture that has eroded is the idea of excellence and the commitment to professionalism. That erosion has affected management; it has also affected the work of those who do things with their hands.)

There are also a number of technical mines beyond the question of culture. Are the immigrants illiterate peasants (like many Mexicans) or educated middle-class people (like many Koreans and the Cubans who arrived in the first waves after the Castro revolution)? To what extent are they motivated to achieve because of class considerations[16] or because of a status in the old country that has made them accustomed to a degree of prestige they will not sacrifice (again, as in the case of the Koreans and Cubans)? Do they plan to sever their tie with the old country, or are they sojourners? Within the ethnic group, is there a predominance of foreign-born or American-born? (Knowing the answer to that question may still leave ambiguity: foreign-born Mexican immigrants are likely to be relatively poor and uneducated; foreign-born Chinese, at least until recent years, and Koreans are likely to be middle class and highly educated.) What is the average age of the ethnic group? (The Mexican-American average is ten years younger than the national average, principally because of high fertility rates. Mexican-American average income thus disproportionately reflects "starting-out" levels.)[17] To what extent is achievement a function of ethnic group solidarity (to be sure, at least in part a reflection of values and attitudes), where those who have made it have helped those who haven't (a frequent contrast is made between Asians and Jews, on the one hand, and blacks, on the other)? To what extent is "achievement" a function of where people settle (income levels are higher in some cities than in others and generally higher in cities than in rural areas)? And do immigrants turn to starting small businesses because their access to salaried jobs is blocked (for example, because of language difficulties or prejudice)?

If there is validity to the idea that culture influences how individuals, groups, and nations perform, then we must enter the minefield of ethnic/national group comparison to assess the performance of immigrants in America. I've chosen the Chinese, the Japanese, and the Koreans for this chapter because they are high achievers whose national success stories (if you'll permit the substitution of Taiwan for China) are the subject of previous chapters in this book. I've selected the Mexicans for chapter 6 because I want to examine the thesis of *Underdevelopment Is a State of Mind* in the context of immigration to the United States, and also because Mexicans are by far the largest Latin American immigrant group. Finally, I've chosen American blacks for chapter 7 because I believe that cultural factors are an important part of the explanation for their achievements and problems.

The Chinese

The Chinese were first drawn to the United States by the California Gold Rush. By 1851, some 25,000 Chinese people had made the 7,000-mile voyage across the Pacific in sailing ships, almost all to California.[18] As work opportunities opened up in railroad construction and mining, the flow accelerated: by the early 1880s, close to 300,000 had made the journey—almost all males. Most set out as sojourners; many in fact did return to China.

Almost all of them had been desperately poor in China and proved to be hard workers in their new home, often accepting very low wages. But they lived frugally and saved. They became another instance of an achieving group provoking the resentment and hostility of less successful groups. Physical differences, in this case body size and skin color, made it easier to rouse the rabble. Natural enemies of labor unions, the Chinese were sometimes employed as strikebreakers; many were killed. They were forced out of mining camps and expelled from several West Coast cities, including Seattle, Tacoma, and Vancouver. Some Chinese immigrants were lynched by white mobs.

The laws were also stacked against the Chinese. From 1854 to 1874, they were prohibited from testifying in court against white men, tantamount to open season on the Chinese. The Chinese Exclusion Act of 1882 virtually cut off their access to legal immigration. Other laws prevented them from acquiring U.S. citizenship, and then required citizenship as a prerequisite to enter a number of professions or to own land. Many Chinese people returned to China, but many more who wanted to were unable to come up with ticket money. (It was during this period that the expression "not a China-man's chance" first surfaced.)

Economic conditions in China were sufficiently bad that many Chinese people were willing to run the risk—and the expense—of illegal immigration. With illegal immigration came an improved balance between men and women, which in turn meant a declining percentage of sojourners. The net of the inflow and outflow was a standing population of 60,000 to 80,000 Chinese through the first half of the twentieth century.

The Chinese Exclusion Act was repealed in 1943 as a gesture of solidarity with a wartime ally. But it was not until the 1965 amendments to the Immigration and Nationality Act of 1952 that Chinese immigrants were placed on a nondiscriminatory footing with immigrants from other parts of the world. The result was a surge in Chinese immigration—about 20,000 legal entrants a year and perhaps an equal number of illegal immigrants through the mid-1970s. The surge was a delayed consequence of the Maoist Revolution: many immigrants had fled China to Taiwan and Hong Kong in the late 1940s and 1950s. Their goal in the United States was clearly to establish families and gain American citizenship: of those Chinese who entered legally between 1966 and 1974, more than 50 percent were women, most of whom were of childbearing age. The Chinese community in America now has a substantial capacity to produce native-born Chinese-Americans.

The first wave of Chinese immigrants under the 1965 legislation came under the "skilled labor" and "student" categories and was noteworthy for high levels of education and professional experience. This selectivity eroded in subsequent waves, which entered under the "family preference" category, and many recent Chinese immigrants have little education or professional background. A continuation of the surge of Chinese immigrants at the end of the 1970s, coupled with natural growth, brought the total of Chinese-Americans to slightly more than 800,000 in 1980.[19]

The vast majority of Chinese-Americans live in cities on the east and west coasts and in Hawaii. Many live in Chinatowns, several of which (for example, the one in New York, which has overtaken San Francisco's as the largest Chinese center in America) have grown rapidly in the past few decades. But some have declined even more rapidly. In 1940, more than 60 percent of the Chinese in the greater Boston area lived in Chinatown; by 1970, the figure had dropped below 10 percent.

Prior to World War II, "[t]he Chinese reaction to pervasive discrimination was withdrawal and inconspicuousness, much like the European Jews in the Ghetto or the Pale."[20] Chinese laundries and restaurants were the principal employers of the Chinese, and Chinese commercial activity was substantially confined to intra-Chinatown transactions. Chinatowns developed their own community organizations, including financial and political institutions. Those who ran the Chinatowns did so with a combination of wealth and force, and vice and crime were also a part of the scene, as they are today.

American attitudes about China and the Chinese were affected by the Japanese invasion of China in 1937 and by the U.S. alliance with Chiang Kai-shek. With the post–World War II changes in American society, including the 1965 Immigration and Nationality Act that formalized a national rejection of anti-Chinese discrimination (at a time when the United States was searching its soul over racial issues), the isolation of the Chinese from the American cultural mainstream increasingly broke down. For the many who live in Chinatowns, the contemporary experience is closer to the salad bowl—in which components retain their identity—than the melting pot. But achievement indicators suggest both a considerable Americanization and a considerable drive for advancement on the part of the Chinese.

Chinese-Americans have clearly attached a high priority to education, consistent with the Confucian value system. Betty Lee Sung believes that "[t]he motivating factor is the high esteem accorded men of learning within the Chinese system of cultural values. In the social hierarchy in China, scholars stood at the top. That is why parents continually urge their children to study hard and reach higher levels in school."[21] Estimates based on 1980 census data indicate that, among native-born Chinese-American males between the ages of twenty-five and sixty-four, the average number of years of schooling is 14.9, compared with 12.9 for non-Hispanic American whites.[22] Census data from 1970 indicate that more than 25 percent of Chinese-Americans have completed four or more years of college, more than double the percentage of American whites. Along with other Asian-Americans, they are disproportionately represented in first-rank universities: "In the early 1980s, Asian-Americans amounted to about 1.5 percent of the nation's population and about 5 percent of California's residents, but made up 20 percent of the University of California at Berkeley's student body. They were 9 percent of Harvard's class of 1985 and a similar figure at Columbia, Yale, and Princeton."[23] One-third of the students at New York's Juilliard School of Music are Asians.

High Chinese-American educational levels reflect themselves in occupational distribution. Table 5.1 orders occupations according to the traditional white-collar/blue-collar breakdown that generally reflects class and income. The educational and occupational indicators are consistent with family income data. Average family income for native-born non-Hispanic whites was $26,535 in 1980; for all Chinese-American families, $28,377 ($39,805 for native-born Chinese-Americans, $26,230 for the foreign-born). The advantage enjoyed by Chinese-Americans is not just a function of education and occupation. More family members, particularly wives, work in Chinese-American families than in white families.[24]

In the face of much adversity, discrimination, even cruelty, the Chinese have been among the most successful ethnic groups in the United States, as the overseas Chinese have been elsewhere. The Confucian ethic is apparent in the high levels of educational attainment of Chinese-Americans, in a disproportionate preference for teaching as a career, and in a propensity for hard work. An added motivation for achievement may well have been discrimination itself. The Chinese are a proud people with a tradition of superior self-image. The "I'll-show-*them*" psychology suggested by Everett

TABLE 5.1

OCCUPATIONAL CATEGORIES BY ETHNIC GROUP

Occupation	Chinese American	Japanese American	Korean American	Non-Hispanic White
	(percentage of native-born men)			
Professional	42.6	31.1	40.0	25.9
Technical, sales, administration	26.5	22.4	17.2	18.2
Service	7.5	5.8	5.6	6.1
Farming, forestry, fishing	0.9	7.2	3.9	3.3
Production, craft, repair	12.2	20.1	18.9	21.8
Operators, laborers	7.6	11.1	12.2	20.8
Unemployed	2.6	2.3	2.2	3.9

Source: U.S. Commission on Civil Rights, "The Economic Status of Americans of Asian Descent" (Washington, D.C.: CCR, 1988).

Hagen as a powerful achievement motivator[25] may well have operated for the Chinese in America as it probably has for the Japanese and the Jews.

The Chinese community is not without its problems, however, particularly with respect to recent immigrants, many of whom have entered through the family preference emphasis of current immigration legislation. As one example, Chinese gang activity has increased notably in New York and California. But the successful adaptation of prior generations of Chinese immigrants should leave us hopeful about the acculturation of the new immigrants in the long run. The success of the Chinese in America is testimony to the virtues of an open political and economic system that nurtures opportunity and fair play. But it is also testimony to an immigrant culture, heavily influenced by Confucianism, in which work, austerity, education, family, and community are all highly valued.

The Japanese

The great influence of the United States on Japanese modernization is not commonly appreciated. I am speaking not of the democratization, land reform, demilitarization, and the like imposed on Japan after World War II but of the events flowing in the wake of Commodore Perry's voyages to Japan in 1853 and 1854. Those encounters powerfully accelerated a process of Japanese introspection, self-assessment, and recognition of backwardness that contributed to the overthrow of the Tokugawa dynasty in 1868 and the Meiji Restoration.

As I noted in the previous chapter, the Meiji leadership openly admired many aspects of the United States and its institutions. Domingo Faustino Sarmiento, who coincidentally became president of Argentina in 1868, uttered words that approximated the view of the Meiji leadership: "We must be the United States."[26] Japanese emigration to America was pushed not only by rapid population growth but also by the high esteem in which many Japanese held America. It was pulled by wage rates that were substantially higher than in Japan.

A few hundred Japanese migrated to the United States in the 1860s and 1870s. Some 2,000 came in the 1880s. The number soared to 26,000 in the 1890s and to 130,000 in the first decade of this century. Most came as sojourners—a preponderance were males—

but, as with the Chinese and other immigrant groups, many remained permanently, mostly in California and Hawaii. "The Japanese who migrated . . . were the ambitious young men of limited means, from farming backgrounds." They were hard-working, cooperative, frugal, and uncomplaining, and they had an abiding interest in education, consistent with the Confucian tradition. "One indication of their diligence is that, when they were paid on a piece-work basis in agriculture, they earned up to twice as much as other laborers."[27] As with the Chinese who preceded them, and with whom they were sometimes either confused or lumped together in "the Yellow Peril," the success of the Japanese provoked the envy and resentment of other workers and labor unions.

As the Japanese edged up the ladder to tenancy and, occasionally, farm ownership, their success and competition antagonized influential white farmers. That antagonism led to a spate of discriminatory laws and regulations in California, including the infamous Alien Land Law of 1913, "which forbade the owning of California land by aliens ineligible for citizenship—that is, Asians in general and Japanese in particular."[28] Pressure also built to limit further Japanese immigration. But the Meiji Restoration had transformed Japan from a backward, weak nation to one that had won wars with China (1895) and Russia (1905), and the United States could not unilaterally terminate Japanese immigration as it had Chinese immigration by the 1882 law. In the face-saving "Gentlemen's Agreement" of 1908, the Japanese committed themselves to restrain the emigrant flow, and the United States agreed to allow entry to a disproportionate number of women, to correct the sexual imbalance. (One is reminded of the recent "voluntary" restraints on Japanese automobile exports to the United States, a case where, if you'll excuse the mixed metaphor, the face saving is on the other foot.) In the wake of the 1908 agreement, Japanese immigration dropped from 130,000 during this century's first decade to 84,000 in the second decade, and 33,000 in the 1920s.

California's Alien Land Law of 1913 was followed by a similar law in 1920 that prohibited the leasing of land to persons "ineligible for citizenship" (read Asians). But both laws were substantially circumvented. By 1920, the first-generation Japanese, the *Issei*, had produced a second generation of American-born citizens, the *Nisei*, who were beyond the reach of the Land Laws. "Much land was owned by Japanese families in the names of children. Sometimes, sympathetic white farmers held legal title to land actually farmed as their own by Japanese farmers who bought it. . . . Some dummy corporations were also formed to evade the Alien Land Law."[29] By World War II, Japanese farmers accounted for one-third of the truck crops produced in California.

The excellent reputation of the Japanese as farmers facilitated their movement into commercial or contract gardening. And it was natural for them to market fruits and vegetables, often buying from Japanese producers, a pattern also successfully followed by Japanese immigrants in Brazil (see chapter 1). The Japanese were also successful in other sectors of the economy: they owned hotels, dry-cleaning establishments, commercial fisheries, and lunch counters in West Coast cities and Hawaii.

The Japanese-Americans were model citizens. Their children were diligent and polite students. Their families were stable. Japanese social and mutual aid organizations sprang up wherever the Japanese settled. They almost never applied for public welfare programs: the needs of the poor were met within the family or the association, as with the Chinese and the Jews. While the Issei retained strong emotional ties to Japan, the Nisei were outspokenly proud of their American citizenship, a contrast between first and second generations common to many immigrant groups.

Today, most Americans correctly view the World War II internment of the Japanese on the U.S. mainland* as a gross miscarriage of justice, driven in part by racism, for which the recent indemnification of those who were interned was insufficient. But many who were alive at the time can remember the intense anxiety felt by most Americans, particularly those on the West Coast, following Pearl Harbor: much of the Pacific Fleet, the only real defense against Japanese invasion, had been destroyed; within a few months, the Japanese controlled most of the Asian coast from Vladivostok to the South Asian subcontinent, as well as the Philippines and other American, British, French, and Dutch possessions in the Southwest Pacific; Australia was in mortal danger; and, in Europe, the survival of Britain and the Soviet Union, the only remaining opponents of Nazi Germany, was in substantial doubt. The internment decision received almost universal support within the United States at the time, and that included liberals and Communists as well as conservatives and reactionaries.

---

*Ironically, the freedom of the 150,000 Japanese living in Hawaii was in no way constrained.

The consequences for the Nisei were appalling. Financial and property losses were enormous—the government itself estimated the losses at $400,000,000 in 1942 prices. The family patterns so central to Japanese culture were disrupted. The internment camps were barracks-style, primitive facilities. Yet, as might be expected of model citizens, the Japanese made the best of it. And white American conscience pangs, due process, and work force needs soon started to be felt. As early as mid-1942, Japanese farm and railroad workers were permitted to return to their jobs, and 4,000 Nisei students returned to Eastern and Midwestern colleges and universities. Early in 1943, the army began to recruit Nisei youths, more than 300,000 of whom fought with great distinction and valor, particularly in Europe but also in the Pacific.

By 1944, Franklin Roosevelt, who had signed the 1942 internment Executive Order, was publicly extolling the loyalty of the Japanese-Americans, and at the end of the year, the Supreme Court declared unconstitutional the internment of Japanese who were American citizens (at the same time validating the internment of Japanese who were resident aliens).

The internment had been economically devastating for the Japanese-Americans, most of whose businesses were either bankrupt or in the hands of others by the time the war was over. In a manner reminiscent of the Cuban middle class that fled to the United States in 1959 and subsequent years, most Japanese-Americans had to start at much lower rungs on the economic ladder than they had occupied before the war. As late as 1958, about 75 percent of all Japanese-owned businesses in Los Angeles were in contract gardening. Within a few years, Japanese-American personal income was equal to that of white Americans, and family income was substantially higher. Doubtless the incentive for achievement implicit in loss of status, discussed by Hagen and others (see the subsequent section, "The Koreans"), played a role. And former Senator S. I. Hayakawa has expressed the belief that the internment experience made the Japanese-Americans more mobile and adaptable.[30]

In 1980, 700,000 people of Japanese antecedence were living in the United States, according to the census of that year. Average years of schooling for native-born Japanese men age twenty-five to sixty-four were 13.7, compared with 12.9 for non-Hispanic whites. Strikingly, the average years of schooling for men of this age group born in Japan but living in the United States were much higher: fifteen years. About 60 percent of native-born Japanese-Americans were in white-collar occupations, substantially fewer than Chinese-Americans (77 percent) but substantially higher than non-Hispanic American whites (50 percent—see table 5.1). Interestingly, of the groups listed in table 5.1, the Japanese-Americans account for the highest percentage in the farming, forestry, and fishing category, an obvious consequence of both the agricultural roots of the Issei and the agricultural emphasis of their early employment in America.

Average income for all Japanese-American families was $35,207 in 1980, compared with non-Hispanic whites at $26,535. (Average income of native-born Japanese-American families was $38,324; for those born in Japan—presumably younger—$25,094.) As with the Chinese and the Koreans, married Japanese-American women tend to work more than married white American women.

In their early history in America, the Japanese were almost as cruelly discriminated against as the Chinese. Yet today, they are the second-highest ethnic group, after the Jews, when it comes to family income. (This may be much more than coincidence, in light of the traditional emphasis on education and achievement in both cultures.) The melting pot has probably worked with the Japanese more than with other Asians: they are less likely to live in ethnically concentrated neighborhoods, and, in what Milton Gordon has identified as the last stage of the process of assimilation, fully half of Japanese-Americans now intermarry.[31]

To be sure, more than 70 percent of Japanese-Americans live in California and Hawaii, both high-income states. But notwithstanding this geographic distortion, the self-selection of the more ambitious (implicit in the decision to emigrate), and perhaps the psychological consequences of the loss of status during World War II, it is difficult to avoid the conclusion that many of the same cultural factors that explain Japan's success, not only since World War II but back at least to the Meiji Restoration, lie behind the success of the Japanese in America—and in Brazil. Among these factors are the Confucian emphasis on education, hard work, and excellence; a commitment to risk taking and creativity; an emphasis on frugality, reflecting in part a strong future orientation; and a sense of self as part of a collectivity that extends the radius of trust outside the family to the community.[32] The parallels with the traditional American cultural mainstream, except for the differing balance between the individual and the collectivity, are striking.

I conclude this section with the words of George DeVos:

The Japanese-American evidence confounds the often too facile sociological generalities about the invariably negative effects of social discrimination. The Japanese acculturation to the United States amply demonstrates that the acculturation patterns of immigrants to a new society depend heavily not only on their acceptability to the host society but also on the nature of the cultural response by the immigrant group itself to external social stimulations and challenges. Any ethnic-group response to the possible stresses of acculturation is governed by psychocultural reaction patterns that are characteristic for the specific group. . . . The Japanese-Americans provide us . . . with the case of a group who, despite racial visibility and a culture traditionally thought of as alien, have achieved a remarkable adjustment to middle-class American life because certain compatibilities in the value systems of the immigrant and host cultures operated strongly enough to overcome the more obvious difficulties.[33]

The Koreans

In 1882, the same year that the United States prohibited further immigration from China, it established diplomatic relations with Korea. The two countries signed a Treaty of Amity and Commerce that stated that "subjects of Chosun (Korea) who may visit the United States shall be permitted to reside and rent premises, purchase lands, or to construct residences or warehouses in all parts of the country."[34] It is ironic that these rights were simultaneously denied to the Chinese and that vigorous efforts would be made a few decades later to deny them to the Japanese.

It was not until the first years of the twentieth century that the Korean government, confronting famine, encouraged Koreans to emigrate. At just that moment, Hawaiian plantation owners were faced with acute labor shortages, the result of the Chinese Exclusion Act and unrest among Japanese plantation workers. American Protestant missionaries were a third factor: they had considerable success converting Koreans and commonly encouraged their converts to emigrate.

Upwards of 7,000 Koreans journeyed to Hawaii between 1903 and 1905. Most were sojourners, as is apparent from the male to female ratio of 9:1. The outflow was quickly arrested, however. When the Japanese defeated the Russians in 1905, they established a protectorate over Korea that, as we have seen, was converted into a colony in

1910. Since the Korean plantation workers in Hawaii competed with Japanese workers, the Japanese government forced the Korean government to stop the flow. Except for about 1,000 females and a small number of political refugees and students, there was virtually no Korean immigration between 1905 and 1924. About 2,000 of the original immigrants to Hawaii migrated to the West Coast, however. Interestingly, another 1,000 ended up in Cuba by way of the sugar plantations in Yucatán, Mexico.

After the national origins quota system, which barred immigration from Asia, was adopted by the Congress in 1924, the trickle of Korean immigration ceased until after World War II. By one estimate, there were about 17,000 Korean-Americans in 1950.[35] The Korean War precipitated a new flow of Koreans to the United States. A large number were wives of American soldiers. Many were orphans adopted by Americans. Many Korean "visitors" and students remained permanently. Almost 50,000 entered the country between 1950 and 1965, when the new immigration bill that stressed family ties and skills was enacted. The 1965 act stimulated an even greater flow and, between 1966 and 1984, more than 400,000 Koreans entered. During that period, Koreans were the third most numerous immigrants, after Mexicans and Filipinos.

The achievements of Koreans in America must be viewed against the backdrop of their experience in Korea: "Recent Korean immigrants are exceptional in terms of their pre-immigrant social characteristics. Several case studies highlight the urban, Protestant, middle class origins of Korean immigrants." In one sample survey in Chicago, almost 90 percent of Korean immigrants were found to have an urban background. The same survey found that 66 percent of the respondents were Protestants, more than three times the percentage of Protestants in Korea.[36]

It is thus not surprising that the average number of years of schooling of recent Korean male immigrants—almost 15, about the same as recent Japanese immigrants—is higher than the native Korean-American male average of 13.8 years (about the same as native-born Japanese-Americans). As mentioned previously, the non-Hispanic white average is 12.9 years.

Table 5.1 shows that 63 percent of Korean-Americans are in white-collar jobs, lower than the Chinese-Americans but higher than the Japanese-Americans. (About 50 percent of non-Hispanic white males are in white-collar jobs.) Average family income of Korean-Americans, at $25,234 in 1980, was slightly below the non-Hispanic white average of $26,535. But native-born Korean-American families earned an average of $38,610, even higher than native-born Japanese. As with the Chinese and Japanese, Korean-American wives are more likely to work than are white American wives.

In 1982, Pyong Gap Min interviewed 159 Korean businessmen in Atlanta using a questionnaire of 121 questions. One of his chief goals was to understand why so many Koreans had gone into business for themselves and why they were generally successful (90 percent, by their own evaluation). His conclusions:

> Korean immigrants' anticipation of [upward] economic mobility through business, together with their perception of labor market disadvantages [above all, problems with English], is the central factor in the decision to start a business in this country.
>
>   . . .
>
> [S]tatus inconsistency [having been in a higher status in Korea] is important in understanding Korean immigrants' occupational adjustment in small business.
>
>   . . .
>
> The Chinese and the Japanese in the United States have been described as possessing three cultural characteristics: hard work and frugality; strong family and kin ties; and group solidarity, each of which is favorable to the operation of small business. Our data based on Korean business owners generally support the view that the same three factors give advantages to Korean immigrants for starting up and operating small business. . . . There is strong evidence that hard work and frugal attitudes are influenced by cultural, class, and situational [reduction in status, English language difficulties] factors, particularly by the latter.[37]

Min's conclusions are substantially confirmed by the research of Ivan Light on the Korean community in Los Angeles. In responding to those who have argued that entrepreneurial success by some immigrant groups can be explained largely by the financial resources they bring with them (for example, the Cubans before the Mariel boatlift), Light observes:

> Koreans also worked sixty-hour weeks; saved one-half of their income by dint of painful thrift; accepted the risk of criminal victimization; passed business information among themselves; maintained expected patterns of nepotism and employer paternalism; praised a Calvinist deity; utilized family, alumni, congregational, and network solidarities; thought of themselves as sojourners; expressed satisfaction with poorly remunerated work; and utilized rotating credit associations in financing their small businesses. All of these culturally derived characteristics of the Korean

immigrant community contributed to Korean entrepreneurship, but none required money.[38]

These "culturally derived characteristics" are common also to the Chinese and the Japanese experience. Many flow from the Confucian emphasis on education and merit. Peter Rose has observed, "To most [Asians], meritocratic principles are the norms by which their lives in the United States have been organized in the past and ought to be in the future. It is this ethos—and the publicity their achievements have received—that causes many to look to them (but rarely to the Hispanics) as archetypes of acculturation."[39]

6

The Mexicans

Hispanic people are evolving to a bilingual, bicultural culture.
. . . We could come back in 100 years and the Latinos will not have
assimilated in the classic sense.
—David Hayes-Bautista, Chicano Studies Research Center,
UCLA, 1991

The problem in which the current immigration is suffused is, at
heart, one of numbers; for when the numbers begin to favor not
only the maintenance and replenishment of the immigrants' source
culture, but also its overall growth, and in particular growth so large
that the numbers not only impede assimilation but go beyond to
pose a challenge to the traditional culture of the American nation,
then there is a great deal about which to be concerned.
—*Dallas Morning News* columnist Richard Estrada, letter to
the author, 1991

Mexicans constitute the single largest immigrant group of recent
decades, accounting for more than half the burgeoning Hispanic-
American community. Wages are several times higher in the United
States than in Mexico, and educational opportunity, social welfare
programs, and judicial/police fairness are far greater. Thus a powerful magnet pulls on the U.S. side of a two-thousand-mile-long border,
while a combination of rapid population growth, slow job creation,
and social injustice on the Mexican side gives a powerful push.

I believe that Mexico's failure to build solid democratic institutions, its slow economic development (relative to, for example, Canada and the United States), and its extreme social inequalities all
reflect the Hispanic value system that has been the principal obstacle
to human progress throughout Hispanic America, and indeed in
Spain itself until recent decades. I would not be concerned by the
massive flow of Mexican immigrants, legal and illegal, if there were
evidence that the melting pot was indeed melting, that mainstream
American culture was substantially displacing Hispanic culture. But
the evidence is not reassuring, and it underscores the costs of an

immigration policy more responsive to the failures of other societies than to the needs of our own.

HISTORICAL OVERVIEW:
MEXICANS IN THE UNITED STATES

Long before the United States was an independent nation, Spain had established itself in that part of its Mexican colony that would become the states of Arizona, California, Nevada, New Mexico, Texas, and Utah, and parts of what would become Colorado, Kansas, Oklahoma, and Wyoming. (Indeed, the names of most of these states are of Spanish derivation.) Most of the Spaniards who ventured into these areas were explorers, adventurers, and missionaries. They did not create large cities, but they did establish hundreds of settlements and missions that still bear their original Spanish names, many of which have since grown in size (such as Los Angeles, San Diego, and San Francisco).

When Mexico achieved independence, in 1821, it permitted the establishment of American communities on its soil. One consequence of this policy was Texas's war with Mexico, which led to Texas's independence in 1836 and its annexation by the United States in 1845. In essence, the United States then precipitated a war with Mexico with the goal of acquiring what would become the American Southwest. The Americans decisively defeated the Mexicans, entered Mexico City late in 1847, and then obtained the sought-after territories for $15,000,000. Mexico lost more than a third of its territory, some 525,000 square miles. To this day, that war is a dominant feature of Mexico's psychic as well as its physical geography.

The approximately 100,000 Mexicans who inhabited the territories ceded to the United States after the war[1] were the first Mexican-Americans.* Of Mexico in general at the time, Thomas Sowell

---

*In this chapter, I use the convenient but imprecise term *Mexican-American* to refer to those who have citizenship by birth or naturalization as well as those who are foreign-born Mexicans who retain Mexican citizenship. Where the distinction is important in what follows, it will be made explicit. I might add that the designation of immigrant (legal or illegal) Mexican citizens as Mexican-Americans is particularly imprecise and also troubling to some American citizens of Mexican extraction.

observes that "there was a highly rigid social class system—about 1 percent upper class, 2 percent middle class, and 97 percent lower class."[2] The few members of the aristocracy in the new U.S. territories tended to acculturate rapidly to the American mainstream, in many cases joining the ranks of the American upper classes. The process of acculturation was much slower for the poor; indeed, when I visited a remote area of New Mexico in the early 1970s, I came across substantially unacculturated and very poor Hispanic/ Mexican communities whose antecedents precede the Mexican-American war.

Little immigration from Mexico to the United States occurred during the balance of the nineteenth century. A principal obstacle was the absence of transportation facilities across the great southwest desert, a condition that was transformed by railroad construction on both sides of the border starting in the 1880s. In the first three decades of the twentieth century, intense poverty in Mexico, in part the result of rapid population growth precipitated by improving public health, combined with the instability and bloodshed of the Mexican Revolution, which erupted in 1910, to impel the first of three great waves of Mexican immigration. World War I labor shortages in the United States intensified the magnet effect. Between 1900 and 1930, some 725,000 Mexicans crossed the border with legal papers, many others without.[3] Most came for agricultural work, particularly "stoop" labor, which, while poorly paid by U.S. standards, paid several times the going wage in Mexico. Many came as sojourners, returning to Mexico after accumulating some savings, perhaps subsequently returning to the United States—a pattern that continues to this day. The Mexicans tended to keep to themselves, to avoid official institutions, and to preserve their native language.

The Great Depression arrested the first wave of Mexican immigration, and, with unemployment approaching 25 percent, the U.S. government undertook a massive campaign of expulsions that, by one count, reduced the Mexican population from about 600,000 to about 400,000.[4] But the hiatus proved brief. World War II placed extraordinary pressures on America's labor force, and one consequence was the *bracero* program, which brought about 170,000 Mexican contract workers to the United States during the war years.[5] Many, many more entered illegally. After the war, the Mexicans were generally viewed as competitors for American jobs, and large numbers—Thomas Sowell uses the figure of four million[6]— were deported. The deportations notwithstanding, American employers found the *bracero* program a convenient and cheap way of meeting their labor needs after the war, and it was continued until 1964. Between 1946 and 1965, several million Mexicans participated in the program.

The third wave of Mexican immigration into the United States may well have been under way simultaneously with the mass deportations. From 1950 to 1980, the Mexican economy grew at the impressive average rate of about 6 percent annually. But population growth, averaging about 3 percent during the same period, in effect ate up half the economic growth, which in any event generated only about half the jobs needed by the rapidly expanding labor force. Moreover, not all parts of Mexico participated in the growth. The oil industry boomed toward the end of this period, and Mexico became one of the world's most important producers. Mexico City became the most populous city in the world. And agriculture and industry grew rapidly in the north, aided by the proximity of the U.S. market and, in the case of industry, by the twin-plant *maquila* scheme, under which capital-intensive components or processes were assigned to U.S. plants while labor-intensive components or processes were assigned to Mexican plants.

But the emigration to the United States continued unabated, and, after the drop in oil prices took the wind out of the Mexican economy's sails in the early 1980s, it accelerated. The principal motivator of the flow was the disparity in wages between the United States and Mexico, aggravated by high unemployment in Mexico. The World Bank estimates Mexico's 1988 per capita GNP at $1,760, that of the United States at $19,840—more than ten times larger. As George Borjas observes, "the wage differential between Mexico and the United States is the largest income gap between any two contiguous countries in the world."[7] The real difference may be even greater because of the highly inequitable pattern of income distribution in Mexico (see table 6.1). The income differential is not the only magnet. Social services, including welfare, are far more plentiful and reliable in the United States. Schools are much better, and a Supreme Court ruling has assured the children of illegal aliens access to primary and secondary schools. And due process is a substantial reality, whereas in Mexico, as in most other Latin American countries, it is a rarity: "justice" is often purchased, and the police are often corrupt and brutal.[8]

Illegal immigration—people sympathetic to it in Mexico and the United States refer to it as "undocumented"—has become so mas-

TABLE 6.1
SHARE OF TOTAL HOUSEHOLD INCOME
(*percentage*)

	Mexico (1977)	United States (1980)
Top 20% of households	57.7	39.9
Second 20%	20.4	25.0
Third 20%	12.0	17.9
Fourth 20%	7.0	11.9
Fifth 20%	2.9	5.3
Top 10%	40.6	23.3

Source: Based on information in the *World Development Report 1988* (New York: Oxford University Press, 1988), table 26.

sive that no one knows with any degree of precision how many Mexicans, or indeed other foreign nationals, are living in the United States. Some Mexican politicians and intellectuals see the illegal immigration as a form of recovery of Mexican land lost in the Mexican-American War.[9] A heavy flow back and forth across the porous border continues, and today the Mexican-American population consists of the offspring, perhaps the fifth or sixth generation, of Mexicans who were on the land in 1847; third- and fourth-generation offspring of the first wave; second- and third-generation offspring of the second and third waves; and large numbers of recent immigrants, many seeing themselves as sojourners and as Mexican citizens, but many having brought families with them or having married in America.

MEXICAN-AMERICANS TODAY

How many Mexican-Americans are there today? In the 1970 census, about 4.5 million people claimed to be of Mexican descent. The Census Bureau did a revised count in 1973, and the total had increased to almost 6.3 million. The U.S. Civil Rights Commission subsequently alleged that the Census Bureau had understated the Hispanic-American population by as much as 10 percent. As economic conditions have deteriorated in Mexico until the last few years—principally the consequence of expansionary policies in the 1970s, an unmanageable debt buildup second only to Brazil's, and the drop in world oil prices until the 1990 Middle East crisis—the incentives for emigration to the United States have increased. The Center for Immigration Studies in Washington estimates that the pool of resident Mexican-American immigrants may currently be increasing by as many as 250,000 annually. Border crossings, legal and illegal, by Mexicans may be six or more times that number every year.[10]

The Census Bureau estimates that there were 18,790,000 Hispanics in America in 1988, but over 20,000,000 in 1989 (Hispanics accounted for 6.5 percent of the total population in 1980, 8.2 percent in 1989).[11] Of the 1988 total, 11,762,000, or 63 percent, were estimated to be of Mexican antecedence, an 87 percent increase over the 1973 estimate. That represents about 5 percent of our total population. About 75 percent live in California and Texas. Thus, Hispanic-Americans (predominantly Mexican-Americans) accounted for 12 percent of California's population in the 1970 census, 19 percent in the 1980 census, and 26 percent in the 1990 census. One study projects that the Hispanic component will rise to 38 percent by the year 2030. A similar study of Texas projects Hispanic—presumably even more predominantly Mexican—population ranging from 28 percent to 53 percent by 2035, depending on assumptions about the rate of immigration.[12]

Generalizations about the degree of progress and achievement of Mexican-Americans are difficult because at any given moment the Mexican-American universe comprises a broad range of people of different social classes, different amounts of time in the United States, different degrees of acculturation, and different preferred languages. At one extreme are the offspring of the pre-1847 Spanish-American aristocracy, highly educated, now often intermarried with the mainstream American upper or upper middle class, totally acculturated, and often non–Spanish speaking. At the other extreme is the illegal immigrant who has just crossed the border in search of temporary work (and with every intention of returning to Mexico): often illiterate, monolingual in Spanish (in some cases, speaking only Indian dialects), and monocultural.

Further complicating the task of evaluation is the fact that age composition varies substantially from generation to generation. In one analysis drawn from 1970 census data, 40 percent of first-generation Mexican-Americans (many single), 45 .percent of the second generation, and 63 percent of the third generation were under thirty-five.[13] Obviously, these variations will have telling implications for occupation and income data.

Table 6.2 shows that, using the same white-collar/blue-collar definitions we used for the Asian immigrant groups, 19 percent of the Mexican-born and 45 percent of the U.S.-born Mexican-Americans are in white-collar jobs, compared with 61 percent of all Californians (a figure that includes Mexican-Americans). We cannot be confident of comparability with Asian immigrant performance as depicted in table 5.1, which is based on national data, whereas this table is based on California data. And table 5.1 is limited to men, whereas this table covers both sexes. But the Asian white-collar component (77 percent for the Chinese, 59 percent for the Japanese, 63 percent for the Koreans) is so much larger than the Mexican-American (and the non-Hispanic white—50 percent—in table 5.1) that the comparison has to have some significance, particularly since the educational and income data confirm the contrast.

Kevin F. McCarthy and R. Burciaga Valdez, from whose study table 6.2 is taken, point out that the progress of the Mexican community in California is understated because of the "recency of large-scale Mexican immigration into California, the resulting concentration of the state's native-born Latinos in the first generation, and the low education levels of earlier cohorts of native-born Latinos."[14] On the other hand, the data for Mexican-Americans are compared with data for "all Californians," a category that includes Mexican-Americans, other Hispanics, and blacks, thereby understating the contrast with Asian immigrants, where the benchmark is "non-Hispanic whites." The same is true for the following education and income data.

I have done a rough interpolation from a graph in the McCarthy and Valdez study[15] that suggests that second-generation native-born

TABLE 6.2

OCCUPATIONAL CATEGORIES OF MEXICAN-AMERICANS
(*percentage*)

Sector	Mexican-born	U.S.-born	All Californians
Professional/technical/managerial	5	13	27
Sales/clerical/skilled service	14	32	34
Craft/semi-skilled	21	20	19
Farm	15	6	3
Unskilled	45	29	17

Source: Kevin F. McCarthy and R. Burciaga Valdez, *Current and Future Effects of Mexican Immigration in California* (Santa Monica, CA: RAND, R–3365–CR, 1985).

Mexican-Americans ages twenty-five to thirty-four in California average about 10.5 years of education.[16] All Californians (including all Hispanics and blacks) average about 12 years. Recall that the national average for native-born Chinese is 14.9 years; for native-born Japanese, 13.7 years; for native-born Koreans, 13.8 years. Nearly two-thirds of Mexican immigrants have had no high school education.[17] In this connection, Thomas Sowell observes, "The goals and values of Mexican-Americans have never centered on education."[18]

The accuracy of that observation is underscored by Department of Education data that show a Hispanic high school dropout rate of 35.7 percent in 1988, three times higher than that of white students and more than twice that of black students. Linda Chavez points out that this alarming rate is skewed upward by the inclusion of recent immigrants from Mexico; she adduces data showing the dropout rate for second-generation Mexican-Americans to be 22 percent and for third-generation to be 29 percent (I find the dropout increase from the second to the third generation particularly troubling)—compared with 10 percent for non-Hispanic whites. (The black rate has been declining fairly steadily since 1978; it was 2.2 percent above the white rate of 12.6 percent in 1988.) The overall Hispanic rate is 1.4 percent higher than it was in 1972, when dropout statistics for Hispanics were first recorded.[19]

Sowell analyzed the 1970 census data for family income by ethnic group and developed index numbers as follows (the U.S. average is 100; the number for each ethnic group is a percentage above or below the U.S. average): Japanese-American, 132; Chinese-American, 112; U.S. average, 100; Mexican-American, 76; blacks, 62. He stresses that, in interpreting these numbers, one must consider the youthfulness of the Mexican-American population (about ten years younger than the U.S. average), "lower levels of schooling, in both quantitative and qualitative terms," and the fact that proportionately fewer Mexican-American women work than do Asian-American, black, or white women.[20]

BENEFITS AND COSTS
OF MEXICAN IMMIGRATION

The McCarthy-Valdez study and a similar study done at the same time by Thomas Muller and Thomas Espenshade[21] reach roughly the same conclusion: on balance, the legal and illegal immigration of Mexican-Americans has been economically beneficial, at least for the cities—above all, Los Angeles, where they live in large numbers. They agree that the immigration has helped economic growth and price stability. They agree that wage rates have been depressed only at the lower end of the scale, and McCarthy and Valdez believe that it is other Mexican-Americans—including U.S. citizens—who are most affected, a nonetheless disturbing conclusion confirmed by George Borjas.[22] They disagree on the fiscal impact of the immigrants: McCarthy and Valdez find that they produce more public revenue than they consume—except for the very substantial expense of education;[23] Muller and Espenshade find a substantial deficit, but one that is largely covered by transfers from other areas of California where there are few immigrants (which, they note, may not be gratifying to taxpayers in those areas). But the conclusion of both studies is generally optimistic.

Circumstances in Colorado appear to be different. Eleven percent of the population is Hispanic, principally Mexican-American; one-third of welfare recipients and one-quarter of the prison population are Hispanic.[24] With respect to immigrant participation in welfare in general, Borjas describes the evidence as "worrisome," noting, among other things, that almost 30 percent of female-headed Mexican immigrant families were receiving welfare in 1980.[25]

If I am right in thinking that Latin America's political, economic, and social problems are largely the consequence of a persistent traditional Iberian culture, then the long-term implications of the vast influx from Latin America, a large percentage illegal, should give us pause. To be sure, many Mexican immigrants come from the northern states of Mexico, where the value system and institutions are changing, increasingly influenced—through immigration, television, the *maquila* industries—by American values, attitudes, and institutions, a point emphasized in a 1986 newspaper article by Joel Garreau.[26] Moreover, the very act of emigrating is, for some Latin Americans, a rejection of the traditional value system and a quest for the more humane and progressive value systems and institutions of the advanced democracies. But the vast majority are simply fleeing poverty and seeking economic opportunity and social justice, and they bring with them traditional Iberian values and attitudes.

Even with steady improvement of the Mexican economy, largely the consequence of the policies of the Salinas de Gortari government, and the uncertain fruition of the movement toward genuine democracy (as of this writing), the United States is going to remain an attractive destination for the foreseeable future, particularly since unemployment is likely to remain high in Mexico. The differences in wages, opportunity, and social services are simply too great. Moreover, rising salaries in Mexico could, at least at the outset, aggravate the illegal immigration problem by making it easier for potential immigrants to accumulate the stake necessary to migrate. Short of a concerted effort by the United States to stem the flow, we must expect a continuation of the influx, particularly into the Southwest, possibly even to the point where Leon Bouvier and Ray Marshall's high projection of a 50 percent Mexican-American population in Texas is reached by the year 2025.

The Melting Pot Falters

The population of countries of the Caribbean basin is approaching 200 million. Perhaps half or more live so wretchedly that what we label poverty in the United States would look to them like affluence. And as more of these people settle in the United States, more family networks are created to receive new immigrants, an opportunity enhanced by the family reunification emphasis of recent U.S. immigration legislation. I am reminded of a poll taken by an American anthropologist friend in a rural community in Haiti in the late 1970s in which more than a hundred villagers were asked whether they would migrate to the United States if they could; 100 percent said yes.

This prospect would not be troubling if there were clear evidence that the melting pot is working and that traditional American values will, in due course, substantially supplant the traditional Ibero-American values that most Latin Americans bring with them, as has happened with so many other immigrant groups. But the evidence is not reassuring on this score. The McCarthy-Valdez study demonstrates movement toward the cultural mainstream by

Mexican-Americans as the generations pass. But that movement is slower than that of most other immigrant groups, and dramatically slower than that of the Asians. The speed of acculturation is burdened by the vastness of the immigrant influx and the resultant buildup of large Hispanic communities where the Spanish language and old-country ways persist, particularly in the Southwestern states: "No foreign language has been so persistently retained and is as likely to survive in this country as Spanish. This remarkable 'language loyalty' . . . is attributable primarily to the Mexican-Americans."[27]

Strident Chicano "nationalism" and insistence on bilingual education and bilingual public services are evidence of the "salad-bowl" rather than the "melting-pot" view of the United States. Acculturation is also burdened by the sojourner, back-and-forth nature of a good part of the immigration.

The anthropologists Susan E. Keefe and Amado M. Padilla conducted research in Mexican-American communities in Oxnard, Santa Barbara, and Santa Paula, California. One finding:

> While social assimilation, in formal spheres at least, increases from the first to the second generation, it tends to level off thereafter. Economic assimilation proceeds similarly: dramatic mobility takes place for second-generation Chicanos [defined as synonymous with "Mexican-Americans"] who become integrated into the stable blue-collar labor force, while white-collar jobs continue to remain out of reach for the vast majority of those from succeeding generations.[28]

True to the conventional wisdom of many American social scientists today, Keefe and Padilla imply that discrimination and exploitation are at the root of the limited social mobility experienced by Mexican-Americans. They do not mention the almost total absence of social mobility in Mexico. They go on to assert that "ethnic minority groups undeniably suffer from higher poverty levels,"[29] ignoring the experience of the Japanese, the Chinese, the Koreans, and the Jews, among others. In sharp contrast, by comparing the earnings of native men of Mexican ancestry with demographically comparable white non-Hispanic natives, Borjas concludes that "the U.S. labor market does not tax Hispanics because of their ethnicity"—that there is no significant anti-Hispanic discrimination in the labor marketplace.[30]

Further troubling evidence of slow assimilation over the generations was found by James W. Lamare in a 1982 study of the attitudes reflecting political integration of Mexican-American children in El Paso, Texas. A substantial increase in political acculturation occurred from the first to the second generation. But Lamare observed a significant decline in the third generation.[31] (Recall that Chavez's data indicated an *increase* in the high school dropout rate from the second to the third generation of Mexican-Americans.)

Low levels of political participation are another preoccupying indicator of nonassimilation. From 1972 to 1988, about 39 percent of the Hispanic voting-age population actually registered, compared with 63 percent of blacks and 69 percent of whites. The low Hispanic registration percentage could be explained in part by counting noncitizens, legal and illegal, as part of the voting-age pool. But even of those who registered, the percentage of Hispanics who actually voted (32 percent) was far below that of blacks (52 percent) or whites (61 percent).[32] Grebler, Moore, and Guzman attribute low Mexican-American political participation to "a culture of political passivity," among other factors.[33]

If a third or more of the populations of Texas and California are going to be Hispanic—and predominantly Mexican—in the first half of the next century, the implications of the principal conclusion of Keefe and Padilla are disturbing:

> Acculturation certainly takes place, but it is neither as rapid nor as thorough as implied by most interpretations. . . . Even the fourth-generation Mexican-Americans in our study retain aspects of Mexican culture— significantly, their value of and involvement in large and local extended families. . . . While certain traits such as knowledge of Mexican history and the Spanish language decline significantly from one generation to the next, other traits such as Catholicism tend to be maintained; in some instances, such as extended familism, Mexican traits are strengthened over time in the U.S.[34]

This conclusion is similar to the conclusions of a recent three-year study by David Hayes-Bautista, head of the Chicano Studies Research Center at the University of California in Los Angeles, a study that was the basis of an extensive *New York Times* article. Dr. Hayes-Bautista also says that Hispanic values and attitudes and facility in the Spanish language are maintained through the third generation and beyond. He stresses the ease with which that culture is maintained in places like East Los Angeles, citing the experience of José Hernández, a twenty-six-year-old Mexican who was shocked to discover that the "Mexican community in East Los Angeles is so self-contained that he could not even find anybody with whom he could practice English."[35]

Poor enclave communities not only make it easier for homeland values and language to persist; they also possess the potential for resentment-driven violence, particularly during bad economic times. That is one of the lessons of the rioting in the Mount Pleasant district of Washington, D.C., in the spring of 1991.

As I discussed earlier, the strong familistic element in Hispanic culture excludes the interests of the community and the nation. Moore characterizes Mexican-American familism as "warmth inside the family and hostility to those outside the family."[36] Grebler, Moore, and Guzman point out that familism is an obstacle to cultural change and achievement because it insulates the family member from outside ideas, which by definition are not to be trusted.[37] Family is also central to East Asian culture, but in Korea and China, and above all Japan, the idea of family carries over to the community and the nation. If the process of Mexican-American acculturation in the United States is so incomplete or slow that traditional Iberian values and attitudes continue, generation after generation, substantially unmodified for large numbers of Mexican-Americans—as they have for centuries for most Latin Americans at home—then we must ask to what extent lagging Mexican-American performance in such indicators as education, employment mobility, income, and political participation are the consequence of traditional Mexican/Hispanic culture.

BILINGUAL EDUCATION AND ACCULTURATION

Language is the conduit of culture. Since Spanish persists as the dominant language for many Hispanic-Americans, a slow pace of acculturation for them is virtually assured. And if large numbers of Mexican-Americans are acculturating very slowly, in part because of the sheer size of the immigration flow, then the long-term implications of the vast immigration from Mexico—along with heavy immigration from Latin America in general—are profoundly troubling, particularly at a time of serious value erosion in the broader American society (see chapter 8). The comparison may seem extreme today, but a few decades hence, as the Hispanic proportion of our population continues to expand, California and Texas may experience tensions similar to those between French-speaking and English-speaking Canada.[38]

While his views surely do not reflect those of all or even necessarily a majority of Hispanic-Americans, Dr. Josué González—subsequently President Carter's Director of the Office of Bilingual Education and Minority Affairs—made a comment in 1974 on Canada's bilingualism laws that bears pondering: "If the present rate of growth of Spanish speakers continues, it is not unlikely that we shall have to consider [a comparable bill] as a very definite possibility."[39]

Richard Estrada believes that, in the long run, the language problem in the Southwest may prove to be greater than in the case of Quebec:

> For Quebec . . . does not lie contiguous to France. . . . The Southwest, on the other hand, shares a 2,000-mile-long border with a Spanish-speaking country of at least 85 million people, hundreds of thousands of whom yearly move to the United States, or who reside with one foot in one country, the other in the other. The twin factors of geographic contiguity and rate of immigration must give pause. No one can witness the growth of Spanish-language media in this country and fail to believe that things are headed in the direction of a parallel culture. And that is the point: bilingualism has generally militated against assimilation. It has promoted a parallel culture instead of a subordinate one.[40]

I want to be clear that I don't view the persistence of Spanish, a language in which I am fluent, as intrinsically a negative factor. I think it is unfortunate, although perhaps inevitable, that ethnic languages are lost as the generations pass. Since I see the operation of the melting pot as crucial to the well-being of our society, it is only when Spanish persists as the *primary* language—a condition facilitated by publicly supported bilingual programs—and English is spoken as a *secondary* language (as is the case, for example, with many Puerto Ricans) that I am troubled.

Linda Chavez observes that bilingual education was sold to the Congress and the people principally by Hispanic activists as a means of facilitating the transition to English and improving the quality of education received by Hispanic-American youngsters. But the reality, as documented by several studies, has been very different: bilingual education has proved to be "at its heart a program to help maintain the language and culture of Hispanic children."[41] Rosalie

Pedalino Porter comes to a similar conclusion in her compelling book, *Forked Tongue*. [42]

Hispanic activists succeeded in convincing the Congress that the nonavailability of electoral material, including ballots, in Spanish was the equivalent of the South's use of literacy tests to prevent blacks from voting. Congress ignored the fact of substantial Hispanic voting[43]—and large numbers (relative to blacks) of elected Hispanic officials—long before the Voting Rights Act of 1965 and legislated an automatic requirement for bilingual election materials where voting fell below 50 percent of the Hispanic population. Particularly in the light of a nationwide pattern of low Hispanic voter turnout—which, in my view, may well reflect a cultural indisposition to political participation—statutory requirement of bilingual election materials amounts to pandering to Hispanic activists, which reinforces the divisive bilingualism movement.

Chavez goes on to quote Eduardo Hernández-Chávez, a speaker at a bilingual education conference sponsored by Georgetown University:

> [T]he school . . . bears great responsibility either in the maintenance of the language and culture of Chicanos or in the shift to Anglo-American norms. . . . It must either work as an agent of deculturation and assimilation, or it must work . . . with the ethnic communities to support and develop their language and culture in the education of their children. . . .
>
> We urgently need . . . a policy of bilingualism . . . that supports the maintenance, development, and full flowering of the ethnic languages.[44]

Arthur Schlesinger, Jr., concludes that "bilingual education retards rather than expedites the movement of Hispanic children into the English-speaking world and . . . it promotes segregation more than it does integration. Bilingualism shuts doors. It nourishes self-ghettoization, and ghettoization nourishes racial antagonism."[45] Isolation from the cultural mainstream is likely to have tragic consequences for human beings: a sense of alienation and resentment as well as disproportionate levels of poverty, welfare dependence, drug use, and crime.

There are also grave consequences for the nation. It is not just our future economic well-being that is at risk—as I mentioned earlier, upward economic mobility is not everything; a highly professional blue-collar work force would be a major asset for the United States. The high Hispanic dropout rates suggest, however, that many Mexican-American youngsters are not going to be qualified for the kinds of jobs the American economy ought to generate in the future. A 1989 article in the *New York Times* carried the head-line, IMPENDING U.S. JOBS "DISASTER": WORK FORCE UNQUALIFIED. TO WORK and quoted the chairman of the Xerox Corporation as saying, "More than a third of tomorrow's work force will be minorities, and half of those are kids growing up poor. A fourth drop out and another fourth don't come close to having the skills to survive in an advanced economy."[46]

The Asian immigrants, particularly the Chinese and the Japanese, started out in this country as persecuted pariahs and are now the new American achievers. There are obvious parallels between the success they know in their homelands (for the Chinese, substitute Taiwan) and the success they know as immigrants. It is difficult to avoid the conclusion that culture—positive values and attitudes about work, education, parental responsibility, saving money, self-reliance, com-munity—has played an important role in these success stories.

The Mexican-Americans have also experienced discrimination, but probably no more than the Chinese or the Japanese. Like the Puerto Ricans, whose achievement levels are among the lowest of any minority or ethnic group, they have acculturated slowly and have remained disproportionately in the lower classes.

Beyond attitudes about education, work, and creativity that affect economic performance are such issues as social and civic responsibil-ity, political participation and the responsible use of political power, and fair play, particularly in the judicial process. The performance of Latin America, Mexico included, with respect to these issues must leave Americans uneasy in the face of the massive, largely uncon-trolled immigration and evidence of slow acculturation.

For Mexican-American citizens and immigrants who are here legally, the principal objective must be to assure maximum exposure and access to the cultural mainstream. One of the most effective ways of achieving this is to reduce sharply the flow of immigrants, thus arresting the growth of enclave communities like East Los Angeles. Unless bilingual education is focused on a rapid transi-tion to English, it becomes a major impediment to acculturation, and I would review and revise bilingual programs to assure their consistency with this goal. I would most certainly discontinue the use of bilingual election materials, an innovation that moves us one step closer to the divisiveness that threatens Canada's integrity.

I think that programs such as Head Start, which enhance the educational and social opportunities of children from lagging ethnic groups and improve their access to the cultural mainstream, should have a particularly high priority for Hispanic-Americans. Another part of the problem is to convince low-achieving groups that access *is* available to them, which is one of the reasons I support time-limited affirmative action programs for blacks. (I define "affirmative action" as preferential treatment in the education system and the workplace.) In the following chapter on black Americans, I discuss some of the weighty problems that attach to affirmative action and explain that my support of affirmative action flows principally from the belief that it has been a political and psychological necessity for bridging the racial fissure in America.

I would not have advocated it for Hispanic-Americans, most of whom have come to this country of their own volition, particularly since the discrimination experienced by Hispanics—for example, in voter registration—has been far less severe than that experienced by blacks. But the precedent of affirmative action for Hispanics has been established, and just as it is difficult to limit affirmative action benefits to one minority group (which, by the way, is one telling argument against affirmative action), it is probably politically unfeasible to terminate it piecemeal. While it operates, affirmative action does send the message of mainstream access to Hispanic-Americans. As we shall see in the next chapter, however, the evolution of the emphasis of affirmative action from equal opportunity to equal results over the past quarter-century has strengthened the divisive forces working toward resegregation of our society.

7

The Blacks

Slavery . . . dishonors labor; it introduces idleness to society, and with idleness, ignorance and pride, luxury and distress. It enervates the powers of the mind and benumbs the activity of man.
—Alexis de Tocqueville, *Democracy in America* (1835)

It is not beyond the bounds of possibility that by the end of this century the United States will have become the first multi-racial democracy in history.
—Octavio Paz, *Woodrow Wilson Quarterly* (Spring 1986)

Since the Supreme Court's *Brown v. Board of Education* ruling against segregated schools in 1954, most black Americans have participated in a political, social, and economic revolution. In terms of political participation, education, upward employment mobility, and family income, huge strides have been made toward closing the gap between blacks and whites, above all for the two-thirds of America's blacks who have made it into the mainstream—and into the middle class. The condition of the one-third who have not made it, most of them in the ghetto, is a tragedy for them, in personal terms, as well as for the broader society, in terms of the heavy costs of lost creativity, crime, and welfare and other social programs.

But while racism still exists (there are many reasons to believe that it has declined sharply), in my view it is no longer the principal obstacle to progress for people in black ghettos. The just-cited statistic of two-thirds of America's blacks having moved into the mainstream is one compelling evidence of that assertion. I believe that the principal obstacle today is culture: a set of values and attitudes, strongly influenced by the slavery experience, perpetuated by the isolation enforced, historically, by the Jim Crow laws and, today, by the ghetto. Accordingly, antipoverty policies and programs must emphasize access to the mainstream. Affirmative action has contributed to the achievement of that access for the majority of blacks, but its costs increasingly outweigh its benefits, particularly since its focus has shifted from equal opportunity to equal results. This evolution strengthens the position of those black leaders who, like the Hispanic leaders calling for bilingualism and biculturalism, would subordinate national—American—identity to racial/ethnic identity.

HISTORICAL OVERVIEW:
BLACKS IN THE UNITED STATES

The first blacks arrived in Virginia in 1619. They were not slaves but, like so many whites, indentured servants who, in due course, earned their freedom. Slavery was not introduced in the colonies until the second half of the seventeenth century, by which time there was already an appreciable number of "free persons of color."[1] The number grew as a result of the freeing of slaves by masters, or *manumission,* often following sexual liaisons; the purchase of freedom by slaves who enjoyed a salary or other income; or escape through the underground railway to the North.

By the outbreak of the Civil War, the number of "free persons of color" approached 500,000, more than 10 percent of the total black population at the time. Many lived in the North, particularly in cities, or in the plantation-free Piedmont, and tidewater Virginia and Maryland. Large and dynamic free black (principally mulatto) communities also sprang up in New Orleans, where a third of the "free colored" families owned slaves,[2] and in Charleston, South Carolina. By the Civil War, most free blacks were literate and self-sufficient. Almost all black slaves were illiterate, since most slave owners believed that education would ultimately precipitate slave uprisings. The free blacks were increasingly acculturated to the white cultural mainstream. In many cases, white fathers of mulattoes facilitated their access. Their self-image—and expectation of upward mobility—had to be far more positive than that of the slaves.

Slaves were acculturated to a system that almost totally suppressed the idea of progress, along with any progressive values and attitudes. Moreover, they came to the New World from traditional African societies that practiced both slavery and religions based on magic and the propitiation of spirits. (The roots of Haitian voodoo are in the Dahomey region of West Africa—today called Benin—whence came large numbers of American slaves, many of whom practiced it as slaves, calling it "Hoodoo".)

I accept Herbert Gutman's thesis that slavery did not destroy the black family.[3] But that does not gainsay slavery's inculcation of values that are impediments to work, saving, education, and upward mobility, impediments that operated with comparably stultifying effect for American *and* Latin American slaves.[4] The Venezuelan writer Carlos Rangel has observed, "a number of factors inhibit the development of societies based on slavery: the passive resistance to work that is the earmark of the slave; the absurd prestige of idleness that afflicts his master; and . . . a rhythm of life so little concerned with punctuality."[5] The words of the liberal Brazilian economist Celso Furtado about the consequences of slavery in his country also merit our attention: "Through the first half of the twentieth century, the vast majority of the descendants of slaves continued to live within the limited system of 'necessities.' . . . Able to satisfy their living expenses with two or three days of work per week, [they] found it much more attractive to 'buy' leisure than to continue working when they already had enough to 'live.' "[6]

Thomas Sowell adds, "As workers, blacks had little sense of personal responsibility under slavery. Lack of initiative, evasion of work, half-done work, unpredictable absenteeism, and abuse of tools and equipment were pervasive under slavery, and these patterns did not suddenly disappear with emancipation."[7] According to John Dollard, "The slavery system was . . . a device for getting work done without regard to its effect on Negro personality. . . . The cultivation of dependence reactions by the slavery system . . . is quite extreme."[8] The historian Stephan Thernstrom speaks of a black "cultural pattern—an emphasis on consumption rather than saving, an aversion to risk-taking investment" that would logically have its roots in the slavery experience.[9]

Slavery undermines the focus on the future that is instrumental to planning, saving, and investing. For the slave, the present is the overwhelming reality. And, as Eugene Genovese notes, there are "some important cultural continuities [with Africa]. Traditional African time-reckoning focuses on present and past, not future."[10]

Freedmen and Their Descendants

It should not be surprising, then, that most black leadership and achievement in the nineteenth century and the first decades of the twentieth century came from the descendants of "free persons of color," who got a head start on acculturation to the American mainstream. The first great black leader, Frederick Douglass, had escaped from urban slavery in the South and lived for many years as a free man in the North, married to a white woman. In 1870, free persons of color established the first black high school in the United States, Dunbar High in Washington, D.C., whose students scored higher as a whole than any white high school in citywide tests in 1899 and for years thereafter, and which sent three-fourths of its graduates on to college. W.E.B. Du Bois was a descendant of free blacks. So were or are United Nations official Ralph Bunche, Supreme Court Justice Thurgood Marshall, and the politically prominent Andrew Young, Clifford Alexander, and Julian Bond.

Thomas Sowell notes that, through the first half of the twentieth century, descendants of free persons of color constituted the majority of black professionals and were far better educated and had smaller families than descendants of emancipated slaves. Sowell concludes, "As with other groups around the world, historic advantages in acculturation had enduring consequences for generations to come."[11]

To be sure, many descendants of freedmen are lighter in color, and it is probably true that they were somewhat less discriminated against for that reason. But in the heyday of anti-Negro prejudice in the United States, lighter skin was no guarantee of better treatment. For example, no American black of any shade played in the baseball major leagues until Jackie Robinson broke the barrier in 1947 (although some Latin Americans "of color" did—but they were labeled "Latins").

Except when it has mitigated discrimination and enhanced expectations of upward mobility, skin color is, I believe, largely a coincidence when it comes to the achievements of the descendants of "free persons of color." I believe that the principal reason that they have done better than the descendants of emancipated slaves is that they got a head start of several generations on acculturation. One evidence of this is the extent to which they speak unaccented English. (The broader, more rapid acculturation of the last few decades has made standard English far more common among blacks.)

The West Indians

Further evidence of the significance of culture in black achievement is furnished by West Indian immigrants in America. Substantial

West Indian immigration started in the early years of the twentieth century, principally from Jamaica, Barbados, Trinidad, and the Bahamas. Sowell observes that, by 1920, one-quarter of Harlem's population was West Indian, although West Indians represent only about 1 percent of the national black population.[12] That 1 percent has produced an extraordinary number of leaders and achievers: Marcus Garvey, Stokely Carmichael, Malcolm X, James Farmer, Roy Inness, Shirley Chisholm, Kenneth B. Clark, W. Arthur Lewis, Sidney Poitier, Harry Belafonte, Godfrey Cambridge, and Ford Foundation president Franklin Thomas.

The parents of General Colin Powell, appointed Chairman of the Joint Chiefs of Staff in 1989, were Jamaicans. His father was a clerk, his mother a seamstress. In an interview at the time of his appointment, he said, "The key to opportunity in this country begins with education. My parents expected it. And in my family, you did what your parents expected of you."[13]

But beyond these celebrities, West Indians have also produced a standard of living and educational level that, by the second generation, have exceeded the national average (and average family size, unemployment, and crime rate *below* the national average).[14] Sowell says:

> Despite the rhetoric of "black solidarity," West Indian Negroes and American Negroes have remained quite distinct social groups. . . . in the 1930's . . . 98 percent of West Indian women attending American Negro colleges married West Indian men. A . . . 1972 . . . study showed that 87 percent . . . of Barbadians in New York . . . married other Barbadians. A survey of a middle-class black community in 1962 found that 98 percent of the West Indians . . . had almost all their friendships either with other West Indians or with a few whites.[15]

> The contrast between the West Indians and American Negroes was not so much in their occupational backgrounds as in their behavior patterns. West Indians were more frugal, hard-working, and entrepreneurial. Their children worked harder and outperformed native black children in school.[16]

The black writer James Weldon Johnson, a descendant of West Indians, said in 1930, "[West Indians] average high in intelligence and efficiency, there is practically no illiteracy among them, and many have a sound English common school education. They are characteristically sober-minded and have something of a genius for business, differing almost totally in these from the average rural

Negro of the South."[17] (Native American blacks sometimes refer to Jamaican immigrants as "Jewmaicans.") Nathan Glazer adds, "The ethos of the West Indians, in contrast to that of the Southern Negro, emphasized saving, hard work, investment, education."[18]

The experience of the West Indian immigrants refutes any argument that lighter skin color and consequent reduced discrimination are at the root of the success of the descendants of freedmen. Sowell observes that West Indian blacks are not racially distinct from American blacks. He explains the more progressive values and attitudes of the West Indian immigrants as the consequence of earlier emancipation (1838) and of the fact that, whereas slaves in the United States were usually fed from a common kitchen, slaves in the British colonies were usually given a small plot to grow their own food and a surplus to sell.[19] I think there is truth to those explanations, as well as in the likelihood that West Indian performance in the United States is in part a consequence of the self-selection of achievers and risk takers implicit in any decision to emigrate. But I also think that the postemancipation access to the respective cultural mainstreams was substantially greater for former British slaves, at least those who lived in urban areas, than for former American slaves, particularly as the institution of Jim Crow took hold on the latter. Acculturation by former slaves to British values, attitudes, and institutions has been so complete in prosperous and democratic Barbados that the Barbadians (or "Bajans," as they call themselves) have been referred to as Afro-Saxons and Black Englishmen.[20] Harold Cruse observes, "West Indians are essentially conservatives fashioned in the British mold."[21]

One manifestation of the generally greater postemancipation access of West Indian blacks to the mainstream has been access to the most prestigious public- and private-sector jobs in the West Indian islands. High-achievement role models symbolizing upward mobility have thus been widely visible to young blacks. Until the past quarter-century, comparable role models for American blacks were proportionally much fewer, a point stressed by John Dollard in his 1937 classic, *Caste and Class in a Southern Town*: "A Negro plantation manager, a very rare specimen, said that the Negroes on his plantation tend to improve faster under a Negro manager. They say to themselves that what he can do, they can do; whereas with a white boss they feel that the gulf is too great and make no effort to improve."[22] Harold Cruse notes that Black Power leaders Stokely Carmichael and Lincoln Lynch, both West Indians, "emphasized the fact that in Jamaica and Trinidad there 'is a lot of poverty but we felt proud being black.' Moreover, the West Indians have political power (i.e., black policemen, civil servants, public officials, etc.)."[23]

Compared to 1937, black role models now abound in America, and the broad awareness of black achievement in politics, sports, business, the media, the arts, and other spheres, as well as the movement into the middle class of substantial numbers of blacks, means that a similar demonstration effect is now operating here, no doubt further contributing to the rapid growth of the black middle class.

Racism

In *A Piece of the Pie*, Stanley Lieberson argues that the overwhelming explanation for low levels of black achievement is racism and discrimination.[24] The bulk of his analysis addresses the differences between the experiences of the south, central, and Eastern European (he uses the acronym SCE) immigrants of the late nineteenth and early twentieth centuries—most of whom arrived penniless but most of whose descendants are now substantially established in mainstream America—and American blacks, many of whom are still outside that mainstream. Lieberson is uncomfortable with culture as an explanation for variations in performance between blacks and whites, and one of the criticisms I have of his book is that he fails to address the widely varying performance within the SCE group, for example, between Italians and Jews.

Using extensive data for Providence, Rhode Island, covering the years from 1880 to 1935, Joel Perlmann analyzed the differences in upward mobility among the Irish, Italian, Jewish, and black communities. While he concludes that discrimination is the overriding explanation for the condition of blacks, which is entirely credible to me given the time period of his study, he also concludes that "[t]he Providence data . . . strongly suggest that in the cases of the Italians and the Russian Jews . . . pre-migration cultural attributes cannot be dismissed or even treated as afterthoughts, but rather constitute an important part of the explanation for group differences in behavior."[25] As Stephan Thernstrom explains, "in Boston, the Irish and Italians moved ahead economically only sluggishly and erratically; the English and the Jews, on the other hand, found their way into the higher occupational strata with exceptional speed. . . . there is some basis for believing . . . that the cultures the immigrants brought with them had some effect."[26]

Although I accept Lieberson's thesis that the discrimination problem has been greater and of longer duration for blacks than for Chinese or Japanese, I think he exaggerates the extent of that difference, making it easier to dismiss culture as an explanation of the striking differences in achievement among the nonwhite groups.

But whatever my reaction to *A Piece of the Pie*, Sowell's data on the performance of West Indian immigrants calls into serious question the validity of Lieberson's thesis. I accept that discrimination is an important part of the explanation of the black condition in the United States and was, in fact, the dominant cause, at least in the South, until the 1960s. But circumstances are very different today, and while racism and discrimination still exist, the principal obstacle to continued movement toward racial equality in America in my view is a cultural one, flowing principally from the black slavery experience perpetuated by the isolation and oppression of Jim Crow.

THE CASES OF HAITI AND LIBERIA

There are two useful laboratories for testing the thesis that slave culture, sustained over the generations in substantial isolation, is a major impediment to human progress even in the absence of racial discrimination: Haiti and Liberia.

Haiti was established as an independent republic, the first black nation in the world, in 1804, following the uprising of black slaves against their French masters. I noted in the introduction that, as a French slave colony, "St. Domingue" was, by Adam Smith's judgment, "the most important of the sugar colonies of the West Indies. . . . its produce [was] said to be greater than that of all the English sugar colonies put together."[27] The Haitians were understandably xenophobic following the departure of the French. But Haiti's isolation was intensified by a quarantine of countries practicing slavery, above all the United States, that feared that the rebellion of Haiti's slaves would become infectious.

Haiti's history as an independent country has been disfigured by an almost unbroken chain of corrupt and greedy despots, mulatto and black, of whom the Duvaliers were the most recent; abuse of power at all levels of the society; failure of those with power to improve the lot of their countrymen; almost total absence of institutions of due process, as well as other political, social, and economic institutions; great difficulty in creating viable organizations; monopoly abuse, scant entrepreneurship, and widespread corruption; and a tendency on the part of Haitian peasants, like peasants elsewhere, to view subsistence as the goal of life. Voodoo, still widely practiced, has helped to lock the Haitian masses into the status quo.

Haiti today is among the thirty poorest countries in the world. Perhaps three-quarters of its people are illiterate. The departure of the Duvaliers has not significantly changed the historic pattern of autocracy, abuse of power, and injustice, although there was some hope when Jean-Bertrand Aristide won fair elections held at the end of 1990. (That fair elections were held is due mainly to the intense efforts of international institutions, particularly the United Nations, and the U.S. government.) But Aristide, whose conduct of government was not always consistent with democratic norms, was overthrown by the Haitian military in September 1991.

Liberia was established in 1847 as the first independent black nation in Africa by a group of American blacks, most of them ex-slaves or the offspring of ex-slaves, whose settlement in Africa had been promoted by American whites who had formed the American Colonization Society in 1816. Five years later, the first shipload of settlers landed in West Africa. The colonists were a small minority among far more numerous indigenous tribes: "The settlers . . . associated agriculture with the life of servitude they or their parents had experienced. . . . For most Americo-Liberians, the role of dirt farmer was decidedly beneath their station."[28] Although many of the colonists had little education, they were far ahead of the indigenous tribes in their ability to control their circumstances and soon established themselves as an aristocracy. Eugene Genovese observes about American slavery: "A genuinely aristocratic ethos characterized by something [a quest for dignity] other than a supine quest for identification with the strong emerged among the slaves."[29]

In 1930, the American black sociologist Charles S. Johnson visited Liberia, which had theretofore had little contact with the outside world, as the American member of the League of Nations International Commission of Inquiry into the Existence of Slavery and Forced Labor in the Republic of Liberia. His findings: "Successive generations have developed corrupt leaders, the machinery of government has been clogged with incompetence and vice; education has been neglected. They have lost the capacity for work, resisted reforms, and, in their extremity, turned the native population into virtual slaves."[30]

Notwithstanding a rich agricultural and mineral endowment, Liberia is today among the forty poorest countries in the world. It continues to suffer from political instability: the government of General Samuel K. Doe, a former enlisted man, was recently overthrown in a bloody civil war. Sixty years after Charles Johnson wrote his report, autocracy, abuse of power, and injustice still characterize Liberia.

AMERICA'S RACIAL REVOLUTION

The debate about the condition and future of blacks in the United States is often overgeneralized. Some black leaders so emphasize racism and discrimination that many white liberals have the sense that bigotry and injustice dominate the lives of most blacks—except perhaps certain athletes, politicians, and media and entertainment stars. The heavy media, academic, and political focus on the acute problems of the black ghetto has contributed to a white American view of race issues that is disproportionately influenced by the condition of a minority of blacks and is often accompanied by disproportionately guilty feelings.

Contrary to the image of broadly persistent racism and poverty, a racial and cultural revolution has occurred in the United States over the past thirty-five years on a par with the Spanish miracle of the same period and even the Meiji Restoration, which occurred in a comparable span of years. In 1950, about one of every six blacks was in the middle class. Today, as I mentioned previously, two of every three American blacks are middle class.[31] In response to the vastly increased opportunity available to them, the majority who are in the black middle class have adopted the future-oriented, progressive values of the American mainstream, sloughing off the present-oriented, static values and isolation inculcated by slavery and Jim Crow. A substantial percentage of American blacks now live in the suburbs.[32]

The National Research Council's five-year study, *A Common Destiny: Blacks and American Society*, published in 1989, opens with the following words:

> Just five decades ago, most black Americans could not work, live, shop, eat, seek entertainment, or travel where they chose. Even a quarter

century ago—100 years after the Emancipation Proclamation of 1863—most blacks were effectively denied the right to vote. A large majority of blacks lived in poverty, and very few black children had the opportunity to receive basic education; indeed, black children were still forced to attend inferior and separate schools in jurisdictions that had not accepted the 1954 decision of the Supreme Court declaring segregated schools unconstitutional.

Today the situation is very different. In education, many blacks have received college degrees from universities that formerly excluded them. In the workplace, blacks frequently hold professional and managerial jobs in desegregated settings. In politics, most blacks now participate in elections, and blacks have been elected to all but the highest political offices.[33]*

In addition, there have been some sweeping changes in white American attitudes about race—in part because of the leadership of Harry Truman (who integrated the armed forces), Dwight Eisenhower, Earl Warren, John F. Kennedy, Martin Luther King, Jr., Lyndon Johnson, and the courts; in part because of the efforts of religious, academic, business, labor, and entertainment leaders throughout the society; in part because of the dramatically changed image of blacks on television and in the movies in recent decades; in part because of the black revolution in sports; and indeed as a consequence of desegregation, busing, and affirmative action programs (all of which have also had their costs).

In 1958, 55 percent of white Americans said they would not move if a black family moved in next door; in 1978, the figure had increased to 85 percent.[34] In 1958, 72 percent of Southern parents and 13 percent of Northern parents objected to desegregated schools; in 1980, 5 percent of parents in both South and North objected.[35] In 1958, 4 percent of whites approved of black-white intermarriage; in 1978, 32 percent did.[36] Shelby Steele, a black professor at San Jose State University who has written extensively about race relations from an integrationist point of view—and who is vilified by some black leaders—recently observed, "As a black person you always hear about racists but never meet any."[37]

Black access to political power has increased dramatically. In 1940, 35 percent of voting-age blacks registered; in 1984, 55 percent did. In 1940, 3.1 percent of Southern blacks registered; in 1988, 63.7 percent did. Black political participation and liberalized white atti-

*The book was published before Douglas Wilder was elected as governor of Virginia.

tudes about race have resulted in striking increases in holding of public office by blacks. In 1941, there was 1 black representative in the Congress; in 1988, there were 23. In 1941, there were 33 elected black officials throughout the country; in 1985, there were 6,016. In 1990, a black was inaugurated as the governor of Virginia, a state with an overwhelmingly white electorate, and a black was inaugurated as the mayor of New York City. In 1941, there were 10 black judges; in 1986, there were 841.[38]

Blacks have experienced dramatic improvement in education over the past fifty years, and the gap between black and white educational levels has shrunk impressively. In 1940, the median years of education for black males was 6.5, compared with 10.5 for white males. In 1980, the numbers were 12.5 for black males, 12.8 for white males. Comparable numbers for black females were 7.5 in 1940 and 12.5 in 1980; for white females, 10.9 in 1940 and 12.7 in 1980.[39]

In 1968, 27 percent of blacks dropped out before completing high school; the white rate was 15 percent. In 1989, the black dropout rate was 13.8 percent; the white rate, 12.4 percent. In 1989, proportionally more white males dropped out of school than black females.[40] In recent decades, more than a quarter of American postsecondary-age blacks have attended a college or university—a higher percentage than the national averages of Switzerland and the United Kingdom.[41]

Access to white-collar jobs has also increased significantly in recent decades, although it remains substantially below white levels. In 1939, 5.2 percent of black males and 6.4 percent of black females worked in white-collar jobs; in 1984, the figures had increased to 27.4 percent and 52.2 percent, respectively.[42]

Although the poverty end of the spectrum, which until recent decades dominated the black condition in America, has persisted in the ghetto, the overall economic condition of blacks has improved impressively. In 1940, the average salaries of black men were 41.5 percent of those of white men. In 1960, the figure had increased to 55.3 percent; by 1980, to 68.9 percent.[43] Since 1980, and probably starting a few years before that, however, the trend toward closing the gap has stagnated, with data heavily influenced by the deepening crisis in the ghettos. For example, while the median income for black families in 1986 was 57 percent of the white median, for black married couples it was 80 percent. Average wages have increased more rapidly for blacks than whites, but black unemployment has increased precipitously, principally a ghetto phenomenon.[44] To be sure, the stagnation also in part reflects the policies of the Reagan administration, during which inequality increased in the society as a whole.

Table 7.1 is eloquent testimony to the early impact of the preferential hiring of blacks under affirmative action. The economist Richard Freeman describes the implications of these and other related data as *"a dramatic collapse in traditional discriminatory patterns in the market for highly qualified black Americans"* (his italics).[45] (The rapid black increase was presumably the result of the high demand for the small number of black college graduates in the early days of affirmative action. Since 1973, the income of black college graduates has slipped below that of white college graduates.)[46]

As I noted in chapter 1, the racial transformation of American society recently prompted a prominent Brazilian black to point to the United States as a model for Brazil, which has long prided itself on the harmony of its race relations. If you have trouble accepting that a sweeping transformation of race relations has occurred in the United States during the last thirty years, read E. Franklin Frazier's *Black Bourgeoisie,* published in 1957, at the time a popular indictment of the black middle class and white America. Frazier summarizes the condition of the small minority of blacks in the middle class: "As the result of the break with its cultural past, the black bourgeoisie is without cultural roots in either the Negro world with which it refuses to identify, or the white world which refuses to permit the black bourgeoisie to share its life. . . . [These Negroes] live in a world of make-believe in which Negroes can realize their desires for recognition and status in a white world that regards them with contempt and amusement."[47] While it may have been substantially accurate in the 1950s, today *Black Bourgeoisie* is as archaic as "Amos 'n' Andy" and Rochester in "The Jack Benny Show."

TABLE 7.1

MEAN INCOME IN 1973 DOLLARS FOR COLLEGE
GRADUATES AGED 25–29

	1959	1969	1973
Black college graduates	$6,419	$ 9,120	$11,168
White college graduates	9,158	11,022	10,242

Source: Richard P. Freeman, *Black Elite* (New York: McGraw-Hill, 1976), p. 34.

THE GHETTO TRAGEDY

The racial revolution has transformed the lives and prospects of two-thirds of America's blacks, but it has not significantly affected the lives of the other third, most of whom live in ghettos (see table 7.2). Many of them came North in the vast waves of Southern black migrants of the 1950s, 1960s, and 1970s. They are but a few decades removed from the typically hopeless poverty of sharecropping and tenant farming, or the humiliation and poverty of Jim Crow caste discrimination in towns and cities. They confront the intense stresses of ghetto life that have produced crime and other manifestations of social breakdown in many immigrant groups. They confront those stresses not only with little relevant experience but with the static, dependent, present-oriented culture of slavery perpetuated in Jim Crow.

The indicators of the waste and suffering of human beings in the ghetto are staggering. Unemployment among ghetto youths approximates 50 percent. The principal cause of death of young black males is homicide. The incidence of drug commerce and use in the ghetto appears to be far higher than in the society at large. In 1980, 48 percent of black infants were born to single mothers, compared with 11 percent of white infants. The rate of infants born to single mothers among black women ages fifteen to nineteen was 82 percent.[48] Almost 50 percent of prison inmates are black (blacks account for 11 percent of the population).[49] One in four black males is either in jail, on parole, or on probation.[50]

In *America Now,* the anthropologist Marvin Harris says, "A study of arrests in seventeen large American cities located in every region of the country, conducted under the auspices of the President's

TABLE 7.2

POVERTY STATUS OF AMERICANS IN 1987

Group	Number (in millions)	Percent of Population	Number Below Poverty Line (in millions)	Percent Below Poverty Line
White	203.7	84.6%	21.4	10.5%
Black	29.3	12.2%	9.7	33.1%
Hispanic	19.4	8.1%	5.5	28.2%

Source: U.S. Bureau of the Census, *Poverty in the United States 1987* (Washington, D.C.: Government Printing Office, 1989), table 1, pp. 7–8.

Commission on the Causes of Crime and Prevention of Violence, indicated that the 'race of offenders' was black in 72% of criminal homicides, 74% of aggravated assaults, 81% of unarmed robberies, and a whopping 85% of armed robberies."[51] These figures may exaggerate the extent of black participation in crime because of discriminatory police behavior, but if we could remove that distortion we would still surely be left with a disproportionate black crime rate.

Harris goes on to observe that whereas "we find there are proportionately five times more homicides, ten times more rapes, and eight times more robberies in the United States than in Japan," if one subtracts the crimes perpetrated by blacks and Hispanics from the U.S. total, "America's rates of violent crime are much closer to the rates found in [Japan]" (for example, the homicide rate in the United States would fall from five times to less than twice the Japanese rate).[52]

The Cultural Explanation

The conventional wisdom, typified by *A Common Destiny*, is to blame the persistent ghetto tragedy and racial inequality mostly on racism and discrimination, past and present:

> Foremost among the reasons for the present state of black-white relations are two continuing consequences of the nation's long and recent history of racial inequality. One is the negative attitudes held toward blacks and the other is the actual disadvantaged conditions under which many black Americans live. These two consequences reinforce each other. Thus, a legacy of discrimination and segregation continues to affect black-white relations.[53]

That approximates the explanation of many black leaders, and it reminds us of what Daniel Moynihan has called "a near-obsessive concern to locate the 'blame' for . . . Negro poverty . . . on forces and institutions outside the community concerned."[54] But if the opinion polls are to be believed, racism, and its concomitant, discrimination, have declined sharply in the United States to the point where only a small fraction of whites practices them in ways that impinge on opportunity for blacks. In fact, affirmative action—positive discrimination, if you will—has operated *for* significant numbers of blacks, albeit principally in the middle class. Surely, opportunities for blacks in the era of affirmative action psychology and poverty programs are at least as great as opportunities were for the ethnic groups that lived in ghettos early in this century, for example, the Chinese, the Jews, the Italians.

The black social scientist William Julius Wilson makes an apt observation:

> [I]t is not readily apparent how the deepening economic class divisions between the haves and the have-nots in the black community can be accounted for when [the racism/discrimination] thesis is invoked, especially when it is argued that this same racism is directed with equal force across class boundaries in the black community. Nor is it apparent how racism can result in a more rapid social and economic deterioration in the inner city in the post–civil rights period than in the period that preceded the notable civil rights victories.[55]

An intense debate about the causes of the ghetto tragedy, with strong ideological overtones, has followed in the wake of the 1965 Moynihan report, *The Negro Family: The Case for National Action.*[56] Charles Murray's *Losing Ground* has become the rallying point for what is often referred to as the "conservative" interpretation. Murray adduces extensive data, which have fomented great controversy among social scientists, to make the point that the social breakdown of the ghetto was the consequence of disincentive effects of the expansion of welfare programs, particularly, liberalized Aid for Families with Dependent Children and the introduction of food stamps.[57]

The "liberal" view has continued to emphasize racism and discrimination. But a more pragmatic liberalism has also emerged in the views of William Julius Wilson and others. Wilson suggests several other causes, including the young age profile of ghetto dwellers, the disproportionate impact on blacks of the decline of American industry, the departure from the ghetto of the middle-class blacks who gave the ghetto both structure and stability.

Although I fully acknowledge that some racism and some discrimination still exist, and although I believe there is truth in the views of both Murray and Wilson, another factor may be even more important in explaining the ghetto tragedy: *ghetto blacks still suffer from a world view, and the values and attitudes it propagates, that is significantly influenced by the slavery experience.* Their ancestors were denied access to the cultural mainstream first by slavery, then by Jim Crow. The current generation is barred by the invisible walls of the ghetto. In this respect, the problems of the ghetto are similar to the problems of Haiti, a former slave society that has lived much of its history isolated from the progressive currents that have moved other nations, including some neighboring islands, toward democracy, economic dynamism, and social justice. The problems of the ghetto also evoke, for the same reason of isolation, the acute problems of American Indians who live on reservations. (A few years ago, the actor Kris Kristofferson and an Indian movement leader were interviewed on television at a Black Hills reservation, where they stated that unemployment was 85 percent, life expectancy forty-four years.)[58]

From his studies of poor people, principally in Latin America, Oscar Lewis concluded that people who live in poverty often are embedded in a "culture of poverty." Among the characteristics of that culture, all of which would be inculcated or reinforced by slavery: "The lack of effective participation and integration of the poor in the major institutions of the larger society . . . present-time [orientation] . . . a minimum of organization beyond the level of the nuclear and extended family . . . the absence of childhood as a specially prolonged and protected stage in the life cycle . . . a strong feeling of marginality, of helplessness, of dependence, and of inferiority . . . fatalism and a low level of aspiration."[59] Those characteristics describe the centuries-old condition of the poor majority in Latin America; several of them are also relevant to the higher social strata there.* The difference between Latin America and the United States is that, in the latter, one finds a far more progressive mainstream that embraces the large majority of the population.

"Assimilation" is another way of approaching the question of cultural isolation. Using Milton Gordon's seven measures of assimilation,[60] Calvin Schmid and Charles Nobbe drew the following conclusion in a 1965 study of assimilation by nonwhite groups:

> As far as the cultural and civic dimensions are concerned, Negroes . . . have evidenced a substantial degree of assimilation, but on the remaining five variables they have remained virtually unassimilated. [American] Indians, with an overwhelming proportion segregated on reservations, are even less culturally and "civically" assimilated than Negroes. . . . On the other hand, Chinese and especially Japanese show

*There are close parallels among Lewis's "culture of poverty," Mariano Grondona's typology of development-prone and development-resistant societies, and George Foster's universal peasant culture thesis. See chapter 1.

a higher degree of cultural and civic assimilation than any of the other minority races. Moreover, they have made some headway in the other dimensions of assimilation.[61]

The cultural explanation is largely dismissed in *A Common Destiny*, consistent with the taboo, common in political and academic circles, against anything that sounds like "blaming the victim,"[62] a taboo that surfaced violently in the response to Daniel Moynihan's 1965 study of the breakdown of the black family.* I want to emphasize that a cultural interpretation of conditions in the ghetto is *not* blaming the victim. It is a way of understanding a grave problem that may contribute to the problem's solution. The idea of blame is essentially irrelevant: to the extent that something is to be blamed for the values and attitudes that get in the way of progress for ghetto dwellers, it would have to be slavery and Jim Crow, surely not those who have suffered from those two institutions.

In *A Common Destiny's* chapter on education, we find:

> Another possible reason for black-white achievement differences . . . is a black-white cultural difference in socialization. Studies of transracially adopted children provide empirical support for this hypothesis. [Four studies of] transracially adopted black children . . . found that these black children perform about as well as white children on intelligence tests . . . [and] that scores in measured intelligence were directly related to greater proximity to a white middle-class standard. [One of the social scientists] concluded that variation in the tested intelligence of black children on the basis of rearing in a black middle-class or white middle-class environment *is difficult to explain on any basis other than black-white cultural differences.*[63] [Italics added.]

A few pages later, the authors point to another phenomenon that evokes the "crabs-in-a-barrel" behavior typical of peasant cultures around the world:

---

*A relevant anecdote: In 1989, I was asked to do a paper on Haiti, where I had directed the USAID program from 1977 to 1979, for the congressionally established Commission for the Study of International Migration and Cooperative Economic Development, for which I received a substantial honorarium. The Director of Research appeared quite satisfied with the final product, but subsequently, obviously embarrassed, advised me that the commissioners had decided against publishing the paper "because it might offend the Black Caucus." The paper appears as a chapter in Anthony Maingot, ed., *Small Country Development and International Labor Flows: Experiences in the Caribbean* (Boulder, Colo.: Westview Press, 1991).

Recent ethnographic work . . . suggests that black student peer culture undermines the goal of striving for academic success. Among eleventh graders at a predominantly black high school in Washington, D.C., many behaviors associated with high achievement—speaking standard English, studying long hours, striving to get good grades—were regarded as "acting white." Students known to engage in such behavior were labeled "brainiacs," ridiculed, and ostracized as people who had abandoned the group.[64]

But *A Common Destiny* concludes with the judgment,

> In considering cultural characteristics, it is especially difficult to assess their independent causal significance. In any case the culture-of-poverty thesis by itself is inadequate to account for the most recent changes we are seeking to understand. . . . if cultural differences have diminished over the years when family differences have increased more rapidly, there is at least some doubt that culture of poverty is a sufficient explanation.[65]

I was unable to find any data documenting a narrowing of cultural differences between people in the ghetto and those in the mainstream. I would obviously not be surprised to see a substantial narrowing of value and attitude differences between middle-class blacks and whites. But I would be both surprised and encouraged to note a significant shift toward mainstream values on the part of ghetto dwellers. Nor did I find reference to Thomas Sowell's work on the achievement of West Indian immigrants in *A Common Destiny*.

In dismissing the role of culture, *A Common Destiny* asks a question that I find astonishing: "the conventional notion of culture of poverty implies that given characteristics (values, beliefs, behaviors) are transmitted from one generation to another as self-perpetuating patterns. . . . How frequently does this occur?"[66] My answer, of course, would be, always.

Some may wonder if it is possible that slavery's destructiveness of progressive values and attitudes can still influence the world view of descendants of slaves 125 years—perhaps six generations—after emancipation. If I am right about Latin America's problems, traditional Iberian culture has persisted for *five centuries*, sustained principally by unchanging child-rearing practices, the transference of values and attitudes from parent to child, and the persistence of status quo institutions.

As I said in chapter 6, language is the conduit of culture. Tellingly, there are no adequate synonyms for *compromise* or *dissent* in Spanish.[67] I believe that the persistence of the English dialect of slavery in today's ghetto is further evidence of the persistence of the values and attitudes of slavery in the minds of the people who communicate in that dialect.

Those who blame the agony of the ghetto principally on racism and discrimination perform a double disservice. They send the message to the ghetto inhabitants that they have no control over their destinies, that their salvation depends on the benevolence and charity of whites. "Racism" thus has as paralyzing and destructive effect on the ghetto as "dependency theory"—the view prevailing until recently in academic circles that Latin America's problems are principally attributable to Yankee imperialism—has had on Latin America.

The accusation of racism also increasingly antagonizes whites who have made a sincere effort—often over many decades—not only to live a color-blind life but also to support affirmative action. To those people, "racism" increasingly sounds like, "What have you done for me today?"

Bringing Ghetto Blacks into the Mainstream

If I am right that the black ghetto problem is now principally a cultural one—and I hasten to repeat that I accept that other factors, including discrimination, are also in play—then the solutions must emphasize access and acculturation to the mainstream. The process is obviously complicated, difficult, and time-consuming. But we should take heart from the vast movement from lower to middle class of most blacks in the past several decades, and from the experience of other ethnic groups in the ghetto.

This book is not the place, nor do I have the experience, to provide a detailed analysis of the pros and cons of various strategies and interventions. But permit me a few general observations. My ideas are, in many respects, parallel to those of many civil rights leaders. The main difference is that I want to send this message: "The opportunity is there. If you meet discrimination—and there's a fair chance you won't—you can overcome it. Go for it!" The message that permeates the ghetto is that the opportunity *isn't* there—instead, discrimination is—and that, short of antisocial behavior, ghetto people are impotent.

The kinds of programs that I think stand the best chance—and I appreciate how difficult and costly it can be to make them work—

are those that focus on exposing children to the broader society. My list is far from exhaustive, but includes: Head Start/supervised play/ day-care activities as early as possible; busing to schools where the student body composition includes significant numbers from the cultural mainstream—white and black—along the lines of magnet school programs; summer work and summer camp programs, perhaps combining the two; the use of university students as tutors of ghetto children;[68] courses that better prepare high school youngsters for effective child rearing.

Dr. James Comer, a professor of child psychiatry at Yale, who is black, has developed an approach, consistent with a cultural interpretation of the ghetto problem, that promotes a shared belief in the value of education among teachers, parents, and pupils in inner-city settings. "The program is based on the belief that like all youth, children from poor families must learn proper values and behavior to be psychologically ready for schooling and must want to do well in school."[69] The Comer approach is now being replicated with the support of the Rockefeller Foundation.

I also think that the acculturation process can be facilitated by more involvement by blacks who are in the mainstream culture with those who aren't. Their upward mobility is compelling evidence to ghetto blacks that the opportunity exists. The black middle class is also eloquent testimony to the capacity of human beings to modify values and attitudes.

A TIME LIMIT ON AFFIRMATIVE ACTION

Its costs and inequities notwithstanding, I continue to believe in affirmative action, defined as preferential treatment in the education system and the workplace. I think it has filled a political and psychological need in our society: as a catharsis for white guilt about slavery, segregation, and acts of racism; and as a concrete demonstration to blacks that whites are genuinely committed to the achievement of racial equality.

A recent Roper poll showed that half of all blacks judge conditions for black people to be good or excellent, up from 39 percent in 1978. In a situation in which an equally qualified black and white applied for the same job, 40 percent of blacks today believe that both candidates would have an equal chance, up from 20 percent in 1978.[70]

I believe that affirmative action—as much the psychology as the specific programs—has been an important contributor to this change in attitudes.

But affirmative action has limited popular support (29 percent of all respondents in a 1987 Gallup poll approved of it; 67 percent of whites, 34 percent of blacks, and 47 percent of Hispanics disapproved of it).[71] And it has its costs, as Thomas Sowell has pointed out in a compelling article entitled "Affirmative Action: A Worldwide Disaster."[72] Among other considerations, he points to data that demonstrate that the already advantaged members of beneficiary groups are those who benefit most, and that group polarization tends to increase in the wake of affirmative action programs. He also points out that such programs, even when presented as "temporary," often turn out to be permanent. Beyond the issues that Sowell stresses, it is also true that some black beneficiaries are unable to manage their responsibilities successfully and can give affirmative action a bad name (often unfairly, I might add: when a black fails, the policy gets blamed; when a white fails, the person gets blamed). Other blacks who may or may not be beneficiaries are uncomfortable either because they are insecure about whether they really merited the opportunity or because they fear that others will view them as less qualified and the objects of favoritism.

The reverse side of affirmative action is, of course, discrimination *against* whites, and no euphemism can change that. That kind of discrimination builds up resentments over time—witness the impact of the "quota" issue on Jesse Helms's reelection in 1990—and black leaders have to weigh that resentment in pondering the future of affirmative action. A policy for the long run that depends for its success on whites behaving out of altruism or guilt, or both, is not going to work.

We also have to consider the fact that affirmative action operates against the principal of merit: the society suffers when the best-qualified people do not get the jobs. In this regard, affirmative action can have effects similar to the spoils system, which has often brought unqualified party faithful (and particularly fund raisers and contributors) into high-level government posts.

Affirmative action has reached beyond the school and the workplace into the electoral district. Voting rights legislation and Supreme Court opinion starting with the landmark Voting Rights Act of 1965 have made a major contribution to the sharp rise in black voter participation. But they have also contributed to the evolution of affirmative action from equal opportunity to equal results, above all with respect to federal oversight of redistricting (see page 217), but also, as noted in chapter 6, in the requirement for bilingual election materials where there are significant numbers of Hispanics. The net effect is the strengthening of divisions within our society.

For these reasons, I think that there should be a time limit on affirmative action, ending, say, in the year 2000. If whites see it as a permanent policy, hostility to it will build and the troubling trend toward the resegregation of America will be reinforced.

A number of prominent blacks, Thomas Sowell and Glenn Loury among them, want to modify or terminate affirmative action. In *Reflections of an Affirmative Action Baby,* Stephen L. Carter, a professor at the Yale Law School and the son of a Cornell professor, expresses respect and gratitude for what affirmative action has done for him—he believes it has leveled his playing field. But he also believes, as Sowell does, that affirmative action has not reached those blacks most in need, and that its costs may now exceed its benefits. He calls for its reorientation to the educational needs of blacks in the underclass and stresses that thereafter "the beneficiaries must be held to the same standards as anyone else."[73]

AFROCENTRISM AND
THE RESEGREGATION OF AMERICA

Like many others, white and black, I am profoundly troubled by the current state of race relations and the disunity in our society. Despite the vast improvement in the condition of most blacks, we seem to be losing Martin Luther King's vision of an integrated society in which race and ethnicity are alloyed with the national essence in the melting pot. Perhaps the centrifugal forces that appear to be driving us apart—the process is often called the Balkanization of America—are more apparent than real, the work of unrepresentative leaders and sensationalist media. After all, about half of America's blacks feel good about their circumstances, about half of Hispanic-Americans oppose affirmative action, and intermarriage is on the rise. (The Census Bureau reported 310,000 interracial—mostly black-white—marriages in 1970 and 1,000,000 in 1990.)[74]

But what we see in the universities and the political system, to say nothing of media coverage of bloody racial incidents, is far from reassuring. Racial and ethnic identity, to the extreme of effective segregation in "houses" and fraternities, is the dominant social feature of many universities. Blacks and Hispanics are not the only activists: other ethnic groups, including Asians and Jews, as well as feminists and homosexuals, also behave clannishly in an environment one professor has described as "the cultural diversity of Beirut."[75]

The disintegration process is, I believe, driven by what Michael Meyers, executive director of the New York Civil Rights Coalition, describes as "ethnic chauvinism . . . this means black nationalism in particular, and its polarizing racial rhetoric. This is the latest campus rage, reinforced, supported, and facilitated by administrators and philanthropists who are confused by the demands of the separatists."[76] Meyers is, by the way, black.

Proponents of multicultural curricula disparage the Western cultural tradition that is the wellspring of the American (and European, Canadian, and Australian) value system, insisting on at least equal emphasis on African, Asian, American Indian, and other non-Western traditions. The multiculturalist movement finds sustenance in cultural relativism, the view propagated by many anthropologists that all cultures are of equal value. It will not come as a surprise to readers of this book and my previous book that I consider cultural relativism patently wrong. I think it is obvious that some cultures do a better job than others of nurturing life, liberty, and the pursuit of happiness, and I think that the maverick anthropologist Arthur Hippler was right when he said, "I propose a basic criterion for looking at culture as a human tool: Cultures are better or worse depending on the degree to which they support innate human capacities as they emerge."[77] We are reminded of Max Lerner's words: "the final test of a culture lies in the quality of the setting it provides for the individual personality to form itself."[78]

I certainly believe that other cultures should—indeed, must—be studied. For example, we have a lot to learn, or at least to be reminded of, from Confucius. But the study of other cultures should be subordinated to the study of Western civilization, the wellspring of our value system. This is particularly true with respect to the current Afrocentrism vogue, which argues that African culture powerfully influenced Western culture through Egypt. The theory hinges on the skin color of ancient Egyptians, which to me is irrelevant. One must look at African history and the reality of Africa today to assess the value and significance of African culture. Arthur Schlesinger, Jr., is far closer to reality than are the Afrocentrists:

> Afrocentrists teach children about the glorious West African emperors, the vast lands they ruled, the civilization they achieved; not, however, about the tyrannous authority they exercised, the ferocity of their wars, the tribal massacres, the squalid lot of the common people, the captives sold into slavery, the complicity with the African slave trade, the persistence of slavery in Africa after it was abolished in the West.
>
> . . .
>
> The West needs no lectures on the superior virtue of those "sun people" . . . who still keep women in subjection and cut off their clitorises, who carry out racial persecutions not only against Indians and other Asians but against fellow Africans from the wrong tribes, who show themselves either incapable of operating a democracy or ideologically hostile to the democratic idea, and who in their tyrannies and massacres, their Idi Amins and Boukassas, have stamped with utmost brutality on human rights.[79]

The Afrocentrists will, I'm sure, respond that many of Africa's problems today are the consequence of European imperialism. I think that the renowned economist W. Arthur Lewis, a black West Indian, was far closer to the truth about colonialism in Africa, particularly the former British colonies, when he wrote, "The best empires have added greatly to human happiness; they have established peace over wide areas, have built roads, have improved public health, have stimulated trade, have brought improved systems of law, have introduced new technical knowledge, and so on."[80] Those who blame colonialism should ponder the histories of Haiti, independent since 1804, and Liberia, never a colony.

The reality of Africa today—mostly authoritarian and often abusive governments, average per capita income well below $1,000 per year, adult illiteracy well above 50 percent, life expectancy about fifty years, rampant malnutrition, infant mortality above 150 per thousand births, and staggering incidence of AIDS—should be a compelling reminder of one of history's great ironies: the descendants of the Africans brought to this country in slavery live better, and with greater political, economic, and social opportunity, than do blacks in any other country in the world that has a substantial black population.* The *Washington Post* columnist William Raspberry, a black, has summed up the reality succinctly: "The need is not to reach back for some culture we never knew but to lay full claim to the culture in which we exist."[81]

Afrocentrism rejects Martin Luther King's vision of an integrated American society and encourages the resegregation of blacks. It is not only the more radical black leaders who think black when the word *community* is mentioned. I was disheartened to find a similarly narrow vision in Professor Carter's *Reflections of an Affirmative Action Baby*. He evinces little concern for the broader, national community: when he speaks of "the continuing collapse of solidarity in our community," he is troubled not by the Balkanization of America but by disunity in the black community.[82]

As noted earlier, affirmative action's evolution from equal opportunity to equal results has had disconcertingly divisive political consequences. In *Whose Votes Count? Affirmative Action and Minority Voting Rights,* Abigail Thernstrom traces this evolution, which has brought us to the point where voting districts are being gerrymandered to assure that minorities will be represented by minority candidates, not only foreclosing the possibility of representation by non-minority candidates but also strongly implying that minority candidates cannot adequately represent the majority. One consequence of this packing of racial/ethnic districts is the enhancement of electoral prospects for Republican candidates. As she puts it, "As blacks are drained from white districts, the latter become fertile ground for conservative candidates."[83]

But the most disconcerting aspect of the emphasis on equal results is acceptance of the idea of proportional representation—minority office holding in proportion to minority population. As Linda Chavez says of Hispanics:

> If [they] are entitled to Hispanic elected officials in areas where their proportion of the population is high, what about areas where it is low? The natural corollary to the notion that Hispanics can best represent the interests of Hispanics is that non-Hispanics can best represent the interests of non-Hispanics. This is a dangerous game for any minority to play. . . . Strict proportional representation would bar the election of Hispanic

*Blacks may live better in France and Canada, but their numbers are relatively small. Barbados could conceivably be another exception, but many more Barbadians have migrated to the United States than have Americans to Barbados.

governors, senators, presidents in return for the guarantee of some city council members, supervisors, school board members, and assorted other local officials.[84]

Proportional representation reinforces the salad-bowl view of America. "Categorizing individuals for political purposes along lines of race and sanctioning group membership as a qualification for office may inhibit political integration," Thernstrom observes.[85] She goes on to cite the views of Henry Abraham, a professor of government at the University of Virginia: "a society deeply divided by lines of race, ethnicity, or religion must be organized as a federation of groups. Separate groups are the equivalent of separate nations. But a society in which the horizons of trust extend beyond the ethnic or racial group can become a society of citizens."[86]

The divisive pressures are but one of many forces contributing to the decline of America, a decline that I believe has been precipitated chiefly by the same erosion of American values that has aggravated the distress of the ghetto.

PART III

THE EROSION OF
AMERICAN CULTURE

8

The Fault, Dear Brutus, Is Not in Japan . . .

We don't save, invest, and produce; we spend, borrow, and consume.
—*The New Republic* (9 and 16 July 1990)

This chapter is the personal statement of an American, a lifelong Democrat, who has lived much of his adult life in Latin America, in the process developing a heightened appreciation of and respect for the great virtues of Western values and institutions in general and those of the United States in particular. In that appreciation, my experience is shared, I think, by most Westerners who live in the Third World.

But the experience also furnishes distance from which to view what has been happening in America, and to perceive patterns of individual and societal behavior that evoke the distress of the Third World. I believe that the erosion of traditional American values lies behind our national decline in recent decades. I also believe that America can learn, or be reminded of, much from the success stories in this book.

The chapters on the nations influenced by Confucianism—Taiwan, Korea, and Japan—underscore the intimate link between values and progress, particularly with respect to economic dynamism and international competitiveness. The work/education/merit/frugality emphases of the Confucian/Taoist ethos provide the chief explanation for the extraordinary economic performance of these three countries, as well as for the comparably impressive achievements of Hong Kong, Singapore, the overseas Chinese, the Japanese in Brazil, and the Chinese, the Japanese, and the Koreans in the United States.

Those cultural emphases are similar to the features of ascetic Calvinism that brought Max Weber to conclude that Protestant precepts were the principal engine behind the Industrial Revolution and the prosperity of Western Europe, Canada, Australia, and the United States. Those emphases, also substantially shared by Judaism, are central to the traditional value system. Our loss of economic dynamism, of international competitiveness, strongly implies erosion of those central values.

Future orientation, which encourages saving and planning, is also emphasized in Confucianism, Protestantism, and Judaism, although with different motivations. The East Asian sees the continuum of family—ancestors through descendants—as an extension of the person for whom the person bears a responsibility. "Calling" and "election" force the eyes of the Calvinist toward the future. "Judaism clings to the idea of Progress. The Golden Age of Humanity is not in the past, but in the future."[1]

Future orientation implies a slow, steady approach to economic growth that emphasizes research, saving, and investment, not quick profits. Our low levels of saving and investment; the fact that Japan invests more in research than we do, notwithstanding the fact that the American economy is almost twice as large; the savings and loan debacle; and the scandals on Wall Street all imply that the American time horizon in the "now" generation has receded toward the present.

Several chapters in this book underscore the costs of isolation for progress: Spain's obdurate rejection of the Enlightenment and the Industrial Revolution well into the twentieth century; China's complacency in its Middle Kingdom self-image as evidence mounted that Western culture and technology had overtaken its early lead, in sharp contrast to Japan's dynamic response; the perpetuation of autocracy, exploitation, and poverty in Haiti, a country whose values were molded by the slavery experience and whose isolation was imposed both by itself and by its neighbors.

We have seen how isolation explains the persistence of the culture of slavery in the United States after emancipation through Jim Crow segregation into the contemporary ghetto. I have expressed concern that Hispanic culture, such an important source of Latin America's problems, may be persisting in the United States because of the vastness of the immigrant flow and the isolation of Hispanic communities from the American cultural mainstream. Conversely, we have seen what can happen when heretofore isolated countries or groups open themselves up—or are permitted access—to more progressive cultural currents: Japan after the appearance of Commodore Perry's fleet in 1853; Spain, with its economy forced to the wall in the late 1950s; the majority of American blacks in the wake of court rulings and legislation designed to assure racial equality, actions that reflect liberalizing white attitudes on race.

We have also seen how powerful the impact of immigrants can be on a country's prosperity for good and for bad. The resilience and tolerance of Portuguese culture may help explain the profound influence on Brazil's economic performance—and its national values—of European and Japanese entrepreneurs. The traditional rigidity and intolerance of Spanish culture may help explain why the proportionally larger European immigration into Argentina was forced into the Argentine mold at considerable cost to the Argentine economy and polity.

The Chinese, the Japanese, and the Koreans who have migrated to the United States have injected a dose of the work ethic, excellence, and merit at a time when those values appear particularly beleaguered in the broader society. In contrast, the Mexicans who migrate to the United States bring with them a regressive culture that is disconcertingly persistent. The skill level of immigrants to the United States in recent decades has deteriorated, due in large part to the emphasis of immigration policy on family relationships. The consequence has been a proliferation of low-paying, low-productivity jobs that have contributed both to stagnation in real wages and to the decreasing competitiveness of many American products.

The United States can take considerable satisfaction from its role in several of the success stories in this book. In what may have been the most generous and enlightened treatment of the vanquished by the victor in the history of the world, the United States gave Japan its democratic institutions (their taking root has been facilitated by some pluralist features of Japanese culture, such as group emphasis and the reforms of the Meiji Restoration), a sweeping land reform, aid, and military cover. U.S. advice and pressure were instrumental in the decisions of the Spanish, Taiwanese, and Korean governments to pursue the open economic policies that have served them so well—and that have often been designed and executed by U.S.-trained professionals. The United States also played a constructive behind-the-scenes role in Spain's rapid democratization after Franco's death. U.S. aid kept the Taiwanese and Korean economies afloat during the 1950s, and while the aid had some adverse effects, on balance it was helpful.

But while these countries have moved ahead impressively to strengthen their economies, improve the standard of living of their people, and enhance social equity, the United States has shown unmistakable signs of decline. Behind that decline lies the erosion of the traditional American value system.

THE EVOLUTION OF AMERICAN CULTURE

Historically, America's success is, I believe, based on eight fundamental values: freedom, justice, work, education, excellence, frugality linked to future orientation, family, and community. The seeds of those values were planted during the Colonial period and flowered in the Revolution, independence, and the Constitution. Freedom and justice have flourished and in several respects—for example, the condition of women and blacks, individual liberties—are more robust today than they were two hundred years ago. Work, education, excellence, frugality, family, and community have shown increasing signs of erosion since the 1960s.

The British, with permanent settlements in Virginia (1607) and Massachusetts (1620), were the principal source of an early American culture that was bifurcated: a Southern branch drawn mainly by the opportunities presented for plantation agriculture, above all tobacco, and gracious living; a northern branch motivated by a need for religious expression outside the orthodoxy of the Church of England—and for a more egalitarian society.

Writing in 1835, Alexis de Tocqueville foreshadowed Weber when he observed of the New England settlers:

> One would think that men who had sacrificed their friends, their family, and their native land to a religious conviction would be wholly absorbed in the pursuit of the treasure which they had purchased at so high a price. And yet we find them seeking with nearly equal zeal for material wealth and moral good—for well-being and freedom on earth, and salvation in heaven.[2]

The English in the North were soon followed by the Dutch, Swedes, French, Germans, Scots, Irish Protestants, and even a sprinkling of Sephardic Jews and free blacks. The melting pot, the desirability and effectiveness of which is so hotly debated today, began its work in the seventeenth century. The dominant culture was strongly influenced by Calvinist precepts: self-reliance, enterprise, hard work, austerity, and obligation to community, values that were all reinforced by the rigors of the New England climate and its rocky soil. Those values, along with justice and fair play, that we today associate with the white Anglo-Saxon Protestant tradition, would serve as a launching platform both for democratic political institutions, beginning with the Mayflower Compact, and the economic dynamism of the Industrial Revolution in the American North.

In stark contrast with the Spanish and Portuguese landed aristocracies, the American South produced several leaders who rejected the aristocratic status quo and played a crucial role in the democratic experiment. The three superstars of the first years of independence were all Virginians: George Washington, Thomas Jefferson, and James Madison. Patrick Henry was also a Virginian. (All four men, by the way, publicly advocated the abolition of slavery at one time or another.)[3] So were Chief Justice John Marshall and James Monroe.

The genius of Virginia was the offspring of the genius of Britain as it moved steadily forward on the frontiers of the Enlightenment, its values, ideas, and innovations reverberating through the Empire and the world. One example was the creation of the House of Burgesses in Virginia in 1619, reflecting evolution of the mother country's parliamentary system. (A House of Burgesses was also established in colonial Barbados in 1639.) British thinkers and statesmen who shared the eighteenth century with the Virginia superstars included John Locke, Isaac Newton, Robert Walpole, William Pitt, David Hume, Adam Smith, David Ricardo, Thomas Robert Malthus, Edmund Burke, Thomas Paine, and Jeremy Bentham.

The mainstream value system survived the Civil War and the economic and social crises that followed as the United States pursued its manifest geographic destiny and simultaneously transformed itself into an industrial power. That value system also substantially survived the impact of tens of millions of immigrants, mostly from Europe, immigrants whose children would, in most cases, be swept into the value mainstream, at the same time imparting to it some of their own culture. By World War I, the United States had become one of the great powers. At the end of World War II, it was *the* great power.

The Symptoms of Decline

Americans came out of World War II supremely confident about themselves and their country, clearly the most powerful country in the world. Let's look at the condition of the United States then in terms of the four basic cultural factors that, in my view, drive progress.

Radius of trust, identification, sense of community. The war engendered a high degree of national unity and sense of national purpose. It had been fought by the products of the melting pot, for whom the country came first, ethnic origin second. Only the blacks—and, temporarily, the Japanese—were not embraced by that sense of *unum.* Trust in national leadership was exemplified by the reelection of Franklin Roosevelt to a fourth term.

Rigor of the ethical system. For many Americans, the war was a war of principle: the American way of life based on the liberty, justice, and opportunity values of our cultural mainstream pitted against authoritarianism, racism, and power lust. Our sense of ethics, as well as our sense of community, had been fortified by the war.

The exercising of authority. The combination of a highly popular father-image president/commander-in-chief and the successful waging of a war had strengthened the acceptance of authority by the American people. Yet that authority continued to be largely circumscribed by the law and popular mistrust of concentration of power. Roosevelt's effort to pack the Supreme Court had been rebuffed; one of the great heroes of the war and the Japanese occupation, Douglas MacArthur, would be fired for insubordination during the Korean War.

Attitudes about work, innovation, saving, and profit. The work ethic had been reinvigorated by the war, victory in which depended importantly on America's capacity to outproduce Germany and Japan. The war sparked research that would give the United States a technological edge, most notably the Manhattan Project, which produced the atomic bomb. With so many resources channeled to the war effort, saving became a national imperative, and even children participated in the savings campaign by buying savings stamps and bonds. Profit was, temporarily, looked at askance, but the idea of economic opportunity and an ever-better life was deeply etched on the American psyche.

In stark contrast with the late 1940s, the United States today is a nation uncertain, even anxious, about itself. Many of us believe that a serious erosion of our national confidence, unity, and purpose has occurred during the past few decades. The drug and crime epidemics, the street people, the budget deficit, the penury of state and local government, the trade deficit, the decline in the quality of some American products, the savings and loan disaster, Japan's phenomenal success, our plummet from the world's largest creditor to the world's largest debtor, the sleaze on Wall Street and in Washington—these are just some of the indicators of and contributors to the national malaise.

Traumatic events, particularly the Vietnam War and Watergate, have played an important role. But at the root of that erosion of confidence, unity, and purpose is, I believe, the erosion of six of the traditional values that had brought us so much progress and success: the belief that work is a core element of a good life; the belief that education is crucial to progress; a commitment to creativity, achievement, and excellence; the belief that ostentation is wrong; and a strong sense of family and community. The erosion of these values has expressed itself above all in disappointing economic performance. Four examples:

- According to World Bank statistics, of twenty-four "high-income economies" (mostly, the advanced democratic capitalist countries), the United States ranked twenty-second (at 1.5 percent) in annual per capita GNP growth during the twenty-two years from 1965 to 1987. Japan was the leader, at 4.2 percent. France, Italy, and Canada achieved a 2.7 percent growth rate, West Germany 2.5 percent, the United Kingdom 1.6 percent.[4]
- During the period 1980–87, the United States and two Mideast oil exporters were the only ones of the twenty-four high-income nations to experience negative growth in exports. During the same period, U.S. imports grew faster than any other country's on the list.
- In 1987, savings represented 13 percent of the U.S. gross domestic product, the lowest of the twenty-four high-income nations except for Israel. In the same year, Japan's savings rate was 34 percent, West Germany's, 25 percent.
- Over the last forty years, U.S. consumption has increased from 58.5 percent of GNP to 64.6 percent. Over the same period,

business investment in plant and equipment has decreased by about 20 percent, and government investment has dropped sharply.[5]

We should also note that, in the face of severe balance-of-trade and fiscal deficits, we have been unable to exercise the discipline necessary to increase substantially the tax on gasoline, which could significantly reduce both deficits—and pollution. Americans today pay about half what it costs Europeans and Japanese to buy gasoline.

But the deterioration is also apparent in a qualitative sense. Four more examples:

- Years of consumer complaints and Detroit's assertions of improved quality notwithstanding, *Consumer Reports* rated most 1988 American cars "below average" in reliability, most Japanese cars "above average," which, of course, helps to explain why Japanese cars continue to sell so well in the United States, even in the face of the devaluation of the dollar. A 1990 Power and Associates poll of 100,000 American car owners found that, of the twelve cars with which customers were most satisfied, six were Japanese, four were German, and two (Cadillac and Buick) were American.[6]
- Americans who are frequent international flyers avoid U.S. airlines because service and food are often so much better on foreign lines. The contrast is embarrassing to American travelers who care about the kind of image their country projects to the world.
- Michael Porter notes that "American consumers are no longer the most affluent. They are certainly not the most demanding. They tolerate products and services that no Japanese or German would."[7]
- The United States, which pioneered television and computer technology, has been overtaken by the Japanese in many of the same technologies it invented.

To be sure, value erosion can't be blamed for all our problems and shortcomings. Flawed policies have made their contribution: for example, the supply-side economic policies of the Reagan administration—George Bush referred to them in the 1980 primaries as "voodoo economics"—helped fuel the unprecedented budget and trade deficits; the Reagan social policies increased the gap between rich and poor and further polarized politics; and the Bush "read my lips" tax policy helped to empty our coffers at a time of enormous opportunity—and need—for leadership in the world, a time also of acute needs at home. External events, such as the energy crisis, have adversely affected our economic performance (although, in the case of energy, surely no more than Japan's). And it is true that we have shouldered a disproportionate share of the West's defense burden, although that burden should now decline.

But the malaise goes much deeper than policies, events, crises. Our national morale, our sense of confidence and purpose, have been affected. We must wonder whether we are not following ancient Greece and Rome, sixteenth-century Spain, and modern Britain into decline. And we must increasingly look to our past—admittedly through the haze of romance and nostalgia—to find America at its best. We sense that traditional American values have suffered.[8]

The Costs of Success and Affluence

I believe that the wounds to the American work ethic and the values of education, excellence, and frugality associated with it, have been inflicted principally by affluence. For most of our history, there were few governmental safety nets, and work was a necessity for satisfying basic needs, not to mention upward mobility. Most Americans did not articulate to themselves such ideas as:

- Work is indispensable to the building of self-respect.
- Work well done is one of the most enduring sources of human satisfaction.
- Work teaches self-discipline.
- Work provides a structure for daily life.
- Through work, the individual discharges an obligation to the society.
- Work is the principal engine of progress and upward mobility.
- Human progress is the sum total of everyone's work.

But a combination of increasing real personal income (at least until recent decades) and the welfare programs made possible by affluence has divorced work from the securing of basic needs and made possible the consumption of goods and services that had been accessible only to the upper classes in our earlier history. That is all to the good in terms of the goals of progress, elimination of poverty—

surely a high priority for any decent society—and equity. But the consequences in terms of motivation and performance have been costly.

The turning point was, I believe, World War II. It ended the unemployment that the depression had ushered in. It also left the economies and infrastructure of Europe, the Soviet Union, and Japan devastated, while the United States, blessed by its geography, escaped not only unscathed but with its economy humming, its technologies far ahead. The postwar years found us preeminent, cocky, complacent. As Michael Porter observes, "Industry was an honorable and prestigious calling in postwar America." He goes on to note that in recent decades, "There [has been] a diversion of top talent away from industry."[9]

For prior generations, with the securing of basic needs at stake, work was an end in itself. For the generations that followed the war, work, often made easier by labor-saving devices, has increasingly become a means of acquiring things—cars, houses, boats, clothes, leisure time. Our principal satisfactions now seem to come from acquisitions or leisure, not from a job well done. Our time horizon has receded from the future toward the present, leaving austerity, saving, and long-term investment a casualty. The focus of life increasingly becomes the fast buck. Quality inevitably suffers.

As in Britain since the late nineteenth century, industry and commerce have lost prestige, and as the economist Joseph Schumpeter predicted, professions that are often hostile to business—for example academe, the media—now attract more top talent.

In *The Protestant Ethic and the Spirit of Capitalism,* Max Weber attributed the Industrial Revolution principally, and I believe correctly, to an ethos that combined hard work with frugality, that is, thrift and austerity. When frugality is removed from the equation, hard work and the related values of education and excellence may be compromised. Disrespect for thrift and austerity, driven by increased focus on the present and reduced focus on the future, has a lot to do with our low national levels of saving and investment, the savings and loan scandals, and the likes of Ivan Boesky.

The Negative Impact of Television

Our post–World War II arrival at the level of affluence that substantially divorced work from survival coincided with the advent of television. Television has become the medium of the acquisitive, now rather than later, ethos. In part a reflection of the postwar value erosion, it has also accelerated the erosion. After the parent-child relationship, it is probably the most influential shaper of values in America, ahead of school and church—and probably, in many cases, even the parent-child relationship.

In a 1987 *Washington Post* article entitled "Our Fragile Tower of Greed and Debt," the television producer Norman Lear bemoaned "our deadly obsession with short-term success. . . . Never before has the business of business been such a cultural preoccupation." He went on to suggest "the possibility that American business is the preeminent force in shaping our culture and its values," and quoted a *Wall Street Journal* overview of the American Corporation: "Gone is talk of balanced, long-term growth; impatient stockholders and well-heeled corporate raiders have seen to that. Now anxious executives, fearing for their jobs or their companies, are focusing their efforts on trimming operations and shuffling assets to improve near-term profits, often at the expense of both balance and growth."[10]

There is no doubt some truth in this view of the contemporary business world, particularly after the eight years of a Reagan "business" government that failed to project the image of either high ethical standards or hard work. But there is also a major flaw in Mr. Lear's argument, one that is representative of an antibusiness bias in the media, academic, and religious communities: the implication that the business world takes frugal, work-ethic-imbued MBAs and brainwashes them with fast-buck values. Most people arrive in their mid-twenties with their value system substantially formed. And today, it is Mr. Lear's television that profoundly shapes those values during the formative years. There can be no question that children today are getting a strong fast-buck message from television and the movies. They are also getting a strong—and distorted—antibusiness message, for example in "Dallas" and "Falcon Crest"; in Oliver Stone's movies *Wall Street* and *JFK*.

While there is thus an element of chutzpah in Mr. Lear's article, I have no reason to question his good intentions and concerns about what is happening to America. At the root of the problem is the fact that television, like other businesses, is driven by profit-and-loss considerations. Audience ratings attract sponsors, and mass audiences crave excitement, vicarious pleasure, and fantasy—thus the disproportionate emphasis on crime, immorality, and fast living in television fare. Pete Hamill made a valid criticism in an article in 1988: "In television shows, virtually nobody is ever shown *working* except cops."[11] To repeat, television both reflects and reinforces the erosion of American culture.

In the introduction, I stated my belief that human creative capacity is the real engine of progress and that the society that is most successful in helping its people—*all* its people—realize their creative potential is the society that will progress the fastest. In economics, another name for that creativity is entrepreneurship. In psychology, *achievement* captures the same idea. *Excellence* is yet another formulation.

I have mentioned the work of the psychologist David McClelland in previous chapters. In *The Achieving Society,* he makes the compelling case that children acquire achievement motivation principally between the ages of five and twelve. (My own experience as child and parent tends to bear him out.)[12] Today, television absorbs inordinate amounts of the time of most children between the ages of five and twelve—and their parents. Few television shows promote the ideas of achievement and excellence. Few television shows stimulate intellectual development. Most do little more than entertain, and that often with a message that stimulates acquisitiveness and cheap thrills. And watching television rarely requires effort, which is why it can be so hypnotic. Thus, during what may be absolutely crucial years in human development, television robs time from opportunities for work, experimentation, and achievement, as well as from the parent-child relationship that nurtures achievement motivation. It also inculcates a present-oriented, rapid-gratification view of the world that undermines the long-term, slow-but-sure, plan-and-save current that has been so important a force for progress in America, Western Europe, and East Asia. Television may well have fathered the now generation and played a key role in our national indisposition to savings. Television is also a major contributor to the decline in educational achievement.

In fairness, there is much that television—particularly public television—offers that is constructive, stimulating, and educational. But the audience for quality television fare is small, mostly highly educated, and mostly upper-middle class.

It is those who live in the ghetto who may suffer the most from television. While the American mainstream has opened up for two-thirds of the black population, ghetto dwellers are still influenced by the culture of slavery, perpetuated by the isolation of Jim Crow. The fast-buck, cheap-thrill, acquisitive message of television combines with slavery's antiwork, antisocial preoccupation with *now*[13] in an explosive mixture that begets illiteracy, illegitimacy, drugs, gangs, crime, and, increasingly, the death of young adults and children.

On the Plus Side

The current panorama is not one of unrelieved gloom. The integration of large numbers of blacks into the cultural mainstream is unleashing the heretofore largely suppressed creativity and productivity of a significant minority in our population. The sex-role revolution, whatever its costs, has similarly liberated the creativity and productivity of a far more numerous segment of our population. Our primary and secondary schools suffer by comparison with European and Japanese standards, but our quality universities continue to be the best in the world. And proportionally more postsecondary-age young people are in schools in the United States than in any other country.

One of the greatest virtues of American culture—and the American system—is an openness that invites criticism, identification and definition of problems, and problem solving. With respect to the relative decline of the United States, this process is well under way and discussed in such books as Ezra Vogel's *Japan as Number One— Lessons for America,* Allan Bloom's *The Closing of the American Mind,* and Paul Kennedy's *The Rise and Fall of the Great Powers.*[14] The anthropologist Marvin Harris points to post–World War II business concentration and bureaucratization as the root cause of the national malaise in *America Now,* and the journalist James Fallows, in *More Like Us,* stresses the need for elimination of the barriers to opportunity and mobility implicit in such institutions as licensing and testing.[15]

I discussed the potentially grave costs of our current immigration policies in chapter 5. But it is also true that the immigration of achievement-prone Asians—Chinese, Japanese, Koreans, Indians, Vietnamese (often of Chinese extraction)—and Cubans has injected a vitality that is felt in the economy, the academic world, and the arts and professions.

But . . . Mistrust, Incivility, Divisions, Litigiousness

The absorption of high-achievement immigrant groups and the racial and gender revolutions notwithstanding, there is evidence of an erosion of trust in the society, and with it the sense of community. In *The Civic Culture*, Gabriel Almond and Sidney Verba found a high level of trust in the United States in the late 1950s: 58 percent said, "Most people can be trusted."[16] The same question was asked in the World Values Survey in 1981: 41 percent felt that most people could be trusted.[17] The American Election Study series found that, in 1958, 71 percent of Americans trusted their government to do the right thing; in 1980, the figure was 25 percent.[18] In 1966, according to other surveys, 48 percent of Americans had confidence in ten basic American institutions (such as the executive branch, Congress, the Supreme Court, the media); in 1987, the figure had dropped to 28 percent.[19]

We still suffer the credibility aftereffects of Vietnam and Watergate and of the "sixties generation" that those two traumas, affluence, and television spawned. High levels of mistrust of government and politicians, but also of business and the professions, are apparent. Divisions within the academic community are often bitter. The incivility of dialogue within the Congress, between Congress and the executive branch, between the media and the politicians, and within the academic world now reaches levels of intensity and even hostility far beyond what I remember before the mid-1960s.

I am particularly troubled by the political polarization and rhetorical stridency of the past few decades. For many Democrats, the label "conservative" evokes words like *selfish, greedy, uncompassionate,* maybe even *fascist* * or *evil.* For many Republicans, as was apparent in the 1988 presidential campaign, the label "liberal" implies Utopianism, financial and policy irresponsibility, guilt complexes, "flakiness," even un-Americanism or treason. In most public policy issues, there are legitimate conservative and liberal positions that demand respect if not agreement. My sense is that the tolerant political middle where that debate can constructively take place has diminished measurably during these decades, with more people moving

---

*I was astonished, in 1981, to hear a Spaniard who teaches at Harvard describe Ronald Reagan as a "fascist" as he introduced a Spanish Socialist to an ample audience in Cambridge. The comment was roundly applauded.

toward the intolerant extremes. The same phenomenon is apparent in our universities.

With the erosion of trust comes a reduced identification among people in the society, a movement toward the irresponsible individualism that has characterized the Iberian countries and their former colonies, as has political polarization. Loss of trust is also reflected in the withdrawing into themselves of racial and ethnic groups in the disconcerting process that has been labeled the Balkanization of America, a process that reminds us of societies—rarely peaceful and progressive—dominated by clans, a process that undermines the melting pot.

One "lesser virtue" manifestation of this loss of sense of community is littering, epidemic in the ghetto but commonplace throughout the rest of the society, even in upper-middle-class suburbs. Littering says, "I really don't care enough about you—or the environment we share—to take this candy wrapper to a trash barrel" (which may require a few extra steps).

Much has been made in the wake of Japan's extraordinary economic achievements about the benefits of Japan's "communitarianism" and the costs of America's "individualism."[20] While I am troubled about the erosion of the sense of community in America, I don't think that the contrast between Japan and the United States is nearly as great as it has been made to appear. The United States clearly emphasizes individualism more, including in child rearing (see chapter 4). But from its beginnings in New England and in the uniting force of *e pluribus unum*, the American sense of community has shaped a deeply rooted tendency of people to organize to solve problems and seize opportunities. Team sports, the Boy Scouts and Girl Scouts, extracurricular school clubs, and church groups are some of the symbols of the emphasis on "communitarianism" in acculturation of American children. Nor is participatory management a Japanese invention. Good managers of any nationality (including those at Boeing and IBM) have long known that lone-wolf decision making is both risky and likely to be based on incomplete comprehension of relevant facts.

Another consequence of the erosion of trust and the sense of community, a consequence aggravated by the fast-buck ethic, is the increasing resort of our society to lawsuits. Fair play, the broader interests of the society, and economic efficiency have suffered in the process. Former governor of Colorado Richard Lamm, an attorney himself, has observed:

The international competitiveness of the United States is affected by its litigiousness—the greatest on earth. Japan trains 1,000 engineers for every 100 lawyers; our nation's rate is the reverse. Two-thirds of all the lawyers in the world practice in the United States. . . . This litigiousness adds to the costs of American goods [and services, e.g. physicians, I might add] as assuredly as does our inefficient management and labor. . . . Litigation also dampens entrepreneurship. It discourages American business from taking risks, retards innovation and imagination. . . . You can't sue a nation to greatness.[21]

The net of the pluses and minuses decisively favors the latter, in my view. That conclusion is underscored by the innumerable indicators of decline.

TOWARD A CULTURAL RENAISSANCE

What can be done to promote a cultural renaissance in the United States? Six of the seven factors[22] that occurred to me in the Latin American context offer a convenient structure for approaching the value impediments to progress in the United States today: presidential leadership, religious reform, educational reform, the media, reform of management practices, and, above all, improved child-rearing practices.

Presidential Leadership

I find it significant—and reassuring—that George Bush and Michael Dukakis were the presidential candidates in 1988. Both project a commitment to traditional American values, particularly the work ethic. But I think that Bush was more successful in communicating that commitment through his emphasis on revived excellence. Dukakis's penchant for austerity may have made him cartoon bait, but it was a very useful reminder of the importance of one strand of the fabric of traditional American values that has been much neglected in recent years. It was almost as if the electorate was saying, after the California glow of the Reagan years, "It's time to get back to the basics." And so we turned to New England—George Bush seems to me much more like Leverett Saltonstall than Lyndon Johnson, much more Kennebunkport than Houston—the wellspring of the Protestant ethic in our nation.

In his first years in office, President Bush has repeatedly stressed the traditional values in his rhetoric, and he has been far more successful in projecting a commitment to the work ethic and austerity than was his predecessor, who lost all remaining credibility (and dignity) in this respect when he accepted $2,000,000 in return for a visit to Japan. But Bush has failed to communicate a comprehensive vision of what is wrong with America and what it must do to get back on track. He does not appear to understand why we "spend, borrow, and consume" rather than "save, invest, and produce." Hamstrung by a less-than-responsible "read-my-lips" tax policy, he acted too slowly and clumsily to manage the budget deficit crisis and the recession that followed. His successful mobilizing of world opinion and force against Saddam Hussein, in particular, and his skillful conduct of foreign policy, in general, notwithstanding, he seems to be buffeted by a complex of domestic issues without perceiving the underlying patterns and causes that connect the issues—and without developing an agenda to do something about them.

The country needs a president who understands both how and why we have gotten into trouble and what needs to be done to start a broad process of revival. That process must start with a call for a renaissance of traditional American values. It must involve both a reinvigorated government and a reinvigorated private sector.

The philosophy of the Reagan administration was clearly "the government that governs least is the government that governs best." It is patent in the early 1990s that solutions to our problems are not going to be found through that philosophy. While the private sector has an important role to play, and while strengthening the private sector must be a high priority of U.S. policy, much of the leadership for a national renaissance must come from the federal government. That is true of the policies necessary to place the economy on a sounder footing, including the tax increases necessary to compensate for the anti–public sector policies and supply-side economics of recent Republican administrations, as well as incentives for saving, research, and economic use of energy; to resolve the inefficiencies and inequities in the health system; to increase the priority and quality of education; to find humane and effective solutions to the problems of the homeless; to integrate the one-third of America's blacks still outside the mainstream; to get immigration under control; to arrest the movement toward *pluribus* and strengthen *unum*.

President Bush's extensive background in public service should have left him substantially free of the contempt for government that characterized the Reagan (and Nixon) years and that is at least in part responsible for the abuses of power and corruption of those years. That contempt had resulted in increased politicization of public service—for example, in the increased proportion of "political" ambassadors, few of whom are qualified for their jobs—and in a general erosion of quality and morale in the federal government. If you don't think government is important, then you don't mind appointing an unqualified campaign contributor to a high-level job. My impression is that in the Bush administration, political credentials continue to be more important than quality credentials in many appointments.

The contempt for government has also communicated itself to the American people, who hold the government worker—and indeed the function of government—in low esteem, as is evident from the popular outcry when congressional, executive-branch, and judicial salaries are proposed for increase at the repeated urgings of blue-ribbon panels. (The outcry is focused on members of Congress; I doubt that many Americans appreciate that the congressional salary level is essentially a ceiling on federal judges and executives.) Americans appear to have no problem with the seven-digit salaries paid to athletes like Joe Montana, Michael Jordan, and Roger Clemens; to movie and television stars like Robert Redford, Oprah Winfrey (her salary is in eight digits), and Dan Rather. But when the president proposes that the top of the federal salary structure be increased from high five digits to low six digits, the popular reaction is outrage. Ralph Nader, a symbol of the public interest and good government, opposes the raise, pointing out, with irrelevant demagoguery, that members of Congress are already making salaries that put them in the top 1 percent of the population. The handsomely remunerated network television anchormen and reporters—in some cases paid ten or more times as much as cabinet members, members of Congress, and judges—appear convinced that they are that much more important and valuable than the pay-raise recipients. Almost without exception, they overlook the cost to our society when good people either avoid or leave public service because the financial rewards outside are so much greater.

For those Americans who are concerned about the prospect of "Japan as number one," it is well to remember the key role played by the Japanese career government service, consistent with the highest prestige that attaches to public service in the Confucian order of things. Ronald Dore notes, "The Japanese value and honour the public service, and an intelligent industrial policy is one consequence of this."[23] Ezra Vogel elaborates:

> The politicians make many important decisions, but compared to the American government the top politicians have little leverage over the bureaucracy. . . . the person who really runs [a ministry] is the administrative vice-minister, the highest career officer. . . .
> Leading bureaucrats have attended the best universities and have risen through the ranks in a carefully prescribed fashion. . . . The top graduates . . . enter the most prestigious ministries (Finance, International Trade and Industry, Foreign Affairs) and agencies (Economic Planning, Land, Environmental). . . . the elite bureaucrats are not only extremely able but are also protected by an aura of respect, rivaled perhaps only by the elite bureaucrats of France. . . . Japanese bureaucrats are constantly amazed at the power the American government grants to cabinet members and department heads who have so little government experience and so little preparation for the position.[24]

We should note that political appointees are found at least one and sometimes two levels (that is, below assistant secretary) deeper in the American bureaucracy than in the Japanese; also, the pay and perquisites of senior Japanese public officials are proportionally greater than those of their American counterparts.

Federal government philosophy and policies are obviously crucial to an American renaissance. But so are restoration of (1) the prestige of government service, and (2) merit as the principal consideration in high-level appointments.

The American business/financial community has a similar problem, partly self-inflicted, to be sure, but also one result of an antibusiness message projected by the media and the academic community, a message roughly comparable to the low esteem in which business activity was held by the Confucian mandarins. We are reminded of Joseph Schumpeter's prediction that democratic capitalism would be so successful that it would subsidize a large intellectual establishment that would inevitably undermine the system because of its hostility to entrepreneurs.[25] We are also reminded of the declining prestige of industry and business in Britain in the second half of the nineteenth and first decades of the twentieth centuries, which has often been cited as the cause of Britain's decline.[26]

That antibusiness message, which has considerable currency among the liberal elite (for example, Norman Lear's *Washington*

Post article referred to earlier in this chapter), is that the really "good," "compassionate," and "thinking" people seek intellectual/ artistic careers, the media, the professions, social work, and perhaps government (although Hollywood treats government officials with about the same contempt that it treats people in business). The "greedy," the "corrupt," the "clods," the "callous," and the "irresponsible" flock to business, according to that view.

There is a double injustice in this kind of arrogance and snobbery. In my experience, people in the "honored" professions can be as mean-spirited, self-seeking, intolerant, discourteous, and even dishonest in their dealings with others as in other, less prestigious professions. But, more important, the success of our private enterprises, particularly our industries, has financed the expansion and flourishing of the arts and the universities, through either tax revenues or philanthropy. As it is easier to appreciate at a time of recession, with cutbacks commonplace in academe, there is a very direct relationship between the well-being of business and industry and the well-being of our universities.

As we increasingly appreciate today, there are limits to what government policy can do to reverse an economic downturn, to reduce a burgeoning fiscal deficit, to arrest intensifying unemployment. In the end, it is the creativity, professionalism, dynamism, and competitiveness of American business that really counts.

In his rhetoric, example, and actions, the president can help to restore the prestige of public service and business. As one small example, the president could personally accord substantially greater public recognition, along the lines of the annual Kennedy Center awards to artists, to achievement in government and business. It might even make good television.

Religious Reform

My sense is that religion has shifted its emphasis from personal morality, character, and the living of a good life to the correction of social and political ills. I recognize that both personal and social/political emphases are present now, as they were fifty years ago. But whereas the former used to be dominant, it seems to me that a shift toward the latter occurred at about the time— after World War II—when affluence disengaged work from the securing of basic needs and when television became the national obsession.

The values of the liberal religions in America today are similar to those of the academic and media communities. The good life is found more in pursuing causes than in building character and seeking truth and achievement. The churches often feel more comfortable promoting redistribution than growth policies, notwithstanding the overwhelming recent evidence—in, for example, Eastern Europe, China, Cuba, and Nicaragua—that poverty is more effectively attacked by growth than by redistribution, particularly in a democratic context, where politics is inevitably influenced by pressures for social justice. In the redistributive moral context, business looks more like the problem than the solution. Yet, like the arts and the universities, religion is heavily dependent on the philanthropy made possible by business success.

The conservative religions, particularly evangelical Protestantism, appear to be so hung up on their causes, above all the fight against abortion and the winning of souls, that personal morality, character, and the living of a good life are relegated to a lower priority, as with the more liberal religions. One consequence is to contribute to the national trend toward polarization and divisiveness. In their quest for rebirths and money, the evangelical, fundamentalist religions have turned to television, with corrupting consequences comparable to the impact of television on the broader society.

I am not arguing that religion should ignore social and political issues, although I must say that, particularly when exaggerated guilt feelings are in play, the causes can get very dubious—such as support of the Marxist Left in Central America and Cuba at a time when hundreds of millions of Eastern Europeans (including Russians) are proclaiming the failure and abusiveness of the same model. What I am advocating is (1) more appreciation by religion of the crucial role a dynamic, expanding economy plays in improving the conditions and prospects of a society, and particularly its poor; and (2) renewed emphasis on morality, decency, achievement, and social responsibility in the individual—more sermons that stress the personal life well and creatively lived as an effective way for the individual to contribute to the well-being of the society and the world.

Norman Lear attributes the erosion of American values principally to the business community. I see the media, particularly television, more at fault. But religion must also share in the blame.

Educational Reform

The qualitative problems of our primary and secondary schools are the subject of continuing intense debate, which is all to the good. My principal concern is not with the techniques of teaching math, English, and the physical and social sciences successfully, although those are surely important issues. My concern is values and motivation: how to develop a stronger national appreciation of the transcendental importance of education to our future, a link underscored by the success of the Confucian societies; and how to inculcate the value of work, achievement, creativity, and community in our youth. I agree entirely with a recent comment by Amitai Etzioni: "The notion that you can pump more math, more languages, more history into children who do not yet have the capacity to control impulse, defer gratification, or finish a task is really quite foolish. The first assignment of the schools should be to supplement the work of the family in character formation."[27]

More rigorous standards, heavier homework loads, smaller classes, longer school years, and increased incentives for and recognition of achievement can help during those crucial years of personal development when the values and attitudes that make for effective and responsible adults are forged. The idea of merit, so central to the achievements of the East Asians, particularly needs to be strengthened in our society. National testing is common to the East Asian countries and many European countries as well. We should adopt it.

I also believe that the teaching profession is both undervalued and underpaid in the United States. Part of the problem is the destructive and largely erroneous idea that teachers are people who teach because they can't do anything else. The quality of American teaching surely will improve with higher salaries—more capable people will be attracted to the profession, and they are more likely to motivate their students. One of the most striking differences between Japan and the United States is the substantially higher prestige that attaches to the teaching profession in Japan, consistent with the Confucian tradition. And when I say "teaching profession," I am talking about primary and secondary teachers as well as university professors.

We focus our concerns about value erosion, particularly in the wake of Professor Bloom's book, at the university level. We must remember that that is where our primary and secondary teachers are prepared and that many of them leave universities imbued with the relativistic approach to values that is the conventional wisdom in a good part of academe. I agree fully with Professor Bloom that relativism—the notions that value judgments have no real basis, that, for example, all societies are equally good, or bad—constitutes a threat to our view of our own society, our aspirations for it, our ability to bring about constructive change, our ability to define and produce excellence, indeed, in the long run, to the survival of our fundamental institutions.

One of the threatened institutions is the university itself. That threat flows principally from the 1960s generation's view of America—and of democratic capitalism: imperialistic, racist, exploitative, greedy, corrupt, and insensitive. The influence of the 1960s activists is still palpable in academe, the collapse of socialism and Eastern Europe's stampede to democratic capitalism notwithstanding. Many of those who threw in their ideological and emotional lot with Ho Chi Minh, Fidel Castro, and Daniel Ortega now promote multiculturalism, resegregation, suppression of Western studies, and intolerance of dissent. They nurture like-thinking students whose activism and efforts at intimidating university faculty and administrators evoke the polarization and politicization of so many pathetic Latin American universities—pathetic because of the waste of young minds through indiscipline, ideological zeal, and disrespect for learning, for seeking truth, for the rights and views of others.

The influence of the Left in universities has fostered the emergence of an activist Right, comparably incivil in its words and actions, comparably disrespectful of dissent. It will take strong leadership committed to academic freedom, civility, excellence, and the idea of community to reverse the academic deterioration. The process will be facilitated by a stronger national consensus on the direction our society should be taking.

The Media

I have stressed throughout this chapter that the media, above all television, are powerful shapers of values and attitudes. I don't want to leave the impression that I think that the transcendental problem of television is repeated elsewhere in the media, other than in the movies. I think that the better American newspapers and newsmagazines do an excellent and balanced job of reporting and analysis, one that ranks their professionalism at the top by world standards. I only wish that more Americans were reading those newspapers and newsmagazines.

But the overriding problem is television (and the movies), and particularly (1) its undermining of the work ethic, creativity, and excellence; and (2) its promotion of quick gratification and acquisitiveness. Television and the movies also reinforce the trend toward mistrust of the society and its institutions—for example, in the films of Oliver Stone, who continues to see his own society and the world much as the radicals saw it in the 1960s. The problem of television is so enormous, and the difficulties of dealing with it so great in our democracy, that my mind boggles when I think about what might be done to channel television's great power toward more constructive ends. Clearly, a national debate is needed on television's impact on society. The process could be started with the naming by the president of a bipartisan, blue-ribbon panel of television executives and artists, educators, social scientists, politicians, and others to study television's impact and recommend ways, including legislation, of making that impact more constructive, more consistent with the needs and goals of the society.[28]

Management Reform

At a time when the value of work, achievement, and quality has eroded, improved ways of motivating people must be a top priority of management. This is the management dimension in which the Japanese appear to have excelled.

Profit sharing and employee stock-ownership plans are increasingly popular ways of strengthening employee identification with the enterprise and of promoting excellence. But beyond these kinds of financial and ownership incentives lie other motivational avenues. Decentralization strategies, which delegate to the employee responsibilities for analysis of problems and opportunities and encourage the employee to participate in problem solving and policy formulation, are likely to result in a more motivated, creative, and efficient work force. Decentralization and broadening of responsibilities also help subordinates to grow professionally, with attendant long-range benefits for the enterprise through expansion and enrichment of the pool of future managers and supervisors. An enterprise that is managed this way is likely to have high morale, with the further efficiency and creativity that flows from it.

Ethics also bear on morale and efficiency. Unethical behavior by management saps the confidence of employees in management, thus undermining morale. It also sends the message that unethical behavior at lower levels in the organization will be tolerated. Honesty and decency trickle down. So do dishonesty and irresponsibility.

Fifty years ago, many workers felt so lucky to have a job, and the work ethic was so much stronger, that boredom was not nearly as much of a problem as it is today. The problem of boredom is magnified by a labor force that brings substantially more education to the workplace: in 1940, the average American adult had about eight years of education; in 1980, more than twelve years. Although we have major concerns about the quality of American education, particularly at the primary and secondary levels, the fact remains that the United States, with 59 percent, is ahead of all other countries in the percentage of its postsecondary-age population that pursues postsecondary studies.[29] (Canada is second with 55 percent, Sweden third with 37 percent. The figure for Japan is 29 percent.) A labor force this highly educated, and with a wide variety of diversions within easy reach, is clearly not going to find stimulation and satisfaction in repetitive, simple tasks. The goal must be, as Michael Porter and Otis Graham have stressed, a labor force constantly moving toward higher value-added activities requiring higher skills—"as well as substantial labor participation in what are too often considered only managerial decisions."[30]

Improved Child Rearing

Parents are potentially the most important agents of constructive cultural change in any society. It is the parents—by their example, by the techniques they choose in child rearing, and by the way they relate to their children—who principally shape what their children become as adults. Japan's success reflects values that promote progress; it also reflects child-rearing techniques that promote achievement and group consciousness.

The significance of the parent-child relationship can be seen most graphically—and tragically—in the ghetto: teenage mothers, often high school dropouts, who are shackled by the antiprogress, antisocial, antiwork cultural chain that runs from slavery through Jim Crow to the ghetto, and also strongly influenced by the rapid gratification values of the broader society. They pass on those values as single parents to their children. Their sons are at high risk for school dropout, drugs, and crime. Their daughters are at high risk to follow in the footsteps of their mothers: school dropout, teenage pregnancy, welfare.

Better child rearing is a key to the broader revival of the values of work, education, and excellence; frugality; and community. Child-rearing techniques tend to persist unmodified, generation after generation: the principal "training" the parent receives for child rearing is his or her own rearing. Child psychology is a mainline scholarly discipline, and while there is still a lot we don't know about what kind of parenting makes for effective, creative, responsible adults, there is a substantial body of knowledge and understanding that is not getting through to many parents. Research on effective child rearing should have a high priority, but so should ways of communicating to prospective parents the lessons the experts have learned, for example, through courses in child rearing for high school students.

A FINAL WORD

Among nations, power and wealth are obviously far more equitably distributed today than they were fifty years ago, and that is to the good. Western Europe's recovery, integration, and current economic and political dynamism are important gains not only for the Europeans but also for us. The same thing is basically true, if less obvious because of competition, of the Japanese miracle. The recent dramatic liberalization in Eastern Europe is likely to have comparably beneficial results for the world community, and perhaps especially for the United States through the reduction of the defense burden it has borne disproportionately.

The goal of repairing the damage to American culture—of an American renaissance—should not be to restore the overwhelming American dominance of the postwar years. That is not in any event feasible, nor is it desirable. The goal is to assure the progressive evolution of human well-being, justice, creativity, and excellence in our own society, both for its own sake and for the contribution it can make to the progressive evolution of humankind. But if we do not understand the causes of our relative decline in recent decades and act on that understanding, the decline will continue. We have recognized the symptoms for some years, but we have not acted. My fear is that we are now so committed to the self-centered, present-oriented aspects of the postindustrial value system that we will *not* act, short of some cataclysmic event such as a prolonged depression.

Henry Rosovsky, then dean of the Harvard College faculty, said in 1980, more than ten years ago:

> It takes a long time to become aware of decline. Most economic historians agree that Britain's climacteric occurred about one hundred years ago, but this fact did not really become a matter of public concern until World War I. . . . In my opinion, the principal factors were internal and human, and therefore avoidable: British entrepreneurship had become flabby; growth industries and new technology were not pursued with sufficient vigor; technical education and science were lagging; the government-business relationship was not one of mutual support. When we look at our own country today in the perspective of history, the danger signals seem obvious.[31]

It is not just the danger signals that are obvious. The lessons of Japan's, Taiwan's, and Korea's success are obvious, too. Britain lost its leadership because it lost its taste for work, saving, creativity, and risk taking. The East Asians are the envy of the rest of the world because they attach high value to precisely these same qualities. The lessons of the costs of divisiveness—of the failure of melting pots— within nations are equally obvious: in the Soviet Union, in Yugoslavia, in Cyprus, in numerous African countries.

Who prospers? Societies committed to the future, to education, to achievement and excellence, to a better life for all, to community, as well as to freedom and justice. The United States was once the leader of such societies. There may still be time to regain that leadership.

Notes

Introduction

1. Quoted in L. Ronald Scheman, ed., *The Alliance for Progress—A Retrospective* (New York, Westport, London: Praeger, 1988), p. 86.

2. Francis Fukuyama, "The End of History?" *The National Interest* 16 (Summer 1989): 3–18.

3. World Bank, *World Development Report 1990* (New York: Oxford University Press, 1990), pp. 178–79.

4. Ibid., pp. 178, 243.

5. In *Wealth of Nations,* Adam Smith says, "The French colony of [Haiti] . . . is now the most important of the sugar colonies of the West Indies, and its produce is said to be greater than that of all the English sugar colonies put together" (New York: Random House, 1937), p. 538.

6. World Bank, *World Development Report 1991,* p. 205.

7. Ronald Inglehart, *Culture Shift in Advanced Industrial Society* (Princeton: Princeton University Press, 1990), table 1-3, p. 60.

8. United Nations, "Development Without Poverty," cited, with map and graph, by the newspaper *Hoy* of Quito, Ecuador, 1 December 1990, p. 1.

9. Hernando De Soto, *El Otro Sendero* (Lima: Editorial El Barranco, 1986).

10. Max Weber, *The Protestant Ethic and the Spirit of Capitalism* (New York: Scribner, 1950), p. 117.

11. Keith S. Rosenn, "The Protection of Judicial Independence in Latin America," Centre for the Independence of Judges and Lawyers, *CIJL Bulletin* (October 1988): 36.

12. This is a point made forcefully about Argentina by Tomás Roberto Fillol in *Social Factors in Economic Development* (Cambridge: MIT Press, 1961).

13. In *The Unheavenly City Revisited* (Boston and Toronto: Little, Brown, 1974), Edward Banfield emphasizes future orientation as a principal motivator of upward mobility in America.

14. David McClelland, *The Achieving Society* (Princeton: D. Van Nostrand, 1961).

15. On child rearing in Latin America, see Malcolm T. Walker, *Politics and the Power Structure: A Rural Community in the Dominican Republic* (New York and London: Teachers College Press, Columbia University, 1972), p. 107; Robert Rotberg, *Haiti: The Politics of Squalor* (Boston: Houghton Mifflin, 1971), pp. 99–101, 122–27; and Fillol, *Social Factors in Economic Development,* passim.

16. Salvador Mendieta, *La Enfermedad de Centro-América,* 3 vols. (1912; reprint 1936, Barcelona: Tipografía Maucci), vol. 3, p. 357.

17. Herbert P. Phillips, *Thai Peasant Personality* (Berkeley and Los Angeles: University of California Press, 1965); quoted by George M. Foster in *Peasant Society: A Reader,* ed. Jack M. Potter, May N. Diaz, and George M. Foster (Boston: Little, Brown, 1967), p. 298.

18. James Fallows makes some relevant observations about cultural obstacles to development—and cooperation—in the Philippines in "A Damaged Culture," *The Atlantic Monthly* (November 1987): 49–58. For example: "Nationalism can of course be divisive when it sets people of one country against another. But its absence can be even worse, if that leaves people in the grip of loyalties that are even narrower and more fragmented. When a country with extreme geographic, tribal, and social-class differences, like the Philippines, has only a weak offsetting sense of national unity, its public life does become the war of every man against every man. . . . people treat each other worse in the Philippines than in any other Asian country I have seen" (pp. 56–57).

19. I believe that Argentine "development" from roughly 1880 to 1930 was more appearance than reality. In terms of proportion between people and natural resources, Argentina may be the most richly endowed country in the world. Like the United States, Canada, and Australia, Argentina had benefited in the second half of the nineteenth century from high levels of British investment and British technology, also from European immigration (see chapter 1 in this volume). But notwithstanding the prominence of a few notable thinkers and statesmen such as Domingo Faustino Sarmiento and Juan Bautista Alberdi, its political system was manipulated by the landed aristocracy until the Radical opposition was permitted to win in 1916. Thus Argentina's precocious economic development was the consequence of its extraordinary resource endowment and foreign presence, and its political development was far closer to the authoritarian Latin American than the Western democratic mainstream. Carlos Escudé's *The Failure of the Argentine Project* tends to bear out this interpretation (*El Fracaso del Proyecto Argentino—Educación e Ideología* [Buenos Aires: Institute Torcuato Di Tella, 1990]).

20. The typology appears in an unpublished manuscript by Mariano Grondona entitled *The Triangle of Development.*

21. Ibid., p. 84.

22. Ibid., p. 82.

23. Potter, Diaz, and Foster, eds., *Peasant Society: A Reader,* p. 304. The elaboration of the thesis in the next paragraphs derives from pp. 305–18.

24. Edward C. Banfield, *The Moral Basis of a Backward Society* (Glencoe, IL: The Free Press, 1958). Chiaromonte looks very different today—see chapter 2.

25. Melville J. Herskovits, *Life in a Haitian Valley* (New York: Knopf, 1937).

26. Henry Wells, *The Modernization of Puerto Rico: A Political Study of Changing Values and Institutions* (Cambridge: Harvard University Press, 1969).

27. David C. Korten, *Planned Change in a Traditional Society: Psychological Problems of Modernization in Ethiopia* (New York, Washington, London: Praeger Publishers, 1972).

28. Quoted in Potter, Diaz, and Foster, eds., *Peasant Society: A Reader*, p. 298.

29. Frank Moya Pons, "Raices del Problema Dominicano" ("Roots of the Dominican Problem"), an address to the monthly luncheon of the American Chamber of Commerce in Santo Domingo, the Dominican Republic, 27 October 1982.

30. In Potter, Diaz, and Foster, eds., *Peasant Society: A Reader*, pp. 10–11.

31. Inglehart, *Culture Shift in Advanced Industrial Society*, p. 14.

Chapter 1

1. The following statistics are drawn from the "World Development Indicators" section of the International Bank for Reconstruction and Development, *World Development Report 1991* (New York: Oxford University Press, 1991).

2. *World Development Report 1980*, table 1, shows Brazil's adult literacy at 76 percent in 1975.

3. The 1990 *World Development Report* shows Brazil falling behind China and Spain.

4. Clodomir Vianna Moog, *Bandeirantes e Pioneiros* (Rio de Janeiro: Editora Civilizacao Brasileira, 1964).

5. Charles Wagley, *An Introduction to Brazil* (New York and London: Columbia University Press, 1963), p. 9.

6. With its economy in the doldrums, Brazil dropped back into the "lower middle" World Bank category in 1988.

7. In an address to the Luso-American Foundation on 16 April 1986, the former U.S. Ambassador to Portugal Richard J. Bloomfield, who had also served in Brazil, said:

> I would say that the values and attitudes that result in development are those that reward people on the basis of merit rather than their status, family, or social class; that encourage the individual to take initiative and to assume responsibility; that encourage trust in the society's institutions; that emphasize rationality rather than ideology in the solving of problems; that promote teamwork and collegiality rather than authoritarian leadership; in short, values and attitudes that are characteristic of modern societies rather than traditional societies. . . . Portuguese society has been much slower than other Western countries in making the transition from traditional values to modern values.

8. Thales de Azevedo, "Catholicism in Brazil," *Thought* (Fordham University Quarterly) 28 (1953): 257, quoted in Wagley, *An Introduction to Brazil*, p. 234.

9. Wagley, in *An Introduction to Brazil*, observes, "The priests were more traditionally motivated than religiously inclined. Some had a female companion and children" (p. 235). Readers of *Underdevelopment Is a State of Mind* may recall the comment of the Nicaraguan historian José Dolores Gámez: "Wanting to break the chains of their priestly vows, especially that of poverty, a large number of priests came to the colonies hoping to enjoy a new existence, carefree and comfortable, and especially to satisfy their earthly ambitions" (pp. 37–38).

10. It was not until 1933 that the first fully integrated Brazilian University was established, in São Paulo. Wagley observes that he has seen a diploma dated 1922

from "the University of Rio de Janeiro," which was, however, "only a loosely organized group of independent faculties at the time" (*An Introduction to Brazil*, p. 207).

11. Wagley, *An Introduction to Brazil*, p. 206.

12. Robert Wesson and David V. Fleischer, *Brazil in Transition* (New York: Praeger Publishers, 1983), p. 10.

13. Wesson and Fleischer, *Brazil in Transition*, p. 42.

14. For parallel analyses of how Brazil got into its debt hole in the 1970s, see Albert Fishlow, "Latin American Adjustments to the Oil Shocks" (chap. 4, pp. 54–84), and Bolivar Lamounier and Alkimar R. Moura, "Economic Policy and Political Opening in Brazil" (chap. 7, pp. 165–96), in *Latin American Political Economy*, ed. Jonathan Hartlyn and Samuel A. Morley (Boulder and London: Westview Press, 1986).

15. In an interview with *Jornal do Brazil* published on 19 November 1988, Erundina identified Nicaragua as her "favorite country." The Workers' party leader and probable presidential candidate Luis Inácio "Lula" da Silva has referred to Nicaragua as "a new model for Latin America" (*Veja* magazine, 23 November 1988, p. 41).

16. A few months after Erundina's victory, Paulo Evaristo Cardinal Arns, the Archbishop of São Paulo, wrote a "dearest Fidel" letter to Fidel Castro in which he expressed the hope that Castro would always govern Cuba. See Alan Riding, "Brazil Cardinal's Praise of Castro Stirs Protest," *New York Times*, 5 February 1989, p. 20.

17. See Riordan Roett, *Brazil: Politics in a Patrimonial Society* (New York: Praeger, 1978).

18. Eliana Cardoso, "Debt Cycles in Brazil and Argentina, in *Debt and Transfiguration*, ed. David Felix (Armonk, NY: M. E. Sharpe, 1990), pp. 111–40. Japan's per capita GDP growth rate during the period was magnified by a substantially lower population growth rate than Brazil's.

19. World Bank, *World Development Report 1988* (New York: Oxford University Press, 1988), table 2, p. 225.

20. Wesson and Fleischer, *Brazil in Transition*, p. 13.

21. For a description and analysis of Brazil's early industrialization, see Werner Baer, *Industrialization and Economic Development in Brazil* (Homewood, IL: Irwin, 1965).

22. "Recent Brazilian Economic Growth and Some of Its Main Problems," University of Brasilia Economics Department Discussion Paper No. 25, April 1975, p. 2.

23. *World Development Report 1980*, table 3, p. 115.

24. Ibid., table 3, p. 227.

25. *World Development Report 1989*, table 14, p. 190, and table 16, p. 194.

26. Helio Jaguaribe, Wanderley Guilhermedos Santos, Marcelo de Paiva Abreu, Winston Fritsch, and Fernando Bastos de Ávila, *Brasil 2,000* (São Paulo: Editora Paz e Terra, 1986).

27. Wagley, *An Introduction to Brazil*, p. 11.

28. Fernando Díaz-Plaja, *El Español y Los Siete Pecados Capitales* (Madrid: Alianza Editorial, 1966, reprint 1985).

29. Some Portuguese speakers who know English cite *jeito* as a synonym for "compromise." But there is a connotation of cleverness, manipulation, and even illegality to *jeito* that disqualifies it. See also Wesson and Fleischer, *Brazil in Transition*.

30. Gilberto Freyre, *New World in the Tropics* (New York: Knopf, 1959), p. 7.

31. María Alice Aguiar de Medeiros, *O Elogio da Dominação* (Rio de Janeiro: Edições Achiame, 1984).

32. Colonel Jorge da Silva of the Military Police, one of the few highly placed blacks in a public institution, was outspokenly critical of Brazil's race relationships in an interview in *Jornal do Brasil*, published on 20 November 1988 with the headline *"Negro diz que elite nao tem compromisso com a nacao"* ("Black says elite are not committed to the nation"). In the interview, da Silva describes the condition of Brazilian blacks today as "not much better than during slavery," and points to the affirmative action policies of the United States as "a source of inspiration." See also Marlise Simons, "Brazil's Blacks Feel Prejudice 100 Years After Slavery's End," *New York Times*, 14 May 1988, p. 1.

33. The *jen* that Japanese in superior hierarchical positions must show their inferiors in return for their fealty (*chu, ko, giri*) approximates noblesse oblige. *Jen* is usually translated as "benevolence."

34. Wagley, *An Introduction to Brazil*, pp. 184–85.

35. Gilberto Freyre, *The Masters and the Slaves: A Study in the Development of the Brazilian Civilization* (New York: Knopf, 1956), pp. 26–27, quoted in ibid., p. 185.

36. For an analysis of the role of *jeito* in Brazil's judicial system, see Keith S. Rosenn, "The Jeito Revisited," *Florida International Law Journal* (Fall 1984): 1–43.

37. See de Medeiros, *O Elogio da Dominacão*, p. 63.

38. Roberto DaMatta, *A Casa e a Rua* (São Paulo: Editora Brasiliense, 1985), p. 40.

39. José Osvaldo de Meira Penna, *Psicologia do Subdesenvolvimento* (Rio de Janeiro: APEC Editora, S.A., 1972), p. 41.

40. Wagley, *An Introduction to Brazil*, p. 198. The problem persists to the present day, as noted by James Brooke in the *New York Times* on 3 May 1991 ("In Brazil's Congress, Nepotism Is Hanging On," p. A9).

41. Maria Lucia Victor Barbosa, *O Voto da Pobrosa e o Pobresa do Voto* (Rio de Janeiro: Jorge Zahar Editor, 1988), p. 26.

42. Cited by Alan Riding in "Venality So Bald It's Now Intolerable," *New York Times*, 14 January 1989, p. 4.

43. Max Weber, *The Protestant Ethic and the Spirit of Capitalism* (New York: Scribner, 1950), p. 117.

44. The estimate appears in John Marcom, Jr., "The Fire Down South," *Forbes Magazine* (15 October 1990): 57.

45. Wagley, *An Introduction to Brazil*, pp. 248–49. The 1950 census figure is cited by Wagley. The Encyclopedia Britannica *World Data Annual* 1988, uses a figure, presumably based on the 1980 census, of 8,620,000 for 1986.

46. See Harrison, *Underdevelopment Is a State of Mind*, chap. 6, "Argentina and Australia," for a cultural interpretation of what is often referred to as "the Argentine enigma."

47. See Tomás Roberto Fillol, *Social Factors in Economic Development* (Cambridge: MIT Press, 1961). See also Mariano Grondona's typology of progress-resistant and progress-prone cultures in the introduction.

48. Robert F. Foerster, *The Italian Emigration of Our Times* (Cambridge: Harvard University Press, 1919), p. 289.

49. For an interesting and relevant analysis of the experience of Dutch settlers

in Paraná—and in Argentina—see Fred Jongkind, "The Protestant Ethic and Economic Progress: Dutch Agrarian Colonies in Argentina and Brazil," paper presented at the American Anthropological Association Congress in Washington, D.C., 16 November 1989.

50. Marlise Simons, "Japanese Gone Brazilian: Unhurried Workaholics," *New York Times*, 8 May 1988, p. 14.

51. Ibid.

52. Fillol, *Social Factors in Economic Development*, p. 32.

53. Foerster, *The Italian Emigration of Our Times*, p. 264.

54. Ibid, p. 267.

55. Everett Hagen, *On the Theory of Social Change: How Economic Growth Begins* (Homewood, IL: Dorsey Press, 1962).

56. Fillol, *Social Factors in Economic Development*, pp. 34, 39.

57. Carlos Escudé, *El Fracaso del Proyecto Argentino—Educación e Ideología* (Buenos Aires: Instituto Torcuato Di Tella, 1990), pp. 200–201, 206.

58. Thomas E. Skidmore, "Comparing Argentina and Brazil—The Link Between Politics and Economic Development," *New World* 1, no. 1 (1986): 37.

59. Middle-class people "identify with and share the aristocratic social values of the traditional upper class." The lower classes "do not have a culture apart from the upper class—they share in Brazilian culture, although largely in a vicarious way." (Wagley, *An Introduction to Brazil*, pp. 126, 147.)

60. Ibid., pp. 128–29, 131.

61. See figures 9 and 10 in Cardoso, "Debt Cycles in Brazil and Argentina."

62. Quoted in ibid., pp. 128–29.

63. Jaguaribe, des Santos, Abreu, Fritsch, and de Ávila, *Brasil 2,000*.

64. Moog, *Bandeirantes e Pioneiros*, p. 198.

Chapter 2

1. See Lawrence Harrison, *Underdevelopment Is a State of Mind—The Latin American Case* (Lanham, MD: Harvard Center for International Affairs and University Press of America, 1985), chap. 7, "Spain and Spanish America."

2. Octavio Paz, *The Labyrinth of Solitude: Life and Thought in Mexico* (New York: Grove Press, 1961), p. 122.

3. Hernando De Soto's best-selling *El Otro Sendero* (Lima: Editorial El Barranco, 1986) describes Peru's economy today as essentially mercantilistic.

4. Keith S. Rosenn, "The Protection of Judicial Independence in Latin America," in Centre for the Independence of Judges and Lawyers, *CIJL Bulletin* (October 1988): 36.

5. Eléna de la Souchère, *An Explanation of Spain* (New York: Random House, 1964), p. 18.

6. Fernando Díaz-Plaja, *El Español y Los Siete Pecados Capitales* (Madrid: Alianza Editorial, 1966, reprint 1985). *Superindividualism* is on p. 76.

7. José Ortega y Gasset, *Invertebrate Spain* (New York: Norton, 1937), pp. 49–50.

8. Díaz-Plaja, *El Español y los Siete Pecados Capitales*, p. 83.

9. See E. Ramón Arango, *The Spanish Political System: Franco's Legacy* (Boulder, CO: Westview Press, 1978), p. 109.

10. Díaz-Plaja, *El Español y los Siete Pecados Capitales*, p. 79.

11. Ibid., pp. 72–73, 127.

12. Cited by Henry Wells in *The Modernization of Puerto Rico: A Political Study of Changing Values and Institutions* (Cambridge: Harvard University Press, 1969), p. 45.

13. Malcolm T. Walker, *Politics and the Power Structure: A Rural Community in the Dominican Republic* (New York and London: Teachers College Press, Columbia University, 1972), p. 107.

14. Edward Banfield, *The Moral Basis of a Backward Society* (Glencoe, IL: Free Press, 1958), p. 159.

15. Max Weber, *The Protestant Ethic and the Spirit of Capitalism* (New York: Scribner, 1950), p. 117.

16. Wells, *The Modernization of Puerto Rico*, p. 32.

17. Quoted in Carlos Rangel, *The Latin Americans: Their Love-Hate Relationship with the United States* (New York and London: Harcourt Brace Jovanovich, 1977), p. 192.

18. Sima Lieberman, *The Contemporary Spanish Economy* (London: Allen and Unwin, 1982), p. 7.

19. Díaz-Plaja, *El Español y los Siete Pecados Capitales*, p. 25.

20. Ortega y Gasset, *Invertebrate Spain*, pp. 152–53.

21. Lieberman, *The Contemporary Spanish Economy*, p. 4.

22. Arango, *The Spanish Political System*, p. 60.

23. Ibid., pp. 70–71.

24. Quoted in ibid. p. 72.

25. Quoted in ibid., p. 76.

26. Pierre Vilar, *Spain—A Brief History* (Oxford: Pergamon Press, 1967), p. 113.

27. Domingo Faustino Sarmiento, *Facundo: Civilización y Barbarie* (Buenos Aires: Espasa-Calpa Argentina, S.A., 1951), p. 103.

28. In Camilo José Cela, *Conversaciónes Españolas* (Barcelona: Plaza & Janes Editores, S.A., 1987), p. 104.

29. Quoted in Arango, *The Spanish Political System*, pp. 119, 103.

30. For a firsthand account of U.S.-Spanish relations in the 1950s, see J. Carter Murphy and R. Richard Rubottom, *Spain and the United States Since World War II* (New York: Praeger, 1984).

31. Joseph Harrison, *The Spanish Economy in the Twentieth Century* (London and Sydney: Croom Helm, 1985), chap. 7.

32. James W. Cortada, *Two Nations over Time—Spain and the United States, 1776–1977* (Westport and London: Greenwood Press, 1978), p. 234.

33. John Hooper, *The Spaniards: A Portrait of the New Spain* (London: Penguin Books, 1986), pp. 26–27.

34. See Julio Alcaide Inchausti, "La Distribución de la Renta en España," in *España: Un Presente para el Futuro*, ed. Juan Linz (Madrid: Instituto de Estudios Económicos, 1984), pp. 127–48.

35. Hooper, *The Spaniards*, p. 33.

36. World Bank, *World Development Report 1988* (New York: Oxford University Press, 1988), p. 273.

37. *World Development Report 1990*.

38. American Embassy, Madrid, "Economic Trends Report," July 1989, p. 5.

39. In *The Spanish Economy in the Twentieth Century*, Joseph Harrison cites an article by Ángel Alcaide Inchausti as his source for this estimate.

40. Alex Inkeles and David Smith, *Becoming Modern: Individual Change in Six Developing Countries* (Cambridge: Harvard University Press, 1974).

41. Harrison, *The Spanish Economy in the Twentieth Century*, p. 156.

42. Lieberman, *The Contemporary Spanish Economy*, pp. 230–31.

43. Hooper, *The Spaniards*, p. 28.

44. David McClelland, *The Achieving Society* (Princeton: D. Van Nostrand, 1961).

45. Francisco Andrés Orizo, Manuel Gómez-Reino Carnota, Pedro González Blasco, Juan J. Linz Storch de Gracia, and José Juan Toharia Cortés, *Juventud Española 1984* (Madrid: Ediciones SM, 1985).

46. Ronald Inglehart, *Cultural Shift in Advanced Industrial Society* (Princeton: Princeton University Press, 1989), appendix 9, table 9-8.

47. Victor Pérez Díaz, "Políticas Económicas y Pautas Sociales en la España de la Transición: La Doble Cara del Neocorporatismo," in *España: Un Presente para el Futuro*, ed. Linz, pp. 31, 42.

48. Juergen B. Donges, "La Insuficiencia de Productividad en la Economía Española: Causas y Remedios," in ibid., p. 114.

49. Hooper, *The Spaniards*, pp. 171–72.

50. Ibid., p. 173.

51. Ibid., p. 174.

52. Ibid.

53. Quoted by José María Martín Patino, "La Iglesia en la Sociedad Española," in *España: Un Presente para el Futuro*, ed. Linz, p. 153.

54. Richard Gunther, "Politics and Culture in Spain," Center for Political Studies, Institute for Social Research, University of Michigan, Ann Arbor, 1988, p. 14. The source is survey work done by José Ramón Montero Gibert. World Value Survey data show that religiosity breaks sharply by age group: about 30 percent of Spaniards aged fifteen to thirty-four have confidence in the church, about 65 percent of those aged fifty-five to sixty-four and 75 percent of those over sixty-five do. To be sure, religiosity probably increases with age in most societies, but probably not to this extent.

55. Paul Preston, *The Triumph of Democracy in Spain* (London and New York: Methuen, 1986), p. 21.

56. Hooper, *The Spaniards*, p. 37.

57. Quoted in ibid., p. 39.

58. Preston, *The Triumph of Democracy in Spain*, p. 122.

59. Ibid., p. 119.

60. Hooper, *The Spaniards*, p. 43.

61. Ibid., pp. 44–45.

62. In Linz, ed., *Espana: Un Presente para el Futuro*, p. 198.

63. Weber, *The Protestant Ethic*, p. 117.

64. Gunther, "Politics and Culture in Spain," p. 23.

65. Quoted in Hooper, *The Spaniards*, p. 73.

66. Ibid., p. 137.

67. See Tomás Roberto Fillol, *Social Factors in Economic Development* (Cambridge: MIT Press, 1961).

68. Robert Graham, *Spain: A Nation Comes of Age* (New York: St. Martin's Press, 1984), p. 61.

Chapter 3

1. Ambrose Y. C. King and Michael H. Bond observe, "While we fully appreciate that Chinese culture is a far from homogeneous system, it seems to us that Confucian values have played a predominant role in molding Chinese character and behavior" ("The Confucian Paradigm of Man: A Sociological View," in *Chinese Culture and Mental Health,* ed. Wen-Shing Tseng and David Y. H. Wu [Orlando, FL: Academic Press, 1985), p. 29. The following discussion derives principally from Edwin O. Reischauer and John K. Fairbank, *East Asia—The Great Tradition* (Boston: Houghton Mifflin, 1960), particularly chap. 3.

2. Reischauer and Fairbank, *East Asia—The Great Tradition,* p. 70. I should note that I was in error in describing Confucianism as a religion in *Underdevelopment Is a State of Mind—The Latin American Case* (Lanham, MD: Harvard Center for International Affairs and University Press of America, 1985, p. 23). The comments about a "highly anti-rational world of universal magic" clearly do not apply to Confucianism, but do apply to Taoism and the other religions that coexisted with Confucianism.

3. Reischauer and Fairbank, *East Asia—The Great Tradition,* p. 30.

4. Ibid., p. 28.

5. Repeated references to placating ancestors are made in Amy Tan's best-selling *The Joy Luck Club* (New York: Ivy Books, 1989). Fear of the actions of dead relatives is also known in Japan (see chapter 4).

6. Roy Hofheinz, Jr., and Kent E. Calder, *The Eastasia Edge* (New York: Basic Books, 1982), p. 121.

7. Max Weber, *Confucianism and Taoism* (abridged by Michio Morishima) (London: International Centre for Economics and Related Disciplines, 1984), p. 60.

8. Reischauer and Fairbank, *East Asia—The Great Tradition,* p. 74.

9. Ibid., p. 72.

10. Reischauer makes the same point in *East Asia—The Great Tradition*: "Because of the Confucian emphasis on ethics as the basis of good government, opposing policies could not be accepted as the product of honest differences of opinion but were commonly regarded as signs of the depravity of one's opponents. . . . The democratic balance of our own partisan politics would have been unthinkable" (p. 438).

11. Lucian W. Pye, "Tiananmen and Chinese Political Culture—The Escalation of Confrontation from Moralizing to Revenge," *Current Asian Survey* (April 1990), and forthcoming in *The Broken Mirror—China After Tiananmen,* ed. George Hicks (London: Longman).

12. Ibid.

13. In *A Korean Village Between Farm and Sea* (Cambridge: Harvard University Press, 1971), Vincent S. R. Brandt stresses the coexistence of hierarchical Confucianism in the village of Sokp'o with an egalitarian community ethic whose historical roots may be even deeper than those of Confucianism. But, he observes, "Confucian doctrine, as it is expressed in Sokp'o, goes beyond the boundaries of kinship in inculcating values of restraint and moderation as a guide to all interpersonal conduct. In this respect it reinforces the more egalitarian ideals of cooperation, hospitality, and

tolerant accommodation of personal differences" (p. 236)—and we are reminded again of the fifth Confucian relationship.

14. Data are from World Bank, *World Development Report 1980* (New York: Oxford University Press, 1980).

15. Shirley W. Y. Kuo, "The Achievement of Growth with Equity," in *Conference on Economic Development Experiences of Taiwan and Its New Role in an Emerging Asia-Pacific Area*, vol. 1 (Taipei: The Institute of Economics, Academia Sinica, 1988), p. 74. (Hereinafter, this two-volume report will be referred to as Academia Sinica 1988.) Other recent data on Taiwan are from the same conference report unless otherwise indicated.

16. *World Development Report 1989.*

17. The principal source for the very brief historical review is Reischauer and Fairbank, *East Asia—The Great Tradition.*

18. Mark R. Peattie, "Introduction," in *The Japanese Colonial Empire*, ed. Ramon H. Myers and Mark R. Peattie (Princeton: Princeton University Press, 1984), p. 44.

19. Lewis H. Gann, "Western and Japanese Colonialism," in ibid., pp. 522–23.

20. Samuel Ho, *Economic Development of Taiwan, 1860–1970* (New Haven and London: Yale University Press, 1978), p. 40.

21. Dwight Perkins, *China—Asia's Next Economic Giant?* (Seattle and London: University of Washington Press, 1986), p. 18.

22. U.S. Agency for International Development, *U.S. Overseas Loans and Grants July 1, 1945–September 30, 1982* (Washington, D.C.: Government Printing Office, 1982), p. 83.

23. Ho, *Economic Development of Taiwan, 1860–1970*, p. 115.

24. The editor of *International Laboratory* observed, in the May/June 1987 issue (p. 8): "It is significant that while the Taiwan population of about ten million contributed over 20,000 students [in the U.S.] of science and engineering between 1957 and 1974 (or 61% of the total of 35,000 students), the population of some 280–350 million of Latin America contributed 30,000 students of science and engineering (or only 27% of the total)."

25. See Roy L. Prosterman and Jeffrey M. Riedinger, *Land Reform and Democratic Development* (Baltimore and London: Johns Hopkins University Press, 1987), for one assessment of the Taiwanese land reform experience.

26. Ho, *Economic Development of Taiwan, 1860–1970*, p. 120.

27. Kuo, Academia Sinica 1988, p. 111.

28. W.W. Rostow, *The Stages of Economic Growth* (London: Cambridge University Press, 1960), p. 39.

29. Chi-ming Hou, "Strategy for Economic Development in Taiwan and Implications for Developing Economies," in Academia Sinica 1988, p. 56.

30. Tzong-shian Yu, "The Role of Government in Industrialization," in "Academia Sinica 1988," pp. 135, 147.

31. Kuo, "The Achievement of Growth with Equity," p. 85.

32. Ibid., pp. 71–120.

33. See Albert Fishlow, "Latin American Adjustments to the Oil Shocks" (chap. 4, pp. 54–84), in *Latin American Political Economy*, ed. Jonathan Hartlyn and Samuel A. Morley (Boulder and London: Westview Press, 1986). Hong Kong and Singapore, the other two "dragons," were comparably vulnerable to the oil shocks but also took them in stride.

34. We are once again reminded of Everett Hagen's motivational analysis in *On the Theory of Social Change: How Economic Growth Begins* (Homewood, IL: Dorsey Press, 1962).

35. Selig S. Harrison, "Taiwan After Chiang Ching-Kuo," *Foreign Affairs* (Spring 1988): 791.

36. The following historical review derives principally from Reischauer and Fairbank, *East Asia—The Great Tradition*, particularly chap. 10.

37. Ibid., pp. 411–12.

38. Ibid., p. 426.

39. Ibid., p. 432.

40. Ibid., p. 449.

41. Ibid., p. 762.

42. Perkins, *China—Asia's Next Economic Giant?* p. 18.

43. These are Fairbank's estimates—*East Asia—The Great Tradition*, p. 847.

44. Edward S. Mason, Mahn Je Kim, Dwight H. Perkins, Kwang Suk Kim, and David C. Cole, *The Economic and Social Modernization of the Republic of Korea* (Cambridge and London: Harvard University Press, 1980), p. 44. This book is the principal source for the post–Korean War period.

45. Stephan Haggard makes the point that Taiwan's outward-looking policies also importantly responded to the intention of the United States to reduce aid (Academia Sinica 1988, p. 284).

46. Mason et al., *Economic and Social Modernization*, chap. 4.

47. Gregory Henderson, *Korea: The Politics of the Vortex* (Cambridge and London: Harvard University Press, 1968), pp. 193–94.

48. "Seoul Is Planning to Convert Its Raucous Politics into Gray Japanese Model," *New York Times*, 6 February 1990, p. A3.

49. Lucian Pye, *Asian Power and Politics* (Cambridge and London: Belknap Press of Harvard University Press, 1985), pp. 58, 75.

50. King and Bond, "The Confucian Paradigm of Man: A Sociological View," p. 35.

51. Robert A. Scalapino, "The Politics of Development: Perspectives on Twentieth Century Asia," Reischauer Lectures, Harvard University, October 1988, sec. 1, p. 12.

52. Ronald Inglehart, *Culture Shift in Advanced Industrial Society* (Princeton: Princeton University Press, 1990), p. 14.

53. Scalapino, "The Politics of Development," p. 12.

54. Harrison, *Underdevelopment Is a State of Mind*, pp. xvi–xvii.

55. Scalapino, "The Politics of Development," sec. 1, pp. 11–12.

56. Perkins, *China—Asia's Next Economic Giant?* passim and appendix.

57. Ibid., p. 8.

58. Max Weber, *The Religion of China* (New York: Macmillan, 1951).

59. Weber, *Confucianism and Taoism*, pp. 18, 20, 76.

60. Ibid., pp. 33, 79, 76.

61. Ibid., p. 81.

62. Edwin O. Reischauer and John K. Fairbank, *East Asia: The Modern Transformation* (Boston: Houghton Mifflin, 1965), p. 93.

63. Weber, *Confucianism and Taoism*, p. 80.

64. Pye, *Asian Power and Politics*, p. 60. In his unpublished 1987 paper "The

Transformation of Confucianism in the Post-Confucian Era: The Emergence of Rationalistic Traditionism in Hong Kong," Ambrose Y. C. King notes that the absence of "transcendental tension" in Confucianism is contested in an article by S. N. Eisenstadt ("The Worldly Transcendentalism and the Structuring of the World: Weber's 'Religion of China' and the Format of Chinese History and Civilization," in *Max Weber in Asian Studies*, ed. Andreas E. Buss [Leiden: E. J. Brill, 1985], pp. 46–64.)

65. Pye, *Asian Power and Politics*, p. 160.

66. John Kenneth Galbraith, *The Nature of Mass Poverty* (Cambridge and London: Harvard University Press, 1979).

67. *Guanxi*—which Ezra Vogel defines as "the cultivation of personal connections" (*One Step Ahead in China* [Cambridge and London: Harvard University Press, 1989], p. 405) and which is akin to Hispanic *amiguismo*—derives, at least in part, from the obligations of the fifth of the Confucian relationships: friend to friend. As Vogel observes, *guanxi* continues as a major force in business in South China. It is so important in Taiwan that the American Institute in Taiwan (effectively, the U.S. embassy) has published a brochure titled "Kuan-Hsi [the same Chinese word transliterated differently]—The Key to American Business Success in Taiwan."

68. In *The Mandarin and the Cadre: China's Political Cultures* (Ann Arbor: Center for Chinese Studies, University of Michigan, 1988), Lucian Pye captures the authoritarian continuity of Confucianism and Marxism in the term "Confucian Leninism."

69. Mason et al., *The Economic and Social Modernization of the Republic of Korea*, pp. 284–85.

70. King, "The Transformation of Confucianism in the Post-Confucian Era," p. 13.

71. See Vogel, *One Step Ahead in China*, p. 406.

72. Stephan Haggard, Academia Sinica 1988, pp. 284–87.

73. King reaches a similar conclusion in "The Transformation of Confucianism in the Post-Confucian Era": "I am of the view that Confucianism does contain within itself the seeds of transformation and in the right institutional settings these seeds could bear fruit to positively influence the course of economic development" (p. 5).

Chapter 4

1. Edwin O. Reischauer and John K. Fairbank, *East Asia: The Modern Transformation* (Boston: Houghton Mifflin, 1965), p. 33.

2. W. G. Beasley, *The Meiji Restoration* (Stanford: Stanford University Press, 1972), p. 16.

3. Ibid., p. 132.

4. Ibid., p. 14.

5. Ibid., p. 36. Hara Hiroko and Managawa Mieko use data that show a 15 percent level for girls in "Japanese Childhood Since 1600," English manuscript version of a chapter in *Zur Sozialgeschicte der Kindheit*, ed. Jochen Martin and August Nitschke (Frieburg/Munchen: Verlag Karl Alber, 1985).

6. Nathan Rosenberg and L. E. Birdzell, Jr., *How the West Grew Rich* (New York: Basic Books, 1986), pp. 60–61.

7. Beasley, *The Meiji Restoration*, p. 57.

8. Beasley notes that "troubles at home and dangers from abroad" is an English translation of a Japanese translation *(naiyu-gaikan)* of an old Chinese saying. (Ibid., p. 41.)

9. Cited in ibid., p. 89.

10. "The Meiji Ishin in Perspective," in *Meiji Ishin: Restoration and Revolution*, ed. Nagai Michio and Miguel Urrutia (Tokyo: United Nations University, 1985), p. 12.

11. In ibid., p. v.

12. Frank R. Gibney, "Meiji: A Cultural Revolution," in ibid., p. 105.

13. Reischauer and Fairbank, *East Asia: The Modern Transformation*, pp. 244, 267.

14. Beasley, *The Meiji Restoration*, p. 329.

15. Ibid., p. 323.

16. Ibid., p. 371.

17. Reischauer and Fairbank, *East Asia: The Modern Transformation*, p. 272.

18. Ibid., p. 276.

19. Ibid.

20. Ibid., p. 247. I expect that most readers will smile when reading this sentence.

21. Ibid., p. 251.

22. Quoted in Beasley, *The Meiji Restoration*, p. 311.

23. Reischauer and Fairbank, *East Asia: The Modern Transformation*, p. 296.

24. Ibid., p. 298.

25. Ibid., pp. 279, 244.

26. Edwin O. Reischauer and John K. Fairbank, *East Asia—The Great Tradition* (Boston: Houghton Mifflin, 1960), p. 474.

27. Ronald Dore, *Taking Japan Seriously* (Stanford: Stanford University Press, 1987), p. 5.

28. World Bank, *World Development Report 1989* (New York: Oxford University Press, 1989), table 30, p. 223.

29. Ronald Inglehart, *Culture Shift in Advanced Industrial Society* (Princeton: Princeton University Press, 1990), pp. 72, 26.

30. John F. Embree, *Suye Mura—A Japanese Village* (Chicago and London: University of Chicago Press, 1939), pp. 163ff.

31. James Fallows, *More Like Us* (Boston: Houghton Mifflin, 1989), p. 33. In an article about Utah in the *Boston Globe* (5 May 1991), Renee Loth says, "Utah is America's Japan."

32. George A. DeVos, *Socialization for Achievement—Essays on the Cultural Psychology of the Japanese* (Berkeley, Los Angeles, London: University of California Press, 1973), p. 191. We should here note the current of analysis of Japan that identifies the village as a key source of both the group and emotional (in contrast to rational) emphases of Japanese culture. See, for example, Gregory Clark, *Understanding the Japanese* (Tokyo: Kinseido, 1983).

33. DeVos, *Socialization for Achievement*, p. 12.

34. Lucian Pye (*Asian Power and Politics* [Cambridge and London: Belknap Press of Harvard University Press, 1985], p. 170) observes that Japanese mothers often

express "hurt feelings" about the bad behavior of their children in a guilt-inducing pattern that is reminiscent of the stereotypical Jewish mother in Philip Roth's *Portnoy's Complaint.*

35. Takeo Doi, *The Anatomy of Dependence* (Tokyo and New York: Kodansha International, 1971).

36. *Ideology and National Competitiveness,* ed. George Lodge and Ezra Vogel, tends to place Japan at the communitarian extreme of the communitarian/individualistic spectrum, the United States at the individualistic extreme (Boston: Harvard Business School Press, 1987). I think the characterization of the United States is somewhat overdrawn and I elaborate on the point in chapter 7.

37. Jared Taylor, *Shadows of the Rising Sun* (Tokyo: Charles E. Tuttle, 1983), p. 28.

38. The World Bank's *World Development Report 1989* shows the top 10 percent in Brazil accounting for 50.6 percent of household income (1972), the top 10 percent in Japan accounting for 22.4 percent (1979).

39. Inglehart, *Culture Shift in Advanced Industrial Society,* p. 37.

40. DeVos, *Socialization for Achievement,* p. 182.

41. Ruth Benedict, *The Chrysanthemum and the Sword* (Boston: Houghton Mifflin, 1946), pp. 191, 197.

42. The information in this paragraph derives from a table in Benedict, *The Chrysanthemum and the Sword,* p. 116. While her analysis of the reciprocal obligations that are the foundation of Japanese ethics has been widely accepted, Ruth Benedict's conclusion that Japanese are motivated by fear of shame rather than conscience has provoked major controversy.

43. See, for example, Doi, *The Anatomy of Dependence,* pp. 48–49, and DeVos, *Socialization for Achievement,* p. 30.

44. DeVos, *Socialization for Achievement.*

45. Taylor, *Shadows of the Rising Sun,* p. 41.

46. DeVos, *Socialization for Achievement,* p. 37.

47. Pye (*Asian Power and Politics,* p. 169) cites the work of the Japanese social anthropologist Chie Nakane as the basis for this comment.

48. Ibid., pp. 169–71, passim.

49. Taylor, *Shadows of the Rising Sun,* p. 171.

50. DeVos, *Socialization for Achievement,* pp. 67, 106.

51. Pye, *Asian Power and Politics,* p. 68.

52. Merry White, *The Japanese Educational Challenge* (New York and London: Free Press, 1987), p. 21.

53. Benedict, *The Chrysanthemum and the Sword,* pp. 253–54.

54. White, *The Japanese Educational Challenge,* p. 23.

55. Hara and Minagawa, "Japanese Childhood Since 1600," p. 98.

56. Ibid., p. 262.

57. Pye, *Asian Power and Politics,* p. 170.

58. McClelland, *The Achieving Society.* Several researchers have concluded that a prominent paternal role in child rearing (as in some Moslem countries) often suppresses a child's efforts to develop a sense of mastery and the tools of achievement. See, for example, DeVos, *Socialization for Achievement,* p. 176.

59. Hiroko and Mieko, "Japanese Childhood Since 1600," p. 103.

60. See DeVos, *Socialization for Achievement,* chap. 6.

Chapter 5

1. Thomas Sowell, *Ethnic America* (New York: Basic Books, 1981), p. 186. Sowell observes that Brazil imported six times as many slaves as the United States, adding further reason for skepticism about Gilberto Freyre's description of race relations in Brazil (see chapter 1).

2. Oliver MacDonagh, "The Irish Emigration to the United States," *Perspectives in American History* 10 (1976): 405–6; cited in Sowell, *Ethnic America*, p. 21.

3. Vernon M. Briggs argues that even in good times, immigrants compete with citizens ("Immigration Policy Sends Blacks Back to South," letter to the *New York Times*, 1 February 1990). In *Friends or Strangers* (New York: Basic Books, 1990), George Borjas carefully documents his conclusion that the competitive impact of immigrants on native-born Americans is neglible. He does not, however, consider circumstances of rising unemployment.

4. See Michael J. White, Frank D. Bean, and Thomas J. Espenshade, "The U.S. Immigration Reform and Control Act and Undocumented Migration to the United States," The Urban Institute and the RAND Corporation, 19 July 1989; and the "Presentation to the Ninth Annual Briefing Session for Journalists" of Wayne A. Cornelius, Center for U.S.-Mexican Studies and Foundation for American Communications, La Jolla, California, 22 June 1989.

5. Borjas, *Friends or Strangers*, pp. 18–19.

6. Richard Estrada, "The Impact of Immigration on Hispanic Americans," *Chronicles* (July 1991): 24–28; Arthur M. Schlesinger, Jr., *The Disuniting of America: Reflections on a Multicultural Society* (Knoxville, Tenn.: Whittle Direct Books, 1991).

7. Michael E. Porter, *The Competitive Advantage of Nations* (New York: Free Press, 1990), p. 6.

8. Borjas, *Friends or Strangers*, p. 8.

9. Porter, *Competitive Advantage of Nations*, p. 3.

10. See, for example, David Card and Joseph Altonji, "The Effects of Immigration on the Labor Market Outcomes of Less Skilled Natives," in John J. Aboud and Richard Freeman, eds., *Immigration, Trade and the Labor Market* (Chicago: University of Chicago Press, 1991); and Donald L. Huddle, "Immigration, Jobs and Wages: The Misuse of Econometrics" (in press).

11. The Roper Organization, "American Attitudes Toward Immigration," 1990.

12. Alejandro Portes and Alex Stepick, "Unwelcome Immigrants: The Labor Market Experiences of 1980 (Mariel) and Haitian Refugees in South Florida," *International Migration Review* 50 (August 1985): 493–514.

13. Katherine Betts, *Ideology and Immigration* (Carlton, Victoria: Melbourne University Press, 1980), p. 34.

14. Mark Falcoff, "You Are What You Think" (review of my *Underdevelopment Is a State of Mind*), *This World* 13 (Winter 1986): 124.

15. Stephan Thernstrom observes in *The Other Bostonians*: "Throughout the United States for at least the past century . . . there has been a fairly high and relatively constant rate of upward intergenerational mobility, with a very large minority of working class sons moving up at least into the lower echelons of the white-collar class" (Cambridge: Harvard University Press, 1973, p. 249).

16. The role of class has been stressed by Edward Banfield in *The Unheavenly City*

Revisited (Boston and Toronto: Little, Brown, 1974) and by William Julius Wilson in *The Declining Significance of Race* (Chicago and London: University of Chicago Press, 1978).

17. There has been a presumption that the youthfulness of the Mexican-American population is also the consequence of the disproportionately youthful illegal immigrant flow. After careful analysis of census data, George Borjas concludes that "there is little evidence to suggest that the illegal-alien population, whether Mexican-American or otherwise, is dominated by young men" (*Friends or Strangers,* p. 66).

18. Betty Lee Sung, *A Survey of Chinese-American Manpower and Employment* (New York: Praeger Publishers, 1976), p. 1—which, with Sowell's *Ethnic America,* is the principal source for this section. Interestingly, the Chinese were also drawn to the 1851 Australian Gold Rush. According to Russel Ward in *Australia: A Short History* (Sydney: Ure Smith 1979), p. 75, about 40,000 Chinese worked the Australian gold fields. Anti-Chinese riots were sparked by the 4,000 or 5,000 Americans who joined the Australian Rush.

19. This figure, from 1980 census data, appears in table 1.1 of "The Economic Status of Americans of Asian Descent" (Washington, D.C.: U.S. Commission on Civil Rights, October 1988).

20. Sowell, *Ethnic America,* p. 139.

21. Sung, *A Survey of Chinese-American Manpower and Employment,* p. 60.

22. Civil Rights Commission, "The Economic Status of Americans of Asian Descent." The traditional subordination of women in China extended to education, which is the chief explanation for why 10 percent of Chinese-American women over sixteen, almost all of them foreign-born, had not attended school at all.

23. David M. Reimers, *Still the Golden Door* (New York: Columbia University Press, 1985), p. 105. In "The U.S.—Decline or Renewal?" *Foreign Affairs* (Winter 1988–89): 90, Samuel Huntington noted that Asians comprised 14 percent of the 1988 freshman class at Harvard.

24. Sung, in *A Survey of Chinese-American Manpower and Employment,* observes, "A comparison of labor force status with whites, blacks, and Japanese shows that a larger percentage of Oriental women (50 percent) work outside the home than do black (48 percent) or white (41 percent) women" (p. 91).

25. Everett E. Hagen, *On the Theory of Social Change: How Economic Growth Begins* (Homewood, IL: Dorsey Press, 1962).

26. Quoted in Thomas F. McGann, *Argentina: The Divided Land* (Princeton: Van Nostrand, 1966), p. 30.

27. Sowell, *Ethnic America,* pp. 161, 162.

28. Ibid., p. 163.

29. Ibid., p. 166.

30. S. I. Hayakawa, *Through the Communication Barrier* (New York: Harper & Row, 1979), pp. 131–32, cited in Sowell, *Ethnic America,* p. 176.

31. Milton M. Gordon, *Assimilation in American Life* (New York: Oxford University Press, 1964), p. 80.

32. Sowell observes that "like the Chinese, [the Japanese] made use of the revolving credit associations to pool funds to finance new businesses. But this simple institution depended on a whole complex of relationships of trust, based on family and community ties and concepts of honor, which would have made defaults virtually impossible" (*Ethnic America,* p. 167).

33. George A. DeVos, *Socialization for Achievement—Essays on the Cultural Psychology of the Japanese* (Berkeley, Los Angeles, London: University of California Press, 1973), pp. 169, 239. William Caudill is co-author of the chapter that contains the second section of this quote.

34. This clause of the Treaty of Amity and Commerce is quoted in Pyong Gap Min, *Ethnic Business Enterprise: Korean Small Business in Atlanta* (New York: Center for Migration Studies, 1988), pp. 8–9. This book is the principal source for the section on Korean-Americans.

35. E. Y. Yu, "Koreans in America: An Emerging Ethnic Community," *Amerasia Journal* 4 (1977): 120.

36. See Min, *Ethnic Business Enterprise*, pp. 19, 21.

37. Ibid., pp. 135, 129, 131.

38. Ivan Light, "Immigrant Entrepreneurs in America: Koreans in Los Angeles," in *Clamor at the Gates*, ed. Nathan Glazer (San Francisco: Institute for Contemporary Studies Press, 1985), p. 174.

39. Peter Rose, "Asian Americans: From Pariahs to Paragons," in ibid., p. 212.

Chapter 6

1. In *The Mexican-American People* (New York: Free Press, 1970, pp. 43–44), Leo Grebler, Joan W. Moore, and Ralph C. Guzman estimate the Mexican population of Texas and the territories as follows: Texas, 35,000; New Mexico and southern Colorado, 61,000; Arizona, 2,000, California, 7,500.

2. Thomas Sowell, *Ethnic America* (New York: Basic Books, 1981), pp. 247–48. Grebler, Moore, and Guzman state, "Prerevolutionary Mexico had a tiny elite, a small middle class, and an enormous lower class comprising more than 90% of the total" (*The Mexican-American People*, p. 321).

3. Data from *Encyclopedia Americana*, vol. 27, "The People" (Danbury, CT: Grolier, 1989), p. 525. Julian Zamora and Patricia Vendel Simon report that about 50,000 illegal Mexican immigrants were apprehended between 1924 and 1930 (see *A History of the Mexican-American People* [Notre Dame, IN and London: University of Notre Dame Press, 1977], p. 144.)

4. Sowell, *Ethnic America*, p. 254. Other estimates of expulsions in the 1930s run as high as 1,000,000.

5. Zamora and Simon have developed figures on the *bracero* program from its inception to its termination (*A History of the Mexican-American People*, p. 140).

6. Sowell, *Ethnic America*, p. 256.

7. George Borjas, *Friends or Strangers* (New York: Basic Books, 1990), p. 13. The source for per capita data is the World Bank's *World Development Report 1990* (New York: Oxford University Press, 1990), table 1.

8. Americans who romanticize Latin America will cite similar problems in the United States. In most cases, they have not lived for extended periods in Latin America, nor have they had a chance to look behind the surface appearance of life in Latin America, particularly for the poor and powerless. For insights behind the surface appearance of Mexico, see Alan Riding, *Distant Neighbors* (New York: Vintage Books, 1986).

9. See, for example, " 'Mexicanización' del Sudoeste de EU" (" 'Mexicanization' of the U.S. Southwest"), *Excelsior*, Mexico City (15 May 1987): 1.

10. Telephone conversation with David Simcox, director of the Center for Immigration Studies, 11 October 1990.

11. See "Hispanic Population Passes 20 Million," *New York Times*, 12 October 1989, p. A20.

12. California study in Leon F. Bouvier and Philip Martin, *Population Change and California's Future* (Washington, D.C.: Population Reference Bureau, 1985); Texas study in F. Ray Marshall and Leon F. Bouvier, *Population Change and the Future of Texas* (Washington, D.C.: Population Reference Bureau, 1987).

13. Kevin F. McCarthy and R. Burciaga Valdez, *Current and Future Effects of Mexican Immigration in California* (Santa Monica: RAND, R–3365–CR 1985).

14. Ibid., p. 36.

15. Ibid., p. 28. In *Out of the Barrio* (New York: Basic Books, 1991), Linda Chavez includes a table (p. 103) derived from Census Bureau data showing the 1988 median years of schooling for all Mexican-Americans as 10.8.

16. *Essays and Data on American Ethnic Groups* (ed. Thomas Sowell [Washington: Urban Institute Press, 1978]) contains a table (p. 375) derived from the 1970 census that shows median school years for Mexican-Americans ages twenty-five to thirty-four as 10.8, thirty-five years and older as 7.3.

17. Borjas, *Friends or Strangers*, p. 52.

18. Sowell, *Ethnic America*, p. 266.

19. "Hispanic Dropout Rate Is Put at 35%," *New York Times*, 15 September 1989, p. A12; Chavez, *Out of the Barrio*, p. 113.

20. Sowell, *Ethnic America*, pp. 5, 260.

21. Thomas Muller, with Thomas J. Espenshade, *The Fourth Wave* (Washington, D.C.: Urban Institute Press, 1985).

22. Borjas, *Friends or Strangers*, chap. 5. Vernon Briggs, in "Mexican Workers in the United States Labour Market: A Contemporary Dilemma," *International Labor Review* 112 (November 1975): 351–68, argues that the adverse effects of immigration on the American labor force are far more profound.

23. In a 13 January 1991 letter to me, the *Dallas Morning News* columnist Richard Estrada wrote: "to aver as the academics do that immigrants pay more in except when you factor in public education expenses is roughly the same as to have argued during the Reagan years that the national budget was balanced except when you factored in defense expenditures."

24. Richard Lamm and John Love (both former governors of Colorado), "Apartheid: American Style," *Rocky Mountain News*, 18 September 1988.

25. Borjas, *Friends or Strangers*, pp. 150, 153.

26. Joel Garreau, "Mexican Counter-Revolt—The Americanization of the North Threatens the System," *Washington Post*, 25 May 1986, p. C1.

27. Joan Moore, *Mexican-Americans* (Englewood Cliffs, N.J.: Prentice-Hall, 1971), p. 119. Readers of my *Underdevelopment Is a State of Mind* will recall my view that the Spanish language is a conduit for traditional Hispanic culture; for example, there are no apt synonyms for the words *dissent* or *compromise*.

28. Susan E. Keefe and Amado M. Padilla, *Chicano Ethnicity* (Albuquerque: University of New Mexico Press, 1987), pp. 7–8. The 1970 findings of Grebler, Moore, and Guzman are similar but somewhat more optimistic with respect to acculturation (*The Mexican-American People*).

29. Keefe and Padilla, *Chicano Ethnicity*, pp. 20–21.

30. Borjas, *Friends or Strangers*, p. 130.

31. James W. Lamare, "The Political Integration of Mexican American Children: A Generational Analysis," *International Migration Review* 16, no. 1 (1982): 169–88.

32. Bureau of the Census, "Voting and Registration in the Election of 1988 (Advance Report)," series P-20, no. 435 (Washington, D.C.: U.S. Department of Commerce, February 1989).

33. Grebler, Moore, and Guzman, *The Mexican-American People*, p. 569.

34. Keefe and Padilla, *Chicano Ethnicity*, pp. 6–7.

35. "They're in a New Home But Feel Tied to the Old," *New York Times*, 30 June 1991, p. 12.

36. Moore, *Mexican Americans*, p. 105.

37. Grebler, Moore, and Guzman, *The Mexican-American People*, p. 352.

38. For a discussion of some of the parallels between Quebec and the American Southwest, see Joel Garreau, *The Nine Nations of North America* (Boston: Houghton Mifflin, 1981), chap. 7, "Mexamerica," pp. 207–44.

39. Testimony before the House Subcommittee on Education, Committee on Education and Labor, 93rd Cong., 2nd sess. (Washington, D.C.: Government Printing Office, 1974), quoted by Noel Epstein in *Language, Ethnicity and the Schools: Policy Alternatives for Bilingual-Bicultural Education* (Washington, D.C.: Institute for Educational Leadership, August 1977), p. 36.

40. Estrada letter, 13 January 1991.

41. Chavez, *Out of the Barrio*, p. 20.

42. Rosalie Pedalino Porter, *Forked Tongue: The Politics of Bilingual Education* (New York: Basic Books, 1990).

43. In *Whose Votes Count? Affirmative Action and Minority Voting Rights*, Abigail Thernstrom notes that "at least in southern Texas, [Mexican-American] votes had become an important source of Democratic power by the late nineteenth century" (Cambridge and London: Harvard University Press, 1987, p. 51).

44. Chavez, *Out of the Barrio*, p. 28.

45. Arthur M. Schlesinger, Jr., *The Disuniting of America—Reflections on a Multicultural Society* (Knoxville, TN: Whittle Direct Books, 1991), p. 61.

46. *New York Times*, 25 September 1989, p. 1.

Chapter 7

1. The divergent experiences of "free persons of color," emancipated blacks, and West Indians derive principally from Thomas Sowell, ed., *Essays and Data on American Ethnic Groups* (Washington, D.C.: The Urban Institute, 1978). A principal source for his analysis of "free persons of color" is Bureau of the Census, *Negro Population 1790–1915* (Washington, D.C.: Government Printing Office, 1918).

2. See David C. Rankin, "The Impact of the Civil War on the Free Colored Community of New Orleans," *Perspectives in American History* 11 (1977–78): 385, cited in Thomas Sowell, *Ethnic America* (New York: Basic Books, 1981), p. 205.

3. Herbert G. Gutman, *The Black Family in Slavery and Freedom, 1750–1925* (New York: Vintage Books, 1976).

4. In *Slave and Citizen* (New York: Vintage Books, 1946), Frank Tannenbaum argues that Ibero-American slave systems were more humane and less destructive of upward mobility, principally because "the cruelties and brutalities were against the

law" (p. 93). The Spanish, and particularly Portuguese (see chapter 1 of this book), treatment of slaves may have been marginally better than in the English colonies, perhaps in part because of the greater sexual contact inevitable as a consequence of the proportionally smaller numbers of Iberian than English women who made the voyage to the New World. But "the law" has been so irrelevant to reality in Ibero-American societies that it is difficult to take Tannenbaum's argument seriously, particularly in the case of the Spanish colonies. For example, at Padre Las Casas's insistence, Spain enacted laws in the sixteenth century to protect the Indians, who nonetheless continued to be treated with a degree of cruelty that approximated genocide. The streak of cruelty and torture in Hispanic culture that persists to this day is also relevant. One should also ponder the implications of a statement by Eugene Genovese: "The less than 400,000 Africans imported into the North American British colonies and the United States had become a black population ten times greater by 1860, whereas despite much larger slave importations by Jamaica, Saint-Domingue, Brazil, and Cuba, these and other slave countries struggled to balance imports against mortality in order to hold their own in population" (*Roll, Jordan, Roll* [New York: Vintage Books, 1976], p. 57). Brazil's slaves were not emancipated until 1888; in Costa Rica, Hispanic-America's most progressive society, blacks were confined to Limon Province until 1948.

5. Carlos Rangel, *The Latin Americans: Their Love-Hate Relationship with the United States* (New York and London: Harcourt Brace Jovanovich, 1977), p. 193.

6. Celso Furtado, *Formacáo Económica do Brasil*, 4th ed. (Rio de Janeiro: Editora Fundo de Cultura SA, 1961), p. 162; cited in Maria Lucia Victor Barbosa, *O Voto da Pobreza e a Pobreza do Voto* (Rio de Janeiro: Jorge Zahar Editor, 1988), p. 39.

7. Sowell, *Ethnic America*, p. 200.

8. John Dollard, *Caste and Class in a Southern Town* (Madison: University of Wisconsin Press, 1988), p. 417.

9. Stephan Thernstrom, *The Other Bostonians* (Cambridge: Harvard University Press, 1973), p. 217.

10. Genovese, *Roll, Jordan, Roll*, p. 289.

11. Thomas Sowell, *The Economics and Politics of Race* (New York: Quill, 1983), p. 128.

12. Sowell, *Ethnic America*, p. 216.

13. Quoted in *Parade*, 13 August 1989, p. 5.

14. I have heard of some recent preliminary data that indicate retrogression in the indicators of progress of West Indians in the United States, for example, with respect to crime. If this is true, it could plausibly be the consequence of the lower educational and professional levels of recent West Indian immigrants, many of whom have entered through the family preference provisions of immigration legislation or illegally.

15. Sowell, *Essays and Data on American Ethnic Groups*, p. 42.

16. Sowell, *Ethnic America*, p. 219.

17. James Weldon Johnson, *Black Manhattan* (New York: Knopf, 1930), p. 153, quoted in Nathan Glazer and Daniel Patrick Moynihan, *Beyond the Melting Pot* (Cambridge: MIT Press, 1963), p. 35.

18. Glazer and Moynihan, *Beyond the Melting Pot*, p. 35.

19. Sowell, *Ethnic America*, p. 216, 218.

20. See Lawrence Harrison, *Underdevelopment Is a State of Mind—The Latin American Case* (Lanham, MD: Harvard Center for International Affairs and University Press of America, 1985), chapter 5.

21. Harold Cruse, *The Crisis of the Negro Intellectual* (New York: Quill, 1984), p. 119.

22. Dollard, *Caste and Class in a Southern Town*, p. 66.

23. Cruse, *The Crisis of the Negro Intellectual*, p. 427. In contrast, Thomas Sowell observes, "Few children of rising ethnic groups have had 'role models' of their own ethnicity. Some of the most successful—notably the Chinese and Japanese—almost never did" (*Ethnic America*, p. 279).

24. Stanley Lieberson, *A Piece of the Pie* (Berkeley, Los Angeles, and London: University of California Press, 1980).

25. Joel Perlmann, *Ethnic Differences* (Cambridge: Cambridge University Press, 1988), p. 216.

26. Thernstrom, *The Other Bostonians*, pp. 250–51.

27. Adam Smith, *Wealth of Nations* (New York: Random House, 1937), p. 538.

28. J. Gus Liebenow, *Liberia* (Bloomington and Indianapolis: Indiana University Press, 1987), p. 21.

29. Genovese, *Roll, Jordan, Roll*, pp. 113–14.

30. Charles S. Johnson, *Bitter Canaan* (New Brunswick and Oxford: Transaction Books, 1987), p. 223. Interestingly, African religions without ethical content are practiced in both Haiti and Liberia. In reporting a ritual killing by a high government official in Liberia in 1989, the *New York Times* said: "The unfolding of the murder case has forced people of this country . . . to confront the enduring influence of magic, witchcraft and the belief in a universe filled with spirits that can be placated with charms and human sacrifices" (15 August, p. A3).

31. I use Franklin Frazier's definition of middle class, which includes white-collar and skilled blue-collar workers. In *The New Black Middle Class* (Berkely: University of California Press, 1987), Bart Landry's data indicate that black white-collar and skilled blue-collar workers, which accounted for 11 percent of the black population in 1910, accounted for 67 percent in 1981. In the 22 July 1991 *U.S. News & World Report*, the economists James Smith and Finis Welch conclude that "fully two thirds of blacks could be characterized as middle class" (p. 20).

32. In a 1987 *Washington Post* series on the condition of blacks in the Washington area, Joel Garreau reported that, although Washington itself is a predominantly black city, a majority of the Washington area's blacks live in the suburbs.

33. Gerald David Jaynes and Robin M. Williams, Jr., eds., *A Common Destiny: Blacks and American Society* (Washington, D.C.: National Academy Press, 1989), p. 3.

34. Ibid., p. 12.

35. *The Gallup Report*, no. 185 (February 1981): 30.

36. *The Gallup Report*, 1958 and 1978.

37. Shelby Steele, "I'm Black, You're White, Who's Innocent? Race and Power in an Era of Blame," *Harper's* (June 1988): 48.

38. Jaynes and Williams, *A Common Destiny*, pp. 15, 233.

39. Ibid., pp. 240–43.

40. U.S. Department of Education, *Dropout Rates in the United States, 1989* (Washington, D.C.: National Center for Education Statistics, 1990).

41. Jaynes and Williams, *A Common Destiny*, chap. 7; and World Bank, *World Development Report 1990*, table 29, p. 235.

42. Jaynes and Williams, *A Common Destiny*, p. 273.

43. United States Commission on Civil Rights, *The Economic Progress of Black Men in America* (Washington, D.C.: CCR, 1986), p. 11.

44. Jaynes and Williams, *A Common Destiny*, pp. 282, 274.

45. Richard B. Freeman, *Black Elite* (New York: McGraw-Hill, 1976), p. xx.

46. Jaynes and Williams, *A Common Destiny*, report that the black college graduate's income was 74 percent of the white college graduate's in 1985 (p. 301). The Commission on Civil Rights' *The Economic Progress of Black Men in America* shows a black/white college graduate income differential of 20 percent in the South, 11 percent in the North (p. 81).

47. E. Franklin Frazier, *Black Bourgeoisie* (New York: Collier Books, 1957), pp. 27–28.

48. Charles Murray, *Losing Ground* (New York: Basic Books, 1984), pp. 126–27.

49. Jaynes and Williams, *A Common Destiny*, pp. 522, 461.

50. "One in Four," *The New Republic*, 26 March 1990, p. 5.

51. Marvin Harris, *America Now* (New York: Simon & Schuster, 1981), p. 123. Earlier data in this paragraph are from the same source.

52. Ibid., pp. 118, 123.

53. Jaynes and Williams, *A Common Destiny*, p. 5.

54. Daniel P. Moynihan, "The Professors and the Poor," in *On Understanding Poverty*, ed. Daniel P. Moynihan (New York: Basic Books, 1968), p. 33; quoted in Murray, *Losing Ground*, p. 33.

55. William Julius Wilson, *The Truly Disadvantaged* (Chicago and London: University of Chicago Press, 1987), p. 11.

56. Office of Policy Planning and Research, *The Negro Family: The Case for National Action* (Washington, D.C.: U.S. Department of Labor, March 1965).

57. Murray, *Losing Ground*.

58. Kristofferson and Indian movement leader interview, "CBS Morning News," 3 July 1989.

59. Oscar Lewis, *Anthropological Essays* (New York: Random House, 1970), pp. 70–77, passim.

60. Milton M. Gordon, *Assimilation in American Life* (New York: Oxford University Press, 1964), pp. 70–75, lists cultural, structural, marital, identificational, attitude receptional, behavior receptional, and civic indicators.

61. Calvin F. Schmid and Charles E. Nobbe, "Socioeconomic Differences Among Non-White Races," *American Sociological Review* 30, no. 6 (December 1965): 909–22.

62. See, for example, William Ryan, *Blaming the Victim* (New York: Vintage Books, 1976).

63. Jaynes and Williams, *A Common Destiny*, p. 370.

64. Ibid., p. 372.

65. Ibid., pp. 543–44.

66. Ibid., p. 541.

67. I made that observation in a *Washington Post* article in 1986. Claudio Campuzano, a columnist writing in the *New York Tribune* (10 July 1986), subsequently asserted that there *was* a perfectly good synonym for "dissent[er]"—"*disi-*

dente"—and went on to give Anatole Scharansky as an example. Campuzano, of course, failed to capture the difference between *dissent* and *dissidence.*

68. This idea was advocated by William Raspberry in ". . . And a Plan That Just Might Work," *Washington Post,* 19 June 1991.

69. *New York Times,* 24 January 1990, p. B6.

70. Burns W. Roper, "Racial Tensions Are Down," *New York Times,* 26 July 1990, p. A19.

71. Gallup poll, 1987 (Wilmington, DE: Scholarly Resources, 1988).

72. Thomas Sowell, "Affirmative Action: A Worldwide Disaster," *Commentary* (December 1989): 21–41.

73. Stephen L. Carter, *Reflections of an Affirmative Action Baby* (New York: Basic Books, 1991).

74. Cited in Arthur M. Schlesinger, Jr., *The Disuniting of America* (Knoxville, Tenn.: Whittle Direct Books, 1991), p. 80.

75. Quoted in ibid., p. 59. The comment was made by Alan Kors, a professor at the University of Pennsylvania.

76. Quoted in Penn Kemble, ed., *A New Moment in America?* (New York: Freedom House, 1991), p. 79.

77. Arthur E. Hippler, "The Yolngu and Cultural Relativism: A Response to Reser," *American Anthropologist* 83, no. 2 (1981): 393.

78. Max Lerner, *America as a Civilization* (New York: Simon & Schuster, 1957), p. 543.

79. Schlesinger, *The Disuniting of America,* pp. 42, 76.

80. W. Arthur Lewis, *The Theory of Economic Growth* (Homewood, IL: Richard D. Irwin, 1955), p. 371.

81. Quoted in Schlesinger, *The Disuniting of America,* p. 58, from "Euro, Afro and other 'Centrics,'" *Washington Post,* 10 September 1990.

82. Carter, *Reflections of an Affirmative Action Baby,* p. 233.

83. Abigail Thernstrom, *Whose Votes Count? Affirmative Action and Minority Voting Rights* (Cambridge and London: Harvard University Press, 1987), p. 234.

84. Linda Chavez, *Out of the Barrio* (New York: Basic Books, 1991), p. 57.

85. Thernstrom, *Whose Votes Count?,* p. 242.

86. Quoted in ibid., p. 132.

Chapter 8

1. The words of a former Chief Rabbi of Great Britain, quoted in *The Pentateuch and Haftorahs,* ed. J. H. Hertz (London: Soncino Press, 1961), p. 196.

2. Alexis de Tocqueville, *Democracy in America,* ed. Richard D. Heffner (New York and Scarborough, Ontario: New American Library, 1956), p. 48.

3. See Thomas Sowell, *Ethnic America* (New York: Basic Books, 1981), p. 193.

4. World Bank, *World Development Report 1989* (New York: Oxford University Press, 1989), table 2, p. 167.

5. Alfred E. Kahn, "Our Treadmill Economy," *New York Times,* 27 July 1991, op-ed page.

6. *New York Times,* 13 October 1990, p. 31.

7. Michael A. Porter, *The Competitive Advantage of Nations* (New York: Free Press, 1990), p. 523.

8. See, for example, Frances Moore Lappé, *Rediscovering America's Values* (New York: Ballantine Books, 1989).

9. Porter, *The Competitive Advantage of Nations*, pp. 304, 527.

10. "Our Fragile Tower of Greed and Debt," *Washington Post*, 5 April 1987, p. C1.

11. "Breaking the Silence—A Letter to a Black Friend," *Esquire*, March 1988, p. 98.

12. David McClelland, *The Achieving Society* (Princeton: D. Van Nostrand, 1961).

13. Banfield identifies "present orientation" as the principal obstacle to progress for the lower class in *The Unheavenly City Revisited* (Boston and Toronto: Little, Brown, 1974), for example, p. 61.

14. Ezra F. Vogel, *Japan as Number One—Lessons for America* (Cambridge and London: Harvard University Press, 1979); Allan Bloom, *The Closing of the American Mind* (New York: Simon & Schuster, 1987); Paul Kennedy, *The Rise and Fall of the Great Powers* (New York: Random House, 1987).

15. Marvin Harris, *America Now* (New York: Simon & Schuster, 1981); James Fallows, *More Like Us* (Boston: Houghton Mifflin, 1989).

16. Gabriel Almond and Sidney Verba, *The Civic Culture* (Boston and Toronto: Little, Brown, 1963).

17. In Ronald Inglehart, *Culture Shift in Advanced Industrial Society* (Princeton: Princeton University Press, 1990), p. 438. Inglehart uses a table from Almond and Verba, *The Civic Culture*, for the 58 percent figure.

18. Cited in Russell J. Dalton, *Citizen Politics in Western Democracies* (Chatham, NJ: Chatham House Publishers, 1988), p. 230.

19. Ibid., p. 234.

20. See, for example, George C. Lodge and Ezra F. Vogel, eds., *Ideology and National Competitiveness* (Boston: Harvard Business School Press, 1987).

21. Richard D. Lamm, "The Uncompetitive Society," *Dartmouth Alumni Magazine* (May 1987): 32, 34. Vice President Quayle was similarly critical of America's rush to litigation in his comments at the 1991 American Bar Association annual meeting.

22. In chapter 2, I added an eighth: the role of intellectuals, who contributed so importantly to Spain's understanding of the obstacles to progress in the Spanish psyche. As will be apparent from the list of American intellectuals who are mentioned in this chapter (Allan Bloom, James Fallows, Paul Kennedy, Marvin Harris, Henry Rosovsky, Ezra Vogel, and so on), my sense is that we do not lack for influential social critics. The one factor relevant in the Latin American context that is omitted here is "development projects."

23. Ronald Dore, *Taking Japan Seriously* (Stanford: Stanford University Press, 1987), p. 15.

24. Vogel, *Japan as Number One*, pp. 54–58. I am reminded of the comment of the Stanford anthropologist Thomas Rohlen in a conversation in Kyoto in March 1990: "In Japan, the bureaucracy is the clean hand, the politicians the dirty hand."

25. Joseph A. Schumpeter, *Capitalism, Socialism, and Democracy* (New York: Harper Bros., 1950).

26. See, for example, Porter, *The Competitive Advantage of Nations*, p. 503.

27. In Penn Kemble, ed., *A New Moment in America?* (New York: Freedom House, 1991), p. 114.

28. A similar recommendation was made by Robert Gorham Davis in a letter to the editor of the *New York Times,* published on 6 February 1990.

29. World Bank, *World Development Report 1988* (Washington, D.C.: World Bank, 1988), table 30, p. 281.

30. Otis L. Graham, "Re-Thinking the Purposes of Immigration Policy," Center for Immigration Studies, Washington, D.C., May 1991, p. 30.

31. Quoted in Fallows, *More Like Us,* p. 11.

Index

Abe Masahiro, 123
Abraham, Henry, 218
Achieving Society, The (McClelland), 68, 232
Affirmative action, 190–91, 212–14, 216–17
Africa, 4, 41, 150, 193, 194, 200–201, 215, 216
Africans, 151
Afrocentrism, 214–17
Agriculture: in Brazil, 34; in Japan, 88–89, 121–22; in Korea, 99, 102; in Mexico, 178; in Spain, 67–68; in Taiwan, 88–89, 91, 92; in United States, 167–68, 177
AIDS, 216
Alfonso XII, 72
Allende, Salvador, 59
Alliance for Progress, 2, 8
Almond, Gabriel, 234–36
Amato, Mario, 40
America Now (Harris), 205–6, 233
Arango, E. Ramón, 58–59
Argentina, 5, 13, 61, 70, 166, 223; authoritarianism and, 13; Brazil vs., 42–43, 45–49; as development-resistant country, 16–19; economic indicators, 35, 42; geography of, 6; immigration to, 45–47; military in, 53; resource endowment, 5–6, 42
Arias Navarro, Carlos, 73
Aristide, Jean-Bertrand, 156, 200
Australia, 6
Authoritarianism: of African cultures, 215, 216; in Argentina, 13; in Brazil, 28, 30–34, 40; child-rearing practices and, 14; in Confucianism, 115; in Japan, 13, 132, 139–40; in Korea, 13, 82–86, 100, 101, 104, 105; in

Latin America, 12–14; in Spain, 15, 53, 56, 57, 60–65; in Taiwan, 13, 82–86
Authority, 12–13; in United States, 226

Bahamas, 195–98
Bakufu, 120–23, 139
Bandeirantes e Pioneiros (Moog), 29
Banfield, Edward, 20, 56, 80, 135
Barbados, 5, 195–98, 225
Barbosa, María Lucía Victor, 40
Basque provinces, 66
Benedict, Ruth, 137–39, 143
Betts, Katherine, 157
Bilingual education, 177, 184–91
Birdzell, L. E., Jr., 121
Black Americans, 23, 150, 155, 192–217; affirmative action and, 212–14, 216–17; Afrocentrism of, 214–17; culture of, 206–11; discrimination against, 198–99, 202, 207, 210–11; education of, 182, 195, 196–97, 202, 203–4, 211–12; freedmen and their descendants, 194–95; ghettos and, 192–93, 204–12, 245–46; from Haiti, 199–200; historical overview of, 193–201; from Liberia, 200–201, 216; occupations of, 197–98, 203; political participation by, 202–3, 213, 217; racial revolution and, 201–4; racism and, 192, 198–99, 207, 210–11; social indicators of, 196–97, 201–12; West Indians, 195–98; *see also* Slavery
Black Bourgeoisie (Frazier), 204
Bloom, Allan, 233, 242–43
Borjas, George, 152, 154, 155, 178, 183, 185
Brasil 2,000 (Jaguaribe), 50
Brazil, 6, 22, 27–50, 70, 136, 204, 223; Afri-